Women of Congress

The Statue of Freedom stands atop the Capitol dome.

Women of Congress
A Twentieth-Century Odyssey

Rep. Marcy Kaptur
(D-Ohio)

Congressional Quarterly Inc.
Washington, D.C.

© 1996 Congressional Quarterly Inc.
1414 22nd Street, N.W., Washington, D.C. 20037

Printed in the United States of America

Cover design: Debra Naylor, Inc.

Photo credits

Cover: Olympia J. Snowe, Teresa Zabada; Alice Robertson, Mae E. Nolan, and Winnifred M. Huck, Library of Congress; Nancy Landon Kassebaum, Congressional Quarterly; Patricia Schroeder, Paul Conklin; Barbara Boxer, Friends of Barbara Boxer; Jeannette Rankin, Wide World; Carol Moseley-Braun, Congressional Quarterly

Frontispiece: Statue of Freedom, Architect of the Capitol

Portraits: Corinne Claiborne "Lindy" Boggs, Paul Conklin; Frances Payne Bolton, The Western Reserve Historical Society; Martha Wright Griffiths, Congressional Quarterly; Nancy Kassebaum, John Blodgett, Congressional Quarterly; Edna Flannery Kelly, Bettmann; Mary Teresa Norton, Bettmann; Jeannette Rankin, Montana Historical Society, Helena; Patricia Schroeder, Jim Richardson, *Denver Post;* Margaret Chase Smith, Library of Congress

Photo Gallery: Jeannette Rankin, Montana Historical Society, Helena; Rebecca Felton, Library of Congress; Women of the 71st Congress, Library of Congress; Alice Robertson, Mae E. Nolan, and Winnifred M. Huck, Library of Congress; Margaret Chase Smith and Truman, Margaret Chase Smith Library; Cartoon, ©1954 *Courier-Journal and Louisville Times;* Margaret Chase Smith and Kennedy, Margaret Chase Smith Library; Shirley Chisholm, Congressional Quarterly; Millicent Fenwick, Jim Wells, Congressional Quarterly; Patricia Schroeder, Scott Ferrell, Congressional Quarterly; Margaret Heckler, World Wide; Lindy Boggs, R. Michael Jenkins, Congressional Quarterly; Geraldine Ferraro and Tip O'Neill, Terry Zabala, Congressional Quarterly; Marge Roukema, Will Cofnuk

Library of Congress Cataloging-in-Publication Data

Kaptur, Marcy.
    Women of Congress : a twentieth-century odyssey / Marcy Kaptur.
        p.   cm.
    Includes bibliographical references and index.
    ISBN 0-87187-989-1 (hard cover)
    1. Women legislators—United States—Biography. 2. United States.
Congress—Biography.
    I. Title.
    E747.K37   1996
    328.73'092'2—dc20   96-22556
    [B]

With utmost love and gratitude
to my beloved family and truest lifetime friends

My mother and father, Anastasia "Cherie" and Stephen "Kappy" Kaptur
My brother and lifetime pal, Stephen Jacob Kaptur

My grandmother "busia" and grandfather "dziadzia,"
Teofila Carolina Swiecicka and John August Rogowski

My aunts and uncles, Ciocia Esther and Stanley "Skip" Rogowski
Ciocia Stella and Tony Rogowski
Sister Mary Cleopha and Uncle Peter Kaptur
and Monsignor Geno Baroni

CONTENTS

PREFACE

As a member of Congress at the dawn of the twenty-first century, I regard myself and my female colleagues as second-wave pioneers, descendants of the original trailblazers who opened new visitas on America's political horizon. Like all pioneers, the first women who served in Congress shattered convention. Many decided to run for the office they had held briefly as widows; others, especially more recently, ran on their own. For each, deciding to seek elected office also meant resolving to step away from the traditional cultural roles defined by gender alone.

During the election cycle of 1994, fifty-six women won seats in Congress—a doubling since my first election to the House in 1982. During my tenure I discovered that since the founding of our Republic, fewer than two hundred members of Congress have been women. Of these, only forty-two served longer than a decade. Curious about these women, I set out to learn more. Who were they, and what did they accomplish? What issues concerned them, and how did their lives vary from those of the men who dominated—and still dominate—this institution? Did any of them chair important committees? Could their experiences enlighten future officeholders about the role of women in politics? As I sought answers to these questions, I found unpublished autobiographies, scattered newspaper and magazine stories, and a wealth of historical material waiting to be organized and presented.

Women of Congress: A Twentieth-Century Odyssey was written to illustrate the triumph of women's perseverance over adversity in politics. In it I have paid special attention to these spirited women who devoted much of their lives to advancing the welfare of the nation and improving the lives of its citizens. The book includes profiles of fifteen tenured congresswomen and provides overviews of other women lawmakers during three periods of the twentieth century. The first section, "Early Women in Congress: 1917 to World War II," includes such pioneers as Jeannette Rankin and Mary Teresa Norton. "The Greening Years," which covers World War II through the 1960s, features long-serving Frances Payne Bolton and Margaret Chase Smith. "The Modern Era" profiles some important contemporary leaders—Shirley Chisholm, Lindy Boggs, Pat Schroeder, Cardiss Collins, and Nancy Kassebaum.

I wish to extend warmest appreciation to the individuals who made this book possible: Jeanne Ferris, formerly with Congressional Quarterly Books, who worked with me to produce this comprehensive account; Joanne S. Ainsworth, whose attention to detail, good humor, and style yielded a more polished volume; Ann Davies and Jackie Davey of Congressional Quarterly, whose enthusiasm and interest took the volume to press and to the public; Katherine McGraw, whose vigilance as research assistant and manuscript typist moved raw material into a readable script; and David Tarr, editor in chief of Congressional Quarterly Books, who was always responsive and helpful. I also want to thank the dedicated library staff members at Western Reserve University, the Margaret Chase Smith Library, the Jeannette Rankin Collection at the University of Montana, and the Jersey City Public Library and its librarian, Joan Lovero.

I also wish to mention wonderful friends whose constant support and encouragement give me the strength and inspiration to serve in public life. As a Polish-American, Roman Catholic daughter of blue-collar America, I have been buoyed by their constancy: Carol and Frank Marsh; Ed and Virginia Marciniak; Joe and Rose Hebda; Mrs. Josephine Baroni; Theresa and Joe Kaptur; Congressman Frank Guarini; Mrs. Clara Fox; Hank and Jackie Kalinski and family; Mrs. Josephine Koziol; Al and Becca Baldwin/Ferguson; Lois and Ray Shuster; Mrs. Lora B. Cunningham; the Reverend Martin Hernady; Jerry Hagstrom; Charles and Sally Livermore; Scott and Jama Hayes; Godson Alexander Hayes; Dr. Jack Devany; Carol Murphy; Patti Skaff; Sandra Solomon; Roseann and Ken Koperski and family; Ted and Peggy Mastroianni; Harry and Laura Kaiser; Blanche and George Hull; Dr. Pat Choate; Betty and George Dixon; Norbert and Ula Gorwic; Michael Billick; Bill and Phyllis Boyle; Gail Austin; Sheila Schwartz; Jan Helfrich, Gay Deiger, and the Romaine Helfrich family; Shannie Barnett; Speaker Jim Wright; Sisters of St. Francis at Sylvania, especially Sisters Mary Damien and Mary Norbertine; Sisters of St. Ursula, especially Sisters Mary Lelia, Kathleen Padden, Justine Hill, Mary Clarence, and Mary Bernice; the Little Flower Parish family; Peter and Elizabeth Ujvagi and family; Godson Andrew Ujvagi; the United Auto Workers family; Manette Seady; Professor Kate Warner; Mrs. Mercedes Wells; Francey Werve and the Werve family; Marion and Maryann Wojciechowski; Mrs. Blanche Zalipski; Ron and Pat Zielinski; John Zerbo; Ray and Thelma, Howard and Eleanor Zwyer; and all our loyal staff members in Ohio and Washington, D.C., who diligently have served the citizens of Ohio's Ninth District: Steve Katich, Fariborz Fatemi, Roberta Jeanquart, Lindsay Potts, Norma Olsen, Susan Rowe, Dan Foote, Karen Harris, Theresa Morris, Deron Roberson, George Wilson, Lisa Konwinski, Julie Michalak, Susan Role, Jamie Wimberly, and Rob McClintic.

Special gratitude is certainly due to the women members of Congress: they permitted their professional and personal lives, which reveal great sacrifice, to be put on display for the benefit of the next generation.

Finally, as this book goes to press in mid-1996, it seems fitting to note that the U.S. Senate, at the urging of David Pryor and Dale Bumpers, both Democratic senators from Arkansas, has decided to hang an official portrait of the first woman elected to the Senate. Until the unveiling of the portrait of "Silent" Hattie Caraway, the only other painting of a woman in the Senate's collection was of Pocahontas. Onward!

Introduction

If you asked the average American how many women currently serve in the U.S. Congress, most would probably guess that about one-third of the members are women. In fact, only 11 percent of the members of Congress today are women (see figure 1). This figure is an all-time high; it has taken nearly a century to reach this threshold.

For myself and the other women in Congress the rite of passage in this century-long odyssey of increasing liberties for women has been possible largely because of the spirited women and supportive men who understood the promise of American life for all our citizenry. Expanding educational opportunities, a developing body of law that gave women status and value beyond "property," longevity, and changing cultural norms that allow women to choose their life's pursuits—all these factors moved women toward equal partnership with men in shaping the progress of humankind.

All 176 women who have served in Congress since the founding of our republic make up merely 1.5 percent of the approximately 11,600 members who have taken the oath of office. Twice as many of these women have been Democrats as Republicans. In fact, since women's suffrage was first granted in 1920, only 38 women have served for more than ten years, and just 13 women have served longer than two decades.

A total of 156 women have been elected to the House of Representatives. Of the 24 who have served in the Senate, 11 were appointed (6 of them to fill vacancies caused by their husbands' death) and 13 were elected. Four women have served in both houses—Margaret Chase Smith of Maine, Barbara Mikulski of Maryland, Barbara Boxer of California, and Olympia Snowe of Maine.

Defining the Women of Congress

Who are the women of Congress? How did their journeys to the center of America's political life differ from the journeys of the men with whom they served? What were their families like? Who helped them along the way? What drove them? What sacrifices did they make? How did they win election with such enormous odds stacked against them? From the first woman to serve in Congress—Jeannette Rankin of Montana, elected to the House in 1917—to the fifty-eight women who serve today, their personal stories have varied tremendously. More than one-third of these women were

Figure 1   Women in the 104th Congress (1995 - 1997)

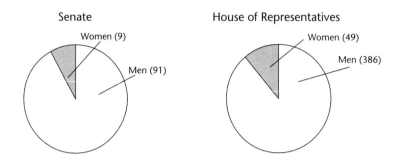

Source: Center for the American Woman and Politics, Rutgers University.

Note: There are 535 members of Congress, 100 in the Senate and 435 in the House.

widows who succeeded their husbands in office and went on to surpass them. Some were self-actualized women who either rose through the ranks of political parties and institutions or took them on and got elected to Congress on their own. Most encountered and rose above incredible adversity and tragedy; a few were blessed with vast wealth. All exhibited insight into the human condition, a persevering determination to overcome obstacles, and a conscience formed in the knowledge that women have always been, and may always be, charged with nurturing, teaching, and enlightening the human race.

The roles that women have been able to play in Congress have also varied widely and assumed greater significance over time. Some women served for just weeks or months, while others served for many years. Only a handful rose to positions of seniority and chaired important legislative committees.

A key reason that women so seldom were able to reach positions of power is that most did not run for office until they were in their late forties or fifties—after their children were grown or their husbands had died. Most men entered Congress at a younger age and served longer, gaining the seniority required to become a committee chair or leader. This pattern has shifted ever so gradually as more women have won election to Congress. Their lives reveal an America of expanding freedom, opportunity, steady advancement, impelling force, and deep conscience.

Jeannette Rankin was thirty-six when she became the first woman elected to the House. The first woman to serve in the Senate was also the oldest woman to serve in Congress—Rebecca Felton of Georgia, appointed to the Senate in 1922 at eighty-seven years of age. She served one day and resigned. Women lawmakers for the nation plowed new paths, broke many barriers, and stood on one another's shoulders—as well as on their mothers' and grandmothers'—as the twentieth century progressed.

This story of the women of Congress is presented in three segments: "Early Women in Congress: 1917 to World War II," "The Greening Years: World War II through the 1960s," and "The Modern Era: Toward the Twenty-first Century." Since women first won the right to vote in 1920, California and New York have led the states in having sent, respectively, twenty and eighteen women members to our nation's Capitol. Illinois has elected nine. The congressional careers of most of the tenured women who are the subject of this book extended two decades or more. Their legislative records are sufficiently rich to illustrate their era. The tables that make up the Appendixes contain detailed information about all the women who have served.

The Changing Status and Social Roles of Women

The Nineteenth Amendment to the U.S. Constitution granting women the right to vote was ratified in 1920. Custom being what it is, it is not surprising that fewer than three dozen women were elected or appointed to Congress during the early years before World War II. Except for Jeannette Rankin, no women were sworn in before the adoption of the suffrage amendment.

In 1789, when the U.S. Constitution was ratified, women did not possess the right to vote. The law treated women as property, not as persons with individual liberties. But in the mid-1800s the status of women slowly began to change. In 1848, New York granted women the right to own the property that they brought into their marriages. Then, in 1860, New York passed the Married Women's Property Act, giving women the right to their own earnings and possessions and making women the joint guardians (with their husbands) of their children. Many other states soon followed suit. About the same time, in my home state of Ohio, Oberlin College became the first college in America to admit women. No doubt that precedent of openness to women's advancement accounts for more women having been elected to public office from northern Ohio than from many other regions of the state and nation.

In 1917, Montana, which had granted women the right to vote in 1914, became the first state to elect a woman to serve in Congress. Only in 1920 did the United States grant all women the vote. Two years later, Congress passed the Independent Citizenship for Married Women Act, granting women rights of citizenship not dependent on their husbands. Only two women elected in this pioneering period made careers for themselves in

Congress: Mary Norton and Edith Nourse Rogers. Both were widows; nei-ther had children.

During World War II, as 16.5 million of the nation's young men were draft-ed and enlisted into military service, women replaced them in America's fac-tories, offices, and farms. These jobs formerly had been limited to men. But women now proved they could serve in the armed forces as pilots and nurs-es, work in factory production lines, and drive trucks while still bringing up children. Whether they chose to do so or not, women were forced to confront independence. Life in the United States was never to be the same again.

After World War II, women moved naturally into the workplace in greater and greater numbers. At the same time, women were becoming better edu-cated. During the prosperous 1950s, returning male veterans established their families and built America's suburbs with the help of the GI Bill. Many of their spouses worked to help pay for their living expenses. And women who had never thought of going to college were encouraged to gain more educa-tion to pursue the American dream. The explosion of post–high school edu-cational advancement for the middle class became an imperative for the post-war era.

Since 1970, even more women, including married women with young children, have pursued degrees beyond high school and have entered the American work force. The United States has faced growing global competi-tion and slower economic growth at home, resulting in flat or declining incomes. The majority of women thus have worked outside the home not only for personal fulfillment but also from economic necessity. Still others chose to pursue careers previously off-limits to women. As a result, women's social roles have been transformed in this last third of the twentieth centu-ry. In 1972, about a quarter of the people who served as bartenders were women; today more than half are women. In 1972, about a third of Ameri-ca's bus drivers were women; today they number nearly half. In 1972, only 4 percent of the attorneys in the United States were women; today that fig-ure is 22.9 percent, and women's enrollment in law schools now equals men's. In 1972, 10 percent of physicians were women; today that percentage has doubled.

Today 55 percent of all college graduates are women, up from 40 percent in the early 1970s. Women also are awarded more than half of all master's degrees. In the 1970s about 14 percent of doctoral degrees were awarded to women; today 39 percent of them are. As to medical degrees, women have moved from 28 percent in 1970 to 36 percent today. And women now earn a third of the dental degrees awarded, as opposed to 1 percent in 1970.

The feminist movement of the early 1970s, mainly driven by college women, freed women to choose whether to raise a family, build a career, or do both. Medical science advanced to the point where women could control the timing and number of children in the family, and by 1994 women made up over 45 percent of the full-time work force. Counting those who had part-time employment as well as those who worked full time, nearly 75 percent of American women worked outside the home, including the majority of women with children. Women's presence in Congress gradually, but solidly, increased from a post–World War II average of perhaps ten.

The Changing Status of African Americans

When I first met Shirley Chisholm in her Washington congressional office in 1982, just before she retired at age fifty-eight after a fourteen-year career, she opened the right drawer of her desk and produced a well-worn, billfold-size copy of the U.S. Constitution. In 1789, when the nation was founded, that Constitution would have viewed her, being both black and a woman, as chattel, or property, and defined her as three-fifths of a person (U.S. Constitution, Article I, Section 2). Nearly two centuries later, she became the first black congresswoman in the United States. In every sense, her journey embodied both an anomaly and an unprecedented achievement, akin to landing a woman on the moon.

The course of African Americans to federal office has been fraught with shipwrecked dreams. To date, sixteen African American women have served in Congress of a total of ninety-seven African Americans who have served, ninety-three in the House and four in the Senate. In a legal sense, only with the enforcement of the post–Civil War Reconstruction Act of 1867 and ratification of the Fifteenth Amendment to the U.S. Constitution in 1870 were "rights of citizens to vote … not … denied or abridged by the United States or by any State on account of race, color, or previous condition of servitude." The law was clear, but its execution fell far from the mark. The vicissitudes of racial discrimination in America, based on a social structure of class distinctions, cast a pall over the new America. Much of the nineteenth century in this country, including the Civil War, was spent in attempting to overcome these divisions.

Hiram Revels of Mississippi became the first black to serve in Congress when he took his seat in the U.S. Senate in 1870 to fill the unexpired term of Jefferson Davis. But shortly thereafter, in 1876, the pace of blacks elected to Congress regressed. The removal of federal troops from the South meant the effective repeal of the Reconstruction Act, and an era of brutal intimidation of black voters by the Ku Klux Klan and other racist groups began. In states like Mississippi, South Carolina, and Louisiana, black voter participation dropped to almost nothing.

It was only in 1928 that another African American, Oscar DePriest, a Republican from Chicago, was elected to the House of Representatives.

African Americans, however, even members of Congress, were still not treated as full citizens.

Until the mid-twentieth century, black Members of Congress like all black Americans, faced the restrictions of legalized segregation. In travelling from their districts, they rode on separate train cars, and in Washington, D.C., they confronted segregated theaters, hotels, and restaurants. Even the restaurants in the Capitol segregated facilities for white and black staff.[1]

The world at war in the first half of the twentieth century thrust black Americans into battle, in segregated units, and into the nation's war factories. Uncle Sam became an equal opportunity employer on the battlefield and in the workplace. The movement of millions of underemployed blacks from the rural South to the North during the war years and the intervening Great Depression transformed American cities, as ethnic and racial pluralism tugged at the edges of civil order. As organized labor slowly included blacks into its ranks, some black Americans moved into steady jobs and onto the first rung of the ladder of economic independence.

Still, it took forty years after DePriest was elected and almost one hundred years after the election of the first black congressman, for the first black congresswoman, Shirley Chisholm, to be sent to Congress.

The Increasing Visibility of Women in Congress

After World War II the number of women elected to Congress began to increase, and the advent of the mass media put a few of them in our living rooms. Sen. Margaret Chase Smith of Maine became known beyond the boundaries of her home state because of television. As a youngster, I remember thinking it was normal for a woman to do what she was doing. I did not fully appreciate at the time that she was the only woman in the hundred-member Senate. In fact, from 1940 to 1970 just seventeen women served more than ten years in Congress. So it is not surprising that when I first came to Congress I could find just one woman—Julia Butler Hansen of Washington—who had chaired any of the thirteen subcommittees of the exclusive House committee on which I now serve, the Appropriations Committee. Hansen capped a four-decade career in public service with her election to Congress at age fifty-three in 1960. At age sixty she rose to chair the Appropriations Subcommittee on Interior and Related Agencies from 1967 to 1974. She remained the only woman to chair one of the subcommittees until 1995, when Barbara F. Vucanovich—in her last term in Congress at age seventy-three—rose to chair the Subcommittee on Military Construction for one term. To date, no woman has ever chaired the full Appropriations Committee. Nor has any woman chaired the other two exclusive House Committees—Ways and Means (or any of its subcommittees) or Rules.

The uncertainty and upheaval of the late 1960s and 1970s, fraught with pent-up anxiety for political reform—coupled with slow economic growth, lingering angst over the Vietnam War, the scandal of Watergate and resignation of President Richard M. Nixon, the oil crisis, and American hostages in Iran—brought more women to Congress, including a number whose careers have been significant. Women were regarded as reformers, breaths of fresh air in a political environment in which trust in government was on the decline. Even President Jimmy Carter of Georgia said the nation suffered from "a deep malaise." He went on to lose the election of 1980. One of these women, Shirley Chisholm of New York, ran for president of the United States in 1972; Margaret Chase Smith had done so a few years before, in 1964. Another, Geraldine Ferraro, also of New York, was the first woman ever selected on a national ticket as the Democratic candidate for vice president a few years later, in 1984.

The early 1990s marked a watershed for women in Congress. More than twice as many women were elected in 1992 as had been just four years earlier, the vast majority from districts redrawn as a result of the 1990 census. Part of the drive for election of more women in that year can be attributed to the reaction of women to the Senate grilling of the witness Anita Hill, who had worked for the Supreme Court nominee Clarence Thomas and objected to his nomination based on his alleged sexual harassment of her. The Senate confirmed Thomas and in the process inflamed many women voters who had believed Hill. The elections of 1994 brought the number of women in the House and Senate to fifty-six (increased in 1996 to fifty-eight after Rep. Juanita M. McDonald of California and Sen. Sheila Frahm of Kansas were sworn in), an all-time high in spite of retirements and election losses by incumbents.

Women and Positions of Leadership in Congress

Despite the increase in numbers, it is still unusual for women in Congress to achieve leadership positions. Julia Butler Hansen and Barbara Vucanovich are still the only women to have chaired House Appropriations subcommittees; both did so at the end of their careers. Barbara Mikulski of Maryland is the first and only woman thus far to chair a Senate Appropriations subcommittee, and no woman has yet chaired any other of the Senate's exclusive committees, or subcommittees—on Appropriations, Rules, or Finance. To date, no woman has ever been hired as a staff director for one of these leadership committees. It was not until the mid-1980s that the first woman was hired as a clerk (an influential policy-driven position) for an exclusive subcommittee (Veterans, Housing and Urban Development, and Independent Agencies, called VA-HUD) of the House Appropriations Committee). This occurred at the urging of supportive male members like Bob Traxler, a former representative from Michigan, who had a young daughter named Sarah. He urged "women to be hired because he wanted all opportunities to be available to Sarah when she grows up."

No woman has ever served as Speaker of the House or as majority or minority leader. Lynn Martin of Illinois won election as vice chair of the Republican Caucus in 1984 and 1986; Susan Molinari of New York won the position in the 104th Congress. This position, the third rung on the ladder up to House leadership, is the highest any Republican woman has achieved. (In 1990, Martin left the House to run an unsuccessful campaign for the Senate in Illinois; she was appointed secretary of labor by President George Bush in 1991.) Barbara Kennelly of Connecticut has been elected to a similar position in the Democratic Caucus, and former representative Mary Rose Oakar of Ohio ran for chair of the Democratic Caucus during the mid-1980s but was unsuccessful.

Why have so few of the women in Congress risen even this high? One reason has already been mentioned: age at election. The majority of women who have served either succeeded their husbands or were elected after their children were grown. In fact, before 1940, more than half the women who were elected succeeded their husbands in office. Thus most women were elected too late in life to establish the seniority that is so important in this conservative institution, marked by its respect for tradition and tenure. Some other women, who were elected at a younger age, chose not to stay long enough to develop seniority or were defeated in their bids for reelection. Two younger women, elected more recently—Blanche Lambert of Arkansas, elected in 1992, and Enid Greene (Waldholtz), elected in 1994—became pregnant during their early tenure and decided to leave Congress. Greene's decision was influenced significantly by a political scandal involving her former husband. Molinari, elected in 1990, bore a child in 1996 and ran for reelection.

Another reason for women's inability in general to reach the most powerful positions in Congress has been their lack of education and political experience compared with the education and experience of male members. Only relatively recently have female members been career women instead of homemakers, had significant education or legal training, and been elected to or served in other public offices or professional positions before running for Congress.

The Changing Profile of Women in Congress since 1970

Since 1970, more women have been elected to Congress at an earlier age, with only about 20 percent succeeding their husbands.[2] Elizabeth Holtzman of New York, Patricia S. Schroeder of Colorado, and Susan Molinari of New York are the youngest women ever elected to Congress; they were all thirty-two when first elected, Holtzman and Schroeder in 1972 and Molinari in

1990. Margaret Heckler was thirty-five when she was sworn in in 1967. Claudine Schneider of Rhode Island, Jill L. Long of Indiana, and Maria Cantwell of Washington took the oath of office in 1981, 1989, and 1993, respectively, at ages thirty-four, thirty-seven, and thirty-six, and I was sworn in at age thirty-six in 1983. Schneider was defeated in a bid for the U.S. Senate in 1990; Long was defeated in a bid for reelection to the House in 1994; and Cantwell was defeated in her first reelection bid in 1994.

Of the married women who were elected, very few reared young children while serving in Congress. When Pat Schroeder was elected in 1972, she was the mother of two young children, ages two and six; she has now served more than two decades in Congress but announced that the 104th Congress (1995–1997) would be her last. Yvonne Brathwaite Burke of California was elected in 1972 and became the first woman in history to bear a child while serving in Congress, but she left Congress shortly thereafter to pursue a legal career. Only since the late 1980s and early 1990s, with the election of such women as Jane Harman and Zoe Lofgren of California, Cynthia A. McKinney of Georgia, Carolyn B. Maloney of New York, Marjorie Margolies-Mezvinsky of Pennsylvania, Patty Murray of Washington, Deborah Pryce of Ohio, and Ileana Ros-Lehtinen and Karen Thurman of Florida, has it become somewhat more common, but still atypical, for women to rear young children while serving in Congress. This tendency is in stark contrast to the male members' family situations.

Before 1940, more than half the women who were elected to Congress succeeded their husbands. As we have noted, this percentage has leveled out during the contemporary period. There also has been a steady decline in the percentage of congresswomen whose families possessed vast wealth or were socially or politically well known, from 85 percent in the early years to approximately half today.[3]

Changes in Society and Their Implications for Women

Politics has been chosen as a career by a growing number of women. During the 1960s, there was an average of 15 women members per session of Congress. That average rose to 16 during the 1970s, 23 during the 1980s, and more than 40 during the 1990s. But why is it still such a small percentage of the 535 members of Congress? Why have seven of our states—Alaska, Delaware, Iowa, Mississippi, New Hampshire, Vermont, and Wisconsin—never sent a woman to Congress? Why have only 4 women in history—Hattie Caraway of Arkansas, 1931–1945; Margaret Chase Smith of Maine, 1949–1973; Nancy Kassebaum of Kansas, 1979–1997; and Barbara Mikulski of Maryland, 1987–present—served more than two terms in the Senate and only 38 women served more than ten years in the House? Why, in spite of being able to vote since 1920, was it not until 1980 that women voted in presidential elections in proportion to their numbers in the population—that is, over half?

The post–World War II revolution in work and education precipitated the need for fundamental changes in our society—changes that are still in process. How does society rear children in families where all adults work? Families have not come to terms with this development, as evidenced by rising rates of divorce, teenage pregnancy, and juvenile delinquency. Schools have not changed to accommodate the different nature of family schedules and vacations. And workplaces still behave as if worker performance and absenteeism have no relation to children or the care of sick relatives. Unfortunately, much of the burden of adjusting a modern life to a still-traditional society remains on women's shoulders as society's chief caregivers. For change to occur in the future and a more representative Congress to result, men and women must adjust their expectations to meet the demands of career and family, in the public and private realms.

Successes of Women in Congress

In spite of the obstacles, some women have pursued long congressional careers. In 1940, Margaret Chase Smith succeeded her husband in the House. She went on to serve in the Senate from 1949 to 1973. Still remembered today for her "Declaration of Conscience" speech against the demagogue Joseph McCarthy, she declared her candidacy for the Republican presidential nomination in 1964 and received twenty-seven votes on the first ballot at the Republican National Convention that year. Frances Payne Bolton of Ohio, who succeeded her husband and whose grandfather had been a representative, served from 1940 to 1969; her son, Oliver Payne Bolton, also served in Congress from 1953 to 1957 and from 1963 to 1965. Leonor Kretzer Sullivan of Missouri, who also succeeded her husband, served from 1953 to 1977; she concentrated her legislative energies on agriculture and consumer affairs.

A few women who served in the House eventually rose to chair full committees. Mary Teresa Norton of New Jersey served from 1925 to 1951 and chaired the Education and Labor Committee from 1938 to 1947. During Franklin D. Roosevelt's presidency, she succeeded in passing legislation on fair labor standards and equal pay. Edith Nourse Rogers of Massachusetts served for thirty-five years, from 1925 to 1960, and remains the longest-serving woman in Congress. She chaired the Veterans' Affairs Committee from 1947 to 1949 and from 1953 to 1955, passing legislation for the Women's Army Corps, the GI Bill, and the Korean Benefits Act. Edna Flannery Kelly of New York served in the House of Representatives from 1949 to 1969 and rose to chair the Subcommittee on Europe of the Committee on Foreign Affairs.

Nine other women have chaired minor committees or nonlegislative committees: Mae Ella Hunt Nolan of California chaired the House Committee on Expenditures in the Post Office (1923–1925); Hattie Caraway of Arkansas, the Senate Committee on Enrolled Bills (1931–1945); Caroline O'Day of New York, the House Committee on the Election of President, Vice-President, and Representatives in Congress (1937–1943); Leonor Kretzer Sullivan of Missouri, the Merchant Marine and Fisheries Committee (1953–1955 and 1965–1977); Yvonne Brathwaite Burke of California and Martha Wright Griffiths of Michigan, the House Select Committee on the House Beauty Shop (1967–1975 and 1975–1979, respectively); Pat Schroeder of Colorado, the House Select Committee on Children, Youth, and Families, a nonlegislative committee (1987–1993); Nancy L. Johnson of Connecticut, the House Ethics Committee (1995–present); and Jan Meyers of Kansas, the House Committee on Small Business (1995–present).

Some women have chaired subcommittees of full committees. For example, Pat Schroeder, a member of the House Armed Services Committee since she was first elected, chaired its Subcommittee on Research and Technology. Schroeder has also been responsible for legislation to gain equity for women serving in the military and to make physical improvements to bases throughout the world. Cardiss Collins of Illinois, first elected in 1973 to fill the vacancy created by the death of her husband, has risen to chair a key subcommittee of the House Energy and Commerce Committee, the Subcommittee on Commerce, Consumer Protection and Competitiveness; she has focused her career on consumer protection. Marilyn Lloyd of Tennessee was elected in 1974 and chaired the Subcommittee on Energy Research of the House Science and Technology Committee. Her district encompasses the Oak Ridge atomic energy facility, and she devoted her career to scientific and technological advancement. Until 1992, when she was defeated in a reelection bid after fourteen years of service, Mary Rose Oakar of Ohio chaired the Subcommittee on Economic Stabilization of the House Banking Committee and the Subcommittee on Personnel and Police of the House Administration Committee. She fought hard to achieve pay equity for women and to improve benefits for congressional employees. As noted earlier, Barbara Vucanovich chairs the Military Construction Subcommittee of the Appropriations Committee, and Julia Butler Hansen chaired the Interior and Related Agencies Subcommittee (now the Interior Subcommittee) of the Appropriations Committee. I chaired the Subcommittee on Housing and Memorial Affairs of the Veterans' Affairs Committee and wrote legislation that revised the veterans' housing loan program and reduced its cost to the taxpayers by more than $100 million.

Some of these women and others who may have been less prominent found the road to Congress easier because of supportive men. Mary Norton of New Jersey found an early male champion in Mayor Frank Hague of Jersey City, while Hattie Caraway of Arkansas received valuable campaign help from Rep. Huey Long. Ruth Bryan Owen of Florida was the daughter of William Jennings Bryan, a Democratic presidential candidate. Barbara Bailey Kennelly of Connecticut, one of four women in history to serve on the House Ways and Means Committee, is the daughter of John Bailey, a former chair of the Democratic National Committee. Nancy Pelosi of California is the daughter of Thomas D'Alesandro, who served in the House from 1939 to 1947 and subsequently became mayor of Baltimore. Susan Molinari, one of the youngest women ever elected to Congress, won a special election to fill a seat vacated by her father, Guy Molinari, in 1990 when she was thirty-two. Many women have had trusted advisers during their careers: for example, Jeannette Rankin of Montana turned to her brother, Wellington Rankin, and Margaret Chase Smith confided in her administrative assistant, William Lewis, an expert in military matters. Supportive males clearly were not the only reason for these women's success in politics. But their example, encouragement, advice, and assistance opened doors to help these women navigate what was an almost exclusively men's world.

The Influence of Women in Congress

Do the women who reach that male world of Congress differ significantly from men in the legislation they sponsor or their voting records? A greater percentage of the legislation women introduced fell into "traditionally feminine" areas of interest, compared with the legislation introduced by men—but not a majority.[4] Interestingly enough, as the number of women in Congress has increased, their voting has become more conservative. This may be because women now see greater opportunity to advance in politics and thus a greater need to conform to the mainstream of views.[5] After having served in Congress for fourteen years, I have noted that women members are often less concerned with the attainment of a position or self-promotion and more concerned with the well-being of the nation than are their male counterparts.

As women are elected to public life in still greater numbers, will their feminine attributes help to transform politics, Congress, and the nation, or will they merely follow masculine roles? Will women place principle before power, self-sacrifice before self-aggrandizement, and understanding before confrontation? Can women's involvement help tame politics? Many of the stories in this book suggest that this is possible. The pursuit of a more decent, humane, and peaceful country and world will require more of women in the next century, and more of men, both personally and professionally. Former representative Frank J. Guarini of New Jersey noted, "As America moves into the uncharted waters of the twenty-first century, it will be America's women, unleashed from previous conventions that bottled their potential, whose new energy will be responsible for the nation's survival and advancement."[6] The true test of women's influence, however, will come only with greater involvement and the exercise of their expanding political power.

Even at this writing, near the close of the twentieth century, citizens struggle when introducing women members of Congress. Are they to be called congress*women?* congress*ladies?* congress*men?* congress*persons?* House rules experts argue whether the term of reference afforded to women members when they are recognized for debate—"Gentlelady"—is a modern-day redundancy. For if one is a lady, is not one "gentle"? However, male members are addressed as "gentlemen," since it is presumed they are not gentle and, therefore, need to be reminded to keep order in the institution. At the close of the twentieth century, it is time for a book about the women of Congress—past, present, and future—all gentleladies, all congress*women* and senators.

NOTES

1. Bruce A. Ragsdale and Joel D. Treese, *Black Americans in Congress: 1870–1989* (Washington, D.C.: U.S. Government Printing Office, 1990), 2.
2. Irwin N. Gertzog, "Changing Patterns of Female Recruitment to the U.S. House of Representatives," *Legislative Studies Quarterly* 4 (August 1979): 431.
3. Ibid., 434.
4. Frieda Gehlen, "Women Members of Congress: A Distinctive Role," in *A Portrait of Marginality: The Political Behavior of the American Woman*, ed. Marianne Githins and Jewel Prestage (New York: McKay, 1977), 315.
5. Susan Welch, "Are Women More Liberal than Men in the U.S. Congress?" *Legislative Studies Quarterly* 10 (February 1985): 132.
6. Frank J. Guarini, interview by author, Washington, D.C., February 1994.

Part 1: Early Women in Congress

1917 to World War II

Early Women in Congress
Overview

W orld War I and the uneasy peace that followed shaped the first half of this era, through the decade of the 1920s. The effect of the war on the heretofore isolationist United States was profound. When the fighting ceased, 116,000 Americans had been killed in heavy fighting and trench warfare; more than 234,000 had been wounded. Coming to terms with the magnitude of the carnage, much of it due to more lethal weaponry such as machine guns, consumed America, as it did the rest of the Western world.

In the United States, the presidential campaign of 1920 was dominated by international affairs and debate about U.S. involvement in any foreign entanglement, such as the League of Nations, which President Woodrow Wilson had inspired. When the votes were counted in November, a complete reversal of political parties—Democrat to Republican—upended the White House and both houses of Congress. Wilson's dream of a League of Nations with U.S. leadership to stop future wars was carried fruitlessly into the unsuccessful campaign by the Democratic candidate, James Cox of Ohio, following the defeat of the Treaty of Versailles in the Senate in November 1919. America had had enough of war and of foreign entanglements.

Republicans, who held a strongly isolationist position as a party, held sway in Washington for more than a decade, until Franklin D. Roosevelt broke their lock in 1932. The presidential election of 1928 had pitted the urban, Catholic, Democratic governor of New York, Alfred E. Smith, against the Republican Herbert Hoover, who won a stunning victory. Yet the influence of new voters, including immigrant Catholic voters, on such races was to remain a feature of national politics for the rest of the century.

Domestically, immigration, industrialization, and urbanization throughout the 1920s began to alter the political landscape. Urban America was booming. By 1920, farmers had become a minority group in the United States, and the rise of industrial centers of manufacturing began to change the face of Congress.[1] Immigrants, who had been streaming to America by the millions during the three previous decades, had first settled along the coast within sight of the Statue of Liberty in places like Jersey City, or migrated inward to places like Lowell, Massachusetts, a booming textile town. A new America was dawning in these gritty cities, as in Jeannette Rankin's mining towns. The volatility of population expansion and the pace of life created conditions ripe for political expression.

The disruptions to life and the horror caused by World War I propelled the first women to Congress. Pioneering women like Jeannette Rankin, Mary Teresa Norton, and Edith Nourse Rogers were among those who began to open the path for others. These congresswomen, who had not envisioned early in their lives their future as lawmakers, faced the task of proving that women were to be taken seriously. As columnist Ellen Goodman observes, "A first is expected to be a role model without ever having had one."[2] The average age of women elected during this pioneering era was about fifty years. Their average length of service, except for Norton and Rogers, was just over two years, far less than their male counterparts; congress*men* served an average of eight years, and those who rose to positions of power served two decades or more. Nearly half of the twenty-six women who served in Congress before 1940 were widows who succeeded their husbands or daughters who followed in their fathers' footsteps. A notable exception was Rankin, who, at the strikingly young age of thirty-six, became the first woman elected to Congress. She shaped her own future, albeit with her brother's encouragement, never married, and bore no children. She dedicated her expeditionary life to such humanitarian causes as antiwar activism, equal voting rights, and the peaceful resolution of conflict.

In 1920, Alice Robertson, at age sixty-six, became the second woman elected to Congress. A Republican from another frontier state, Oklahoma, which had granted women suffrage in 1918, she served only two years, from 1921 to 1923. Like Rankin, Robertson came from a pioneer background, but her political philosophy and beliefs differed markedly. She opposed women's suffrage, believing that women who wanted to trade their woman's privilege for a man's right were "bartering the birthright for a mess of pottage."[3] She also refused to support a bill for women and children's health care because she thought it invaded personal privacy. Her support of tariffs and immigration quotas appealed to the xenophobia of her constituency. Having taught Indian children in Oklahoma, however, she was a strong advocate for Native Americans and served on the Indian Affairs Committee in Congress. A woman of high principle, her campaign slogan was "I cannot be bought, I cannot be sold, I cannot be intimidated."[4] Robertson was defeated in her bid for reelection in 1922, largely because she had opposed a bonus for soldiers who fought in World War I.[5]

In that year, 1922, Rebecca Latimer Felton, a Democrat from Georgia, became the first woman to serve in the U.S. Senate. Felton's husband, William H. Felton, had served three terms in the House, and she was chosen by Gov. Thomas Hardwick in early October as a temporary replacement for Sen. Tom Watson, who died in office.[6] She was eighty-seven at the time of her appointment and served for one day, having persuaded the senator-elect, Walter George, to delay taking the oath of office so that she could be seated for the sake of history.

The two longest-serving women during this early period—Mary Teresa Norton and Edith Nourse Rogers—were sworn into office in 1925, during a period that historians Henry Steele Commager and Samuel Eliot Morrison describe as extravagant, pretentious, and voluble. "Postwar abandon turned inward" in the nation when stock market futures skyrocketed.[7] Yet these women were serious and dutiful. Both were widowed during their middle years, at ages fifty-nine and forty-four, respectively. Neither had any living children. Both were thrust into politics by the convergence of tragedy and opportunity that led them accidentally but methodically to careers in the nation's Capitol. By personality, neither seemed to fit the flapper image of the time, which the dictionary defines as "bold and unconventional."[8] But, in fact, both were daring women of rare courage and dedication. The sheer span of their service is impressive—from the mid-1920s through World War II and the subsequent election of Harry S. Truman. Norton served twenty-six years, until 1951, and Rogers served a decade more, until 1960.

Although the backgrounds of the two women were vastly different, both represented the fast-growth, industrializing towns of the nation, where the bold possibilities of a newly emerging America were being forged. Rogers, a Republican, hailed from Massachusetts, home of the new Republican president, Calvin Coolidge. Mary Norton was a Democrat from New Jersey, a state that also was home to Woodrow Wilson while he served as president of Princeton University and then governor of the state before his election as president of the United States. Both women, no doubt, were more politically aware because of the presence in their home states of men, their contemporaries, who became presidents of the United States.

In 1931, Hattie Wyatt Caraway, a Democrat from Arkansas, joined Norton and Rogers in the Capitol, first as the appointee chosen to fill out her late husband's senatorial term and then in 1932 as the first woman elected to the Senate. Running against four seasoned politicians, she had been given little chance to win the Democratic primary. With the help of the renowned Louisiana senator Huey Long, however, Caraway won the nomination and then the election in November. Many suspected that she would be "Huey's echo."[9] But she responded to the charge, saying, "Nothing was ever farther from the truth.... I told him straight out that it must be my campaign, not his, and that I wouldn't stand for attacks on his personal enemies.... 'Mr. Long,' I said, 'I wouldn't give a dime for my seat in the Senate if I couldn't vote according to my convictions and my conscience.'"[10] And she did vote according to her conscience, refusing, for example, to vote with Long against establishing the World Court. Caraway was reelected in 1938 and served until

1945. A prohibitionist and the cosponsor of a proposed Equal Rights Amendment to the Constitution, she, like most of her southern colleagues, voted against the anti-lynching law of 1938 and a proposed bill in 1942 to eliminate the poll tax.[11] She was the first woman to chair a Senate committee, the Committee on Enrolled Bills; the first woman to conduct a Senate hearing; the first woman to preside over the Senate; and the first woman to become a senior U.S. senator.[12] Nevertheless, she felt acutely, as many women have subsequently, the marginal role of women in the Senate. She noted in her journal, "I have the same desk as the one used by Mrs. Felton. I guess they wanted as few of them contaminated as possible."[13]

In the House of Representatives, both Norton and Rogers carved out roles for themselves. During the Great Depression in the 1930s, each was a party to the enlarging role of the federal government in steadying the economic and social rudders of the nation and its families. Mary Norton's proudest legislative achievement as chair of the Labor Committee was passage of the landmark Fair Labor Standards Act, which granted dignity to America's workers by including in our laws a national minimum wage, assurance of time-and-a-half pay for overtime, and prohibition on child labor. Edith Nourse Rogers, "Mother of Veterans," rose to chair the Veterans' Affairs Committee in 1947 and steered to passage the GI Bill of Rights, which economically empowered millions of veterans and their families to obtain education and a low-interest home mortgage in recognition of their wartime service. Together, the Fair Labor Standards Act and the GI Bill, perhaps as much as any other legislation, have been credited by historians with helping to build a solid middle class in the United States in the last half of the twentieth century.

NOTES

1. *World Book Encyclopedia*, s.v. "Wilson, Woodrow."
2. Ellen Goodman, "The Second Line," *Boston Globe*, August 5, 1993, 19.
3. Susan J. Tolchin, *Women in Congress, 1917–1976* (Washington, D.C.: U.S. Government Printing Office, 1976), 71.
4. Hope Chamberlin, *A Minority of Members: Women in the United States Congress* (New York: Praeger, 1973), 42.
5. Annabel Paxton, *Women in Congress* (Richmond, Va.: Dietz Press, 1945), 2.
6. U.S. Congress, Office of the Historian, *Women in Congress, 1917–1990* (Washington, D.C.: U.S. Government Printing Office, 1991), 66.
7. Samuel Eliot Morrison and Henry Steele Commager, *The Growth of the American Republic: 1865–1950* (New York: Oxford University Press, 1960), 520.
8. *Webster's New World Dictionary*, 3d college ed., s.v. "flapper."
9. Chamberlin, *A Minority of Members*, 92.
10. George Creel, "The Woman Who Holds Her Tongue," *Collier's*, September 18, 1937, 22.
11. House, *Women in Congress, 1917–1990*, 42.
12. Paxton, *Women in Congress*, 20.
13. Hattie Wyatt Caraway, *Silent Hattie Speaks: The Personal Journal of Hattie Caraway*, ed. Diane D. Kincaid (Westport, Conn.: Greenwood Press, 1979), 44.

Jeannette Rankin

Republican Progressive–Montana
(1917–1919 and 1941–1943)

First Congresswoman

> *I want to be remembered as the only woman who voted to give women the right to vote.*
> Jeannette Rankin, in conversation with Rep. Pat Williams,
> D-Mont., 1968

Jeannette Rankin, the first woman to be elected a member of Congress, fought against war and the diminution of human beings all her life. A pioneering daughter of a pioneering family, she boldly cut a high-water mark for political advancement in her devotion to the causes of peace, humanitarianism, and the empowerment of women. She led the suffrage movement that enfranchised Montana women in 1914. Five years later, at age thirty-six, as a strikingly young member of the U.S. Congress, she introduced legislation that led to the enfranchisement of all women citizens of the United States. Her life's path twice moved into congressional office and then out again, and in each of her terms in Congress she followed deeply held beliefs, twice voting against America's entry into a world war. At age eighty-eight, she remarked to Rep. Pat Williams of Montana, "I want to be remembered as the only woman who voted to give women the right to vote."[1] At the end of her life she mused: "If I had my life to live over, I would do it all again, but this time I'd be nastier."[2]

Rankin was born June 11, 1880, near the remote pioneer town of Missoula, Montana, the eldest of seven children. Missoula, deep in the rugged Bitterroot Range of the Rocky Mountains, bore no resemblance to Boston, New York, or San

Francisco, where Brahmins prided themselves on their aristocratic back-grounds, influential connections, and access to political channels. Missoula was the new America—a sparsely populated, frontier corner far from Wall Street and other havens of power. The mining town world that Rankin knew brimmed with gold and silver prospectors, vast and lonely ranges, wild horses, vigilantes, and ponderosa pine. Centered on the far western side of Montana, Missoula lies near the jagged border with Idaho, along the banks of the Blackfoot River. Adjacent to the Flathead Indian Reservation, it is situated a stone's throw from picturesque settlements like Rattlesnake, Milltown, and Lolo Hot Springs. The arduousness and possibility associated with this pioneering territory ultimately lifted the first of America's daring congressional daughters to serve the nation.

Rankin's lifelong friends, like Belle Winestine, mused that Jeannette gained the strength to become the first woman elected to Congress by leading the cows home by lantern in the pitch black of the mountain night. Her father, John Rankin, described as a hotheaded silver Republican, was a successful rancher and lumber merchant whose family had migrated from Scotland to Canada about 1800.[3] He ventured west during the gold rush era in search of work and labored as a carpenter building homes for settlers who also were moving west. Her shy but adventurous mother, Olive Pickering, of English ancestry, was an elementary school teacher who set out from New Hampshire with one sister in 1878 to find work in Montana.[4] The next year she met and married John.

Their stories alone would inspire a child to courage, and their eldest daughter shared their urge, as she wrote in her journal in 1902, to "Go! Go! Go! It makes no difference where just so you go! go! go! Remember at the first opportunity go!"[5] All the Rankin children heard that message. According to the historian Joan Hoff-Wilson,

The Rankin household represented a curious amalgam of western informality, individualism, and self-reliance, along with upper middle-class aspirations. As a result, most of the Rankin children successfully pursued professional careers; Harriet became dean of women at the University of Montana; Mary an English instructor at the same institution; Edna a lawyer and pioneer in the field of planned parenthood; and Wellington [the only son], one of Montana's most famous trial lawyers and one of the country's largest land owners.[6]

Wellington Rankin eventually rose to serve as state attorney general and associate justice of the Montana Supreme Court, although he narrowly lost an election for the U.S. Senate in 1924.

Montana was not yet a state when Rankin was growing up. Much of the territory was wild and untouched, and even Missoula was in its infancy. Few houses in town had the finishing touches that enterprising John Rankin added for his family, like hot and cold running water, a woodburning stove, and a new bathtub.[7] The Rankins' ranch was outside the settlement, however, and it was there that their firstborn grew to appreciate the freedom and opportunity of this wide open, challenging land.

In 1898, Jeannette Rankin set off for the University of Montana, ultimately majoring in biology. Characterized as an indifferent student, she had no clear idea what she wanted to do with her life when she graduated in 1902.[8] She taught school briefly in Whitehall, about 150 miles southeast of Missoula but saw conventional schooling as tedious and academic. At age twenty-four, in 1904, after the death of her father, she decided to go to Boston to visit her brother, Wellington, who had enrolled as a student at Harvard Law School. It was on this trip that she awakened to social injustice and political realities. In the urban tenements of Boston, Rankin saw a world she had never before experienced, where people lived in squalid conditions, lacking the freedom and skills of practical living she had known on the Montana ranch.[9] The sights, especially the poverty of women and children, motivated her to discover ways to make life more humane for others. She tried to place homeless children in decent living conditions and embarked on a path of discovery both personal and political. She pursued graduate study in Boston briefly and occupied herself with odd jobs.

By 1908, she determined to travel again, this time to San Francisco to familiarize herself with the political reform and suffrage movements brewing on the West Coast. She worked in the fledgling settlement house movement there and again encountered the poverty that afflicted so many women and children. She volunteered to work in a shelter for homeless women but soon decided that she could do more by working to address the conditions that prevented women from supporting themselves.[10]

In the fall of 1908, Rankin left for New York and enrolled at the New York School of Philanthropy, later the Columbia University School of Social Work. During this period, she met Katherine Devereaux Blake, a New York school principal, who much later would join her for the suffrage campaign in Montana. She joined the suffrage movement and resided on East 86th Street in the Suffrage League House. She was influenced by the sociologist Benjamin Kidd, whose *Science of Power* theorized that women prefer principle over narrow interests. After graduating from this school in 1909, she searched again to find the right channel to apply her efforts. She first went home to Missoula to gain perspective and then worked for a while in Spokane, Washington, at the Children's Home Society. Frustrated by this work, as well as her social work in other places, she enrolled at the University of Washington in Seattle and simultaneously joined the state's woman's suffrage movement. It was while working among the poor of Seattle that Rankin realized what other public-spirited women had also realized: without the vote, women's efforts on many issues would be marginal. She helped push at the edges of political change, and one year later the state of Washington enacted woman's suffrage.

The experience helped transform Jeannette Rankin, who became a major political figure in the suffrage movement, traveling across the country to organize and exhort. She worked for suffrage in other states and in 1913 served as field secretary for the National American Woman Suffrage Association. Her next target was Montana, where she organized ceaselessly. She helped kick off parades in which children carried signs reading, "I Want My Mother to Vote."[11] Her part in the Montana campaign took her thousands of miles—on horseback, in cars, and on trains—back and forth across the state so much that she built a political base that resulted in her decision to run for office herself. Thanks in large part to Rankin's efforts, Montana women obtained suffrage on November 3, 1914, six years before it became the law of the United States. The vote was 41,302 to 37,588. Rankin once spoke of the process of gaining women's suffrage in Montana as easier than other struggles because "the spirit of pioneer days was still alive. Men thought of women in the same terms as they thought of themselves."[12] Shortly thereafter, in 1915, she lobbied for women's suffrage in Washington, D.C., and traveled to New Zealand, which in 1893, had become the first nation to grant women full suffrage rights. For several months she observed women using ballots and worked as a seamstress in order to learn firsthand about the plight of women workers. She was inventive in seeking new ways to help others become self-reliant, at one point taking a correspondence course in furniture design.[13]

During this time the West was becoming more of a part of America. In 1910, two years after Theodore Roosevelt had completed his presidency with its emphasis on confronting the wilderness, Congress established Glacier National Park in Montana, just 300 miles north of Missoula, flat against the international border with Canada. Roosevelt, who had lost the presidency to William Howard Taft in 1908, launched the Progressive Party as the base from which to make a third try at the presidency in 1912. At the Republican National Convention in Chicago, he declared, "I'm feeling like a Bull Moose," a term thereafter that was applied to members of the new party. Roosevelt's candidacy lurched toward change, but failed. The president of Princeton University, Woodrow Wilson, a Democrat, became president of the United States. Tragically, wars consumed many of this erudite and gentle man's years as president—a revolution in Mexico that threatened U.S. territorial interests, the Russian Revolution in 1917, and America's entry into the war in Europe in 1917. Wilson's herculean efforts to draft the Fourteen Points that underlay the peace treaty in Europe and his dream of forging a League of Nations to make future wars impossible left him a broken man.

Rankin's life embodied the crosscurrents of the era. A Republican by heritage, she had joined the "social justice wing of the Progressive Movement" and from there went on to embrace suffrage and pacifism.[14] In 1916, she decided to run for the U.S. Congress. She knew many people and had a statewide network of women ready to turn out to help her.[15] Her brother, who became her campaign manager, encouraged her to run and offered his financial and moral support, as he would do throughout her life. Wellington Rankin was active in Progressive Party politics in Montana but would later become one of the leading Republicans, and wealthiest men, in the state.

Nevertheless, Jeannette Rankin's campaign was wholly her own. For example, she cited the fact that the federal government spent $300,000 a year to study hog fodder, while it spent only $30,000 a year to study the needs of children. "If the hogs of the nation are ten times more important than the children, it is high time we [women] made our influence felt," she admonished.[16] Asked why a woman should be elected to Congress, she replied, "There are hundreds of men to care for the nation's tariff and foreign policy and irrigation projects. But there isn't a single woman to look after the nation's greatest asset: its children."[17] Arguments like these won her the votes of the newly enfranchised Montana women, and in 1916 she won election as a Republican by 6,354 votes, even though Montana voted Democratic, giving President Woodrow Wilson approximately a 26,000 vote margin over Charles Evans Hughes, his Republican challenger. On the day she was sworn into Congress, April 2, 1917—still three years before women in thirty-six of the forty-eight states were allowed to vote—Rankin received a standing ovation while carrying a bouquet of yellow and purple flowers given to her that morning at a suffrage rally.[18] "What Miss Rankin remembered best from that day was a white-haired gentleman from Michigan, a seasoned Representative, whom she felt she could sit next to without accusation of flirting. She also recalled the abundance of fancy brass spittoons and the lack of bathrooms for women."[19]

Rankin's college degree, and her subsequent education, made her better educated than most of the men elected to Congress as freshmen members in 1916. Most women in those days were not attending college, much less leaving for New York City afterward to study social work. But, as John F. Kennedy later wrote, "Jeannette Rankin was not a woman who shrank from hard and difficult tasks."[20] Although news reports of the day commented that "'the lady from Montana' packed .44 caliber six-shooters and trimmed her skirts in chaps fur," she worked arduously in Congress for women's suffrage and for peace, planting fragile seeds that would grow by century's end into a broad academic and political movement of legitimate peace studies and peaceful resolution of conflict.[21]

Still, Rankin had to consider more than her own ideals in her congressional voting. She had to consider how her votes would reflect upon women. "A first is expected to be a role model without ever having had one," explains the noted columnist Ellen Goodman. "She's considered a queen bee by some and a token by others. She's supposed to be the reason why a company or an electorate wants 'another one.' But she's never entirely sure if she'll become the excuse that 'we tried one.'" Women after Rankin would find the path less steep. Goodman continues, "A second woman can be a person as well as a pioneer. A second woman is the next in what we can assume is a line."[22] Each woman of Congress has been a pioneer. But the early women were rare and courageous indeed, serving in an age when roles were prescribed and when most women did not work outside the home.

Shortly after taking her seat in the House in 1917, Rankin faced one of the most important votes any member of Congress can face. Early on the morning of April 6, four days after she was sworn in, the House of Representatives prepared to vote on the declaration of war that would take the country into World War I. Rankin had campaigned with the promise that she would not vote to send any Montana men to fight in Europe, but as she entered the chamber she was still unsure how she would vote. Friends and acquaintances on all sides had urged her to vote for war. A vote against war, they said, would make women seem weak and unable to deal with tough decisions in Congress and therefore would set back the cause of women in politics. Although women's suffrage and political participation were causes Rankin held dear, she valued peace more highly. As she herself stated during the presidency of Calvin Coolidge and the World War I debate in Congress, "Small use will it be to save democracy for the race if we cannot at the same time save the race for democracy."[23]

When the roll call reached her name, Rankin remained silent, by most accounts noticeably affected by emotion. But when the clerk called her name on the second round, she had no other choice. The first woman in Congress rose to her feet and spoke, "I want to stand by my country, but I cannot vote for war."[24] Accounts differ about whether she managed actually to say "I vote no" or the clerk simply recorded her vote as a "nay." There is also some disagreement about whether she was overcome with emotion and tears or remained calm. Her speech itself was a significant breach of protocol, because speeches are not officially permitted during House roll call voting. Nevertheless, she had cast her vote, and the reaction was almost immediate. Even though fifty-five other representatives—all men, of course—had also voted against war, Rankin's was the only individual vote criticized by the media. None of the men were accused of betraying the innate weakness of their sex or of dooming the future election of members of their gender. Her tears, real or not, were also widely reported. Some people, seeking to determine the truth of the story, asked Rep. Fiorello LaGuardia if she had wept. He replied, "I do not know, for I could not see because of the tears in my own eyes."[25] In short, Rankin was subject to the insidious double standard by which women are judged as representatives of their sex on matters on which men escape judgment. Nevertheless, she had done what she believed right, stating, "All I'm interested in is what they will say 50 years from now."[26]

For all her attempts not to be judged as a representative of her gender, Rankin cultivated a feminine image. One article described her as "not of the militant-suffragist type; in fact, she is gentle, modest, and a bit retiring."[27] A woman who knew her told the *New York Times*, "Miss Rankin ... dances well, and makes her own hats, and sews, and has won genuine fame among her friends with the wonderful lemon meringue pie that she makes when she hasn't enough other things to do to keep her busy."[28] Still, there was one aspect of the traditional feminine image of the early twentieth century to which Rankin did not conform: she never married. Although she had male friends throughout her life, she was never able to reconcile her freedom to move across the country for her suffrage and peace work with the limitations that she believed marriage would impose. Jeannette Rankin was a solitary figure for much of her life, but she had freely chosen to live as she did.

In that tradition, Rankin cast her famous vote, not on the basis of her own chances for reelection, nor on what her friends and supporters urged her to do, nor even on the basis of advancing the cause of women's suffrage and election to Congress. Perhaps her conscience struggled with all of these thoughts, but what matters is what she did, at the risk of becoming an object of scorn and ridicule.

Rankin did not run for reelection to the House in 1918; her district had been redrawn, divided from one at-large district into districts composed of the eastern and western halves of the state. She decided early on that she had little chance running in the less rural western district and instead announced a 1918 campaign for the Senate.[29] Although she lost in the Republican primary, she went on to run as the candidate of the Nationalist Party, a coalition of socialists, progressives, and populists. She came in a distant third.

Rankin devoted the next two decades of her life to developing her theories of political power, which she modeled on the work of Benjamin Kidd. Rankin used his precepts—that women, preferring principle over narrow interest, look to the future rather than the present—to promote the idea that it would be women's responsibility to bring about peace.[30] Women could be the major civilizing force of the future. Her friend Minni Reynolds, from Washington State, had urged her to link the peace movement with the suffrage movement. She believed that the interests of all people, especially women and children, were best served by achieving world peace. During these years, Rankin lobbied for many peace organizations, including the Women's International League for Peace and Freedom, the Women's Peace Union, and the National Council for the Prevention of War, which she resigned from in 1939 as the group edged toward support of U.S. involvement in World War II.[31]

Her struggle to present a view distinct from the prevailing politics of the times was heroic. It was also controversial. As Hoff-Wilson writes, "Economic conditions shaped Rankin's brand of pacifism between the two World Wars."[32] Americans were leaving the rural life for the cities, and a growing consumerism captured the fancy of the nation, aided by a burgeoning motion picture industry. More and more, Rankin turned away from the consumer society. Although she continued to vote and own property in Montana, she found a second home near Athens, Georgia, where she lived a Spartan life, having purchased sixty-four acres there for $500 in 1924. Until 1943 she had no telephone, electricity, or running water. The Georgia Peace Society, which she founded in 1928, became her base for pacifist activities and remained so until it closed on the eve of World War II. In Georgia, she organized "sunshine" clubs for local boys and girls to teach them "peace habits" and founded a foreign policy study group for adults. The Georgia Peace Society, which Rankin had made into one of the first peace action groups in the country, perennially attempted to defeat the defense appropriations bills of Rep. Carl Vinson, Georgia's powerful man in Washington who chaired the House Committee on Naval Affairs. Because of these endeavors, the Atlanta American Legion Post labeled Rankin a "communist" and successfully kept Brenau College in Gainesville from establishing a "Chair of Peace" for her."[33] Her idealistic pursuits often left her in financial hardship and she was forced to rely on her $125,000 inheritance.

Rankin's brother remained her greatest supporter, but the two chose different ways of living. As one of the largest landowners in the country, he dwelt in obvious wealth in Montana, while she chose a life of seeming semipoverty in Georgia. Whereas he ignored the personal suffering brought about by the Great Depression, she embraced the extreme remedies proposed by Francis E. Townsend of the Townsend Recovery Plan and the writer and social reformer Upton Sinclair. Her brother became a Christian Scientist, but she ridiculed all religion. Their sister Edna's involvement in the birth control movement embarrassed him, but Jeannette Rankin encouraged such activities. "Clearly, Wellington had lost his liberal credentials during the interwar years, while Jeannette had become more and more secure in hers."[34]

By 1940, World War II was raging in Europe, and Rankin's pacifist, isolationist sentiments found a Montana audience once again. Although she had spent much of the interim time living in Georgia, she had maintained a residence in Montana. At sixty, her devotion to the cause of peace had not diminished, nor had her stamina and dedication. She decided to make another run for Congress and was one of the eight women elected to the House in the fall of 1940; again she was elected by a margin of fewer than 10,000 votes. She ran on an explicitly isolationist platform, but later she would be attacked for standing by her campaign promise.[35]

The political climate, however, had changed since Rankin had last been in Congress twenty-four years earlier. The peace movement was now regarded as the home of isolationist left-wing sympathizers and ultraconservative Republicans. Because she was a Republican and a pacifist, Rankin was thus perceived as a conservative in 1940; in truth, she had become more liberal in her views on domestic and foreign policy.[36] In fact, she had voted for the socialist Norman Thomas each time he ran for president.

Soon after her arrival in Congress, on December 8, 1941, Rankin was again faced with a decision that would have far-reaching consequences. This time she did not consult with her friends and relatives as she had in 1917.[37] When the time came for the vote on the entrance of the United States into World War II, Rankin tried futilely to gain recognition from House Speaker Sam Rayburn.[38] If he had recognized her on a "parliamentary inquiry" or "point of personal privilege" prior to the vote, she would have been allowed a few moments to communicate her concerns about the pending vote. But the Speaker ignored her, a disconcerting event for any member. With no other choice, she cast the sole negative vote in both houses of Congress. Her colleagues in the House alternated between booing her and trying to persuade her to change her vote to make the declaration of war unanimous. Later she would say, "I felt an overpowering psychological pressure to vote as a woman against war and violence.... I had voted my lifetime commitment against war."[39]

After her term expired in 1942, Rankin did not consider another run. Probably she realized how unpopular she had made herself in the eyes of her constituents, and perhaps she felt that she had done all she could in Congress. Subsequently, she pursued her peace interests freely, traveling to India five times, including a journey in 1967 at age eighty-eight. She was captivated by the work of the Indian nationalist leader Mohandas Gandhi and his devotion to nonviolent social change. Her brother also underwrote three world trips for her. In 1947, she returned to Montana to nurse her dying mother and thereafter continued her peace activism in Georgia. Her self-sufficient lifestyle persisted throughout her career, and by the 1960s she had built a "Round House" in Georgia. The house consisted of ten wedge-shaped rooms around a common area, but it "never attracted the older, female residents she had planned for."[40] Housing for senior citizens supported by federal housing law would not come about until nearly two decades later.

During the late 1960s, Rankin organized the Jeannette Rankin Brigade to protest the U.S. war in Vietnam, and on January 15, 1968, at age eighty-eight, she marched in Washington with 5,000 women from Union Station to the U.S. Capitol. She spoke at a similar antiwar rally on October 15, 1969, at the University of Georgia.[41]

Certainly she had demonstrated her devotion to a cause higher than political expediency and more humane than bloodshed. Her other congressional initiatives now go largely unnoticed in the shadow of her two war votes and antiwar activities, but Rankin also honored her first campaign promise to work for women's suffrage. She successfully created a thirteen-member Woman Suffrage Committee in the House and became its ranking minority member in 1917.[42] She introduced a resolution in 1919 to support a suffrage amendment, which led to voting rights for all U.S. women citizens (technically the Constitution was amended when she was no longer serving in Congress because three-quarters of the states had to ratify the amendment). She introduced the first bill to grant women citizenship independently of their husbands or whether their spouses were U.S. citizens. She pushed for legislation to ban the exploitation of child labor and to improve working conditions at the Bureau of Engraving and Printing. She promoted legislation giving women a role in commercial food preservation to help with the war effort during World War II, conducted investigations into unsatisfactory labor practices, and sponsored a women's health program bill, which later was enacted as the Sheppard-Towner Act.[43] Years later, she would say with a wry smile, "The government has always offered instruction in the hygiene of pigs."[44] As she herself admitted, however, little could be accomplished while the nation was preoccupied with war, as it was during both her congressional terms.

Jeannette Rankin was not a career politician. But she was highly political in the sense that a labor organizer is political. She built constituencies and she brought new people together to exert their common interest on the political process. Politicians generally broker between existing constituencies. She brought new vitality.

Rankin built her life around causes so closely tied to morality and humanity that no one could accuse her of a mere hunger for power. She sacrificed power for her principles in the cause of world peace, and her congressional career was cut short twice because of her votes cast against U.S. involvement in both world wars. As William Allen White wrote on December 10, 1941, in the *Emporia (Kan.) Gazette*, "When in 100 years from now, courage, sheer courage based on moral indignation, is celebrated in this country, the name of Jeannette Rankin, who stood firm for her faith, will be written in monumental bronze, not for what she did but for the way she did it."[45]

Rankin served only four years in Congress, yet she scored a deep mark on the political landscape as a woman of peace, standing in stark relief to the prevailing political winds. At the close of the twentieth century, she no doubt would be heartened by the achievements of the past half-century that inch the world toward peace—the United Nations, the U.S. Institute for Peace, nuclear arms reduction, a developing body of thought concerned with conflict resolution, and growing attention in the field of psychology to the roots in the human psyche of the "construct of an enemy" and how to transcend it.

Crossing new boundaries was perhaps second nature to those who lived their lives on the frontier. Rankin told stories of "operating her father's sawmill, of sewing up a horse torn by barbed wire."[46] When she was in her eighties, she was building cooperative housing on her Georgia farm for unemployed, homeless women so that they could live and become financially secure and leading a march on Washington against the war in Vietnam.[47] She died of a heart attack in 1973, one month shy of her ninety-third birthday, in her Carmel, California, apartment after a protracted illness.

In May 1985, Jeannette Rankin became the first and only congresswoman in U.S. history to have dedicated in her honor a life-size sculpture in the Capitol Rotunda. Upon its dedication, Sen. John Melcher of Montana paid her the ultimate tribute: "Jeannette Rankin—who gave a new definition to courage."[48] Like the early American pioneers, the first woman in Congress was hardly able to explore all of the new territory, but she set in motion the political journey for women that has become a twentieth-century odyssey.

NOTES

1. Quoted by Rep. Pat Williams, interview by the author, Washington, D.C., July 1995.
2. Joan Hoff-Wilson, Remarks made at the Jeannette Rankin statue dedication, Proceedings in the Rotunda, U.S. Capitol, May 1, 1985, in *Jeannette Rankin Statue Dedication* (Washington, D.C.: U.S. Government Printing Office, 1987), 59.
3. Sen. John Melcher, Remarks made at the Jeannette Rankin statue dedication, Proceedings in the Rotunda, U.S. Capitol, May 1, 1985, in *Jeannette Rankin Statue Dedication,* 34–36; Hoff-Wilson, Remarks at statue dedication, 21.
4. Kevin Giles, *Flight of the Dove: The Story of Jeannette Rankin* (Beaverton, Ore.: Touchstone Press, 1980), 21.
5. Quoted in ibid., 19.
6. Hoff-Wilson, Remarks at statue dedication, 21.
7. Giles, *Flight of the Dove,* 22.
8. M. S. Davis, "Jeannette Rankin—A Time Line," in *Jeannette Rankin Statue Dedication,* 70.
9. Giles, *Flight of the Dove,* 33.
10. Shawn Lake, "Jeannette Rankin: The Woman Who Voted No," *Cricket* 21 (March 1994): 44.
11. Ibid.
12. Hope Chamberlin, *A Minority of Members: Women in the United States Congress* (New York: Praeger, 1973), 6.
13. Giles, *Flight of the Dove,* 33.
14. Hoff-Wilson, Remarks at statue dedication, 22.
15. Chamberlin, *A Minority of Members,* 7.
16. Lake, "Jeannette Rankin," 44.
17. Chamberlin, *A Minority of Members,* 103.
18. Kate Walbert, "Remembering Jeannette," *New York Times,* April 2, 1993, Op-Ed sec.
19. Ibid.
20. John F. Kennedy, "Three Women of Courage," *McCall's,* January 1958, 37.

21. Walbert, "Remembering Jeannette."
22. Ellen Goodman, "The Second Line," *Boston Globe,* August 5, 1993, 19.
23. Chamberlin, *A Minority of Members,* 103.
24. "Pacifists Fight the War Bill to the Bitter End," *Helena (Mont.) Independent,* April 6, 1917, 1.
25. Chamberlin, *A Minority of Members,* 98.
26. Ibid., 95.
27. "Our Busy Congresswoman," *Literary Digest,* August 11, 1917.
28. "Miss Rankin's Vote a Personal Triumph," *New York Times,* November 12, 1916.
29. Giles, *Flight of the Dove,* 116.
30. Cited in Hannah Josephson, *Jeannette Rankin: First Lady in Congress* (New York: Bobbs-Merrill, 1974), 107.
31. Chamberlin, *A Minority of Members,* 13.
32. Hoff-Wilson, Remarks at statue dedication, 24.
33. Ibid.
34. Ibid., 25.
35. Esther Stineman, *American Political Women: Contemporary and Historical Profiles* (Littleton, Colo.: Libraries Unlimited, 1980), 127.
36. Hoff-Wilson, Remarks at statue dedication, 25.
37. Josephson, *Jeannette Rankin,* 160.
38. "Nazis Accused of Pushing Tokyo to War," *Montana Standard,* December 10, 1941, 1.
39. "Stories of Our Times: She Voted No on Two Wars," *Modern Maturity,* December 1983–January 1984.
40. Davis, "Jeannette Rankin—A Time Line," 75.
41. Ibid.
42. Chamberlin, *A Minority of Members,* 10.
43. U.S. Congress, House, Office of the Historian, *Women in Congress, 1917–1990* (Washington, D.C.: U.S. Government Printing Office, 1991), 208.
44. Rep. Claudine Schneider, Remarks made at the Jeannette Rankin statue dedication, Proceedings in the Rotunda, U.S. Capitol, May 1, 1985, in *Jeannette Rankin Statue Dedication,* 15.
45. Quoted in "Stories of Our Times."
46. Walbert, "Remembering Jeannette."
47. Melcher, Remarks at statue dedication, 35.
48. Ibid., 36.

Mary Teresa Norton
Democrat–New Jersey (1925–1951)
First Urban Congresswoman

No novice in politics was ever more innocent than I.

Mary Norton, "Autobiography"

In 1924, Mary Teresa Norton became the first Democratic woman elected to the House of Representatives and the first from an urban center east of the Mississippi River.[1] She thus cut a fresh path for women of ordinary means to gain election to Congress. Of middle-class, Roman Catholic background, she toiled relentlessly, and against great odds, to achieve fair pay and decent working conditions for America's newly industrialized workers and to allow them to bargain collectively for the value of their work. She was the first member of Congress, male or female, to chair three House committees, including the powerful Labor Committee.

Norton's most historic work involved her partnership with President Franklin D. Roosevelt in gaining passage of his New Deal legislation in the 1930s. An American original, she came to champion the cause of blue- and pink-collar working people. She understood instinctively the new America she was asked to represent in the halls of Congress, block by block, family by family. Her career embodied the links in American urban politics between the big-city Democratic machine, the labor movement, and the Catholic Church and its social reform mission that were essential to the passage of the New Deal legislation. For her efforts as chair of the District of Columbia Committee, which resulted in, among other things, a law providing the district with self-government, she became known as the mayor of Washington.

Born in Jersey City, New Jersey, on March 7, 1875, Norton was first-generation American, the eldest daughter of four surviving children (of seven) born to her Irish-Catholic immigrant parents. Her early years were joyful ones, and her autobiography is replete with warm reminiscences of her parents and siblings. Her "worldly and ambitious" mother, Maria Shea, from County Langford, Ireland, had hoped to become a teacher.[2] The eldest of eight children, she had been educated, "as was the custom for well-bred Irish girls."[3] In 1860, at age nineteen, concerned about supporting the family after her father died, she traveled to Liverpool and sailed from there to America. The stormy sailing took three months and left her physically weakened. By the time she arrived at Castle Garden in New York City, she had become seriously ill, having contracted typhoid fever. The doctor who cared for her over several weeks at Bellevue Hospital and learned of her ambition to become a teacher suggested she take the job as governess for his four children. She worked for him for ten years until she married.[4] Meanwhile, with the self-confidence of many Irish women, she paid the way for her two sisters and two brothers to join her in America.[5]

Norton's father, Thomas Hopkins, was the eldest son of a prosperous farmer and, under Irish law, destined to inherit the family farm in County Langford. But he hated farming. At age sixteen, in 1854, he left a note for his parents, borrowed $200 from a family safe, and sailed to America.[6] He worked briefly as an itinerant farmhand, being paid with food and lodging, and as a contractor. After working as a railroad laborer, going into the South and West, eventually he landed a permanent job with his uncle, a contractor in New York. There he became reacquainted with Maria, who had been a childhood playmate in Ireland, and in 1870, Thomas and Maria married. By 1875, when their daughter Mary was born, they had moved to a small frame house that Thomas had bought for $1,000 in Jersey City. Their first home had been near Brewster in New York State, but the couple had lost their first-born child there—and almost Maria's life as well—from the lack of adequate medical attention. In Jersey City four children were born to them: James, then Mary, and after her Anna and Loretta.

Adjacent to New York City and within eyeshot of the Statue of Liberty, Jersey City is perched just about as far east as one can journey along the banks of the Hudson River. In the late nineteenth century, it was a rough-and-tumble, working-class city of immigrants, largely Catholic. It was not part of the "liberal states of Massachusetts or New York, nor was it [one of] the better educated suburbs of New Jersey, reputed to be more enlightened and progressive than working class Hudson County."[7] Jersey City was a town that meant business—Colgate, American Can, the Atlantic and Pacific Tea Company, the Mueller Macaroni Factory were located there. Families in its neighborhoods would bear heavily the wounds of the Great Depression and the casualties that were to come in World War II.

Of the many immigrants who settled in the cities east of the Mississippi, Irish Americans enjoyed the advantages of being able to speak English and of having arrived early on U.S. shores. By 1924, Irish Americans, and notably the powerful Democratic mayor Frank Hague, shaped and dominated the political life of Jersey City—and ultimately New Jersey—by the huge electoral victories his Democratic organization was able to achieve in the northern and eastern parts of the state. Hague established a reputation as one of the most powerful political bosses in U.S. history.[8] First elected mayor in 1917, he held sway until 1947. From humble beginnings he rose from a custodial position at City Hall to become a legend as a patronage politician who, by the time of his death, had accumulated millions of dollars in personal wealth. It was rumored that he had more than $50 million on deposit in overseas bank accounts during the Great Depression, when other families were penniless. But Hague was also a visionary: while he was mayor, Jersey City became the first city in America to introduce fluoridated water and built one of the largest urban hospitals of its day. His influence as a political boss in New Jersey and as vice-chair of the National Democratic Committee also helped Franklin D. Roosevelt win the presidential election of 1932.

Hague saw the power of the women's vote unleashed by suffrage and made an effort to place women in important party positions. As vice-chair of the Democratic National Committee, he declared, "I want to be the first leader in the Democratic Party to help elect a woman to Congress."[9] And he succeeded. But there could have been no more unsuspecting a target of his vision than Mary Hopkins Norton.

As much as Norton's life was inspired by the strength of her parents and love of her brother and sisters, it was also deeply touched by tragedy. At age seventeen, she lost her mother. As the eldest daughter, she was expected to run the household, which she did until her father remarried four years later. She recalled, "If mother [had] lived, [my sisters] probably would have gone on to college, but my father was definitely opposed to women going to college. Since I was the eldest daughter ... the running of the home became my job."[10] After her father remarried, however, Mary and her two younger sisters moved to New York City to live together and attend Packard Business College. "Being together, independent, and free from a stepmother's criticisms meant more to us than living in our father's home and having our bills paid. It certainly did teach all three of us self-reliance."[11]

In the late nineteenth century, women working outside the home was a new phenomenon. But Norton had an extraordinary drive to better her situation. After graduating from the business college, she began her career in a bustle factory as a stenographer for nine dollars a week. Norton disliked the requirement that the employees wear the bustles made by the company. "As nature had taken care of me," she stated, "I felt reluctant to add anything that was obviously unnecessary."[12]

In every job she took, Norton ran up against male prejudice. "It was a time when women were feeling their way and finding new outlets in the labor market," she said later. "They were not accepted freely in positions of responsibility."[13] Norton was clever enough, however, to negotiate her way forward. When she was hired by a large corporation to fill a secretarial position, she was told by its president, "I don't want any woman around here upsetting my business." She gradually learned that the men on the staff resented her presence because it forced them to behave like gentlemen—wearing their suit coats and not smoking. She confronted them directly and eased the situation by telling them that she liked men to be comfortable.[14]

In 1909 she left the business world to marry Robert Francis Norton, a widower eleven years her senior who had two grown children. Robert Norton operated a cooperage business. Their only son—also named Robert—was born the following year, but he died when he was one week old. His death left Mary Norton devastated after a pregnancy complicated by pneumonia and severe physical illness. The loss was deepened when she learned that she could have no more children.

It was the Catholic Church, in the person of Monsignor Patrick Edwards Smyth, that encouraged Norton back to a useful life. Monsignor Smyth needed help in finding a place that would care for the young children of working mothers. After first volunteering to care for the children herself, Norton aided him in establishing the Queen's Daughters Day Nursery in Jersey City.[15] In 1910, she stalwartly "turned from her baby's empty cradle and resolutely forced herself to face the crowded cots in the Day Nursery."[16] This effort may have been the beginning of her career in politics:

Something had to take the place of the children I could not have. I cannot say that politics and Congress ever filled the place. They couldn't. But at least I've had an active life and an interesting one, with the opportunity to do a little to help other mothers more fortunate than I was, and their children.[17]

Norton was elected secretary of the organization and three years later became its president, a position she held for twelve years, until her election to Congress. The day nursery was a forerunner of early childhood learning centers across America and remained a lasting legacy.

Although she was unaware of it, Norton was building a formidable political base. Hundreds of mothers and children came to the nursery. During World War I, Monsignor Smyth persuaded her to organize a Red Cross workroom at her parish—Saint Joseph's—with one hundred sewing machines and an equal number of workers. Because the war effort had forced more women to work outside the home, the nursery constantly expanded and Norton sought financial support from local leaders. She thus met key business leaders in Jersey City, including many Republicans, who never forgot her, nor she them. Ultimately, they would lend their blessing to her candidacy, as would their spouses, and, like the ward heelers in the Democratic machine, contribute to her congressional campaigns.

Norton had a knack for being conciliatory at the right times and for telling stories, an art she learned from her father. When she attempted to raise funds at a Democratic political meeting of men in the Eleventh Ward in 1918, she was told to cool her heels in the waiting room. When she finally was ushered in, she relieved the tension by telling a story:

[O]n election day, years ago, my father was in a bad spot because he did not like the Democratic candidate for President. That morning he was complaining bitterly and saying he'd be damned if he'd vote for that crackpot, when my mother said innocently, "But Tom, I thought you always said the party was bigger than the man." At that he gave her a dirty look and went out, slamming the door behind him. Later in the day when he came home, she asked, "Well, Tom, how did you vote?" "You know damned well how I voted," he replied with a grin.[18]

According to Norton the story was a huge success, with everyone laughing and applauding, and she left with a contribution.[19]

Of course, in Jersey City, the obvious person to turn to for help with the nursery expansion was Mayor Frank Hague. Hague's family background, like Norton's, was Irish, and no doubt he appreciated her Irish heritage, her tenaciousness, and, as a result of the suffrage movement, her political value as a woman. He supported her cause and then became her political godfather. He encouraged a reluctant Norton, first in 1920 to serve on the Democratic State Committee, and in 1923 helped her to earn a seat on the Hudson County Board of Freeholders. Hague, however, had to do a great deal of talking to persuade Norton. Until she became involved personally, she did not understand the relevance of politics to her life and the social welfare work she was doing. When Hague first proposed that she join the state committee in 1920, she replied, "Why don't you ask a prominent suffrage leader to serve? ... I am not a politician."[20] He replied that "[n]o women knew anything about politics. They would just have to learn. I know that you *are* [a politician]."[21] In fact, her first act as freeholder was to draft a resolution creating a maternity hospital with county funds—the only one in the United States to be so financed—named after Hague's mother, Margaret Hague.[22]

Norton guardedly agreed to accept the position, with the understanding that she would have to serve for only one year and would have no substantive duties. Three months later, after the suffrage amendment giving women the vote had been ratified, Norton received a message to call Hague at City

Hall. "I was informed that a meeting was set for next week to organize the women of Jersey City to take part in the campaign for president.... I would have to preside. I was horrified and indignant. I reminded the mayor that he said it was an empty honor, that I would have nothing to do." Hague replied, "Oh, but then you didn't have the vote. We were just anticipating. Now it is a fact and this is your job."[23] Frank Hague had managed to trump her. And so Norton—a capable woman who was not likely to overreach her authority—found herself with a new job.

She sought refuge in the wisdom of her trusted brother, James Hopkins, whom she had always tried to "imitate and whose approval meant everything to me."[24] Stopping by the high school where he was principal, she told him how she had been trapped by Hague and that she lacked the assurance to speak in public. Hopkins advised her that it would be no different from presiding at a nursery board meeting. And remember, he said, "no woman in the audience would probably do the job any better."[25] His words comforted Norton, and she remembered them throughout her career. Shortly thereafter, her brother died at age fifty-seven, after having risen to the position of superintendent of the Jersey City schools. After her brother's death, the grief-stricken Norton told Hague she could not face the county election. He replied brusquely, "So you are yellow. I'm surprised. I thought you had guts, but you are just like most people. You can't take it, and I was silly to think you would make a career in politics. What do you think Jim would think of you now?" Tearfully, Norton told the mayor he was a brute and later revealed that "never in my life did I feel more like striking a person."[26]

Norton's autobiography leaves unstated the connection between her brother and the Hague political network in Jersey City. Hague's tight-fisted control of all appointments, his command over all aspects of Jersey City government, and his generous tax policies, which provided support for public education, meant that James Hopkins was at the center of political life in Jersey City. How ironic it was that he died one year before his sister's election to the U.S. House of Representatives.

As she began her duties as a state committeewoman in 1920, Norton's naiveté was profound. She admits in her autobiography, "No novice in politics was ever more innocent than I."[27] In one of her first campaign appearances, she launched into a heartfelt defense of the League of Nations only to have her audiences run cold. In her autobiography, she reflects:

Irish bitterness, growing out of the long struggle with the Crown, undoubtedly colored the feeling of the Irish toward the League also, and this supposedly would influence many Americans of Irish descent in this country and would affect the outcome of the election in cities with large Irish-American populations. It posed a problem for the Democrats in Jersey City.[28]

Norton was fast learning about interest group politics and the conflicts between official party positions and the views of her constituency.

She continued her political ascension with her election in 1923 as the first woman on the Hudson County Board of Freeholders and the first female freeholder in all of New Jersey. With encouragement and pressure from Frank Hague, despite her mourning, she became convinced that the responsible course of action was to run for the office as her brother had expected her to do. She served one and one-half years, and the lessons she learned enlightened her for the congressional career that was to follow. "In 1923, we did not have old age pensions, nor did we have unemployment insurance, we did not have federal aid for the blind nor for children deprived of parents through death or desertion."[29] She confronted the poverty and need of her constituents at the county level, ultimately transforming those human needs into federal legislation that came to be called Social Security, unemployment compensation, and child welfare. One instance she remembered vividly was of a

nice old couple who, at the end of their resources and very near the end of their lives, entered the county home for the aged. They could not remain together. There was one building for men and another for women. It was the end of their life together. As long as they were able to walk outside, they would meet and walk and talk together. Old age pensions have been a godsend.[30]

Norton was not always treated gently when she gave speeches. During the early 1920s, as she ventured into an industrial district organizing women in her state committee role, she faced a large, male-dominated audience. A man stood up in the back of the hall and said roughly, "Our women are home looking after their children—where you ought to be." Norton replied:

How very fortunate they are to have children! That privilege has been denied to me. If I had children, I'd certainly be at home with them now if they needed me. But since I haven't, I am here to talk to you about a new responsibility that has been given to women [voting].[31]

In 1924, with Hague's help, Norton won nomination and election to the U.S. House of Representatives by a plurality of 17,000 votes. From 1916 to 1940, 56 percent of the women elected to the House were widows succeeding their husbands in office. Norton, in contrast, was elected in her own right. "Hundreds of faithful members of the day nursery" had become her ardent supporters, and Norton commented, "[M]y considered opinion is that nothing else takes the place of a well-disciplined organization in winning elections."[32]

Norton was forty-nine years old when she was elected and fifty when she was sworn in. Little did she realize that a long chapter of her life was still ahead and that her career would proceed in tandem with Frank Hague's; he would leave the mayoralty in 1947, and she the House shortly thereafter.

Their political careers traced the mid-twentieth-century history of New Jersey and Democratic urban politics. "Throughout those years she steadfastly supported Democratic Party positions and Hague's nominees for office. For her loyalty to the party, President Roosevelt acknowledged her by official letter in 1942 after a bitter intraparty squabble: 'Dear Mary, You are a grand girl.'"[33] The relationship between Norton and Hague benefited each of them; Norton gained from Hague's knowledge and influence, and Hague was sometimes accused of using Norton "to give respectability to his machine politics."[34] *Newsweek* at the time referred to them as the duke and duchess of eastern New Jersey.[35]

So few women had served in Congress when Norton was first elected that misconceptions about their role in it were common. The morning after her election, Norton recalled, reporters and photographers started ringing the doorbell early. She counted forty reporters before noon.[36] One photographer had to be rebuffed when he asked her to pose for photographs standing by a stove and hanging clothes on the clothesline. She informed him that she expected to deal with legislation in Congress, adding, "I do not expect to cook, and I do not expect to wash any clothes in Congress." But in a housewifely manner she added, "It took days to get the smell out of my living room curtains," because the "flashlights were taken with powder in those days before smokeless bulbs."[37]

On one occasion after assuming her duties in the House of Representatives, Norton became engaged in debate with a male member of Congress. At one point he said sarcastically that he would "yield to the lady." Norton retorted, "I'm no lady; I'm a member of Congress, and I'll proceed on that basis!"[38] She was nicknamed "Battling Mary" by Republican representative Thomas Blanton of Texas, her nemesis, who, as fellow committee member, used parliamentary tactics to derail her bills concerning the District of Columbia. She referred to him as the most disliked man in the House.

For the first six years of her career, Norton was relegated to minority status in a House controlled by Republicans, although during this time she did not lack for work. During the 1920s she introduced bills to investigate the Eighteenth Amendment, which instituted the prohibition of alcohol, and a few years later the first bill to repeal it; she also introduced a bill to exempt from taxation the first $5,000 of a family's income. Her early legislative interests included measures to create a board of industrial adjustment to mediate the labor-management disturbances common in the coal-mining industry; to permit foreign-born wives and children of citizens to enter the country on a nonquota basis (immigration equality); to provide for more effective enforcement of the Narcotics Drug Act; to improve compensation benefits for mothers who had lost sons during World War I; and to set up a Welfare Board in the District of Columbia that would separate the penal and welfare functions of that city's government. In 1928, at the request of Al Smith, she headed the Democratic Women's National Speaker's Bureau.[39] Smith, also a Catholic and former governor of New York, had lost the presidential election that year and would run against Franklin Roosevelt, current governor of New York, in 1932.

After the election of a Democratic Congress in 1930, Norton became the chair of the Committee on the District of Columbia, the first of the three committees she was eventually to lead. She served in that position from 1931 until 1937, governing a city that at that time had no municipal government of its own. All bills relating to its governance and finances went through Norton's committee.

Although Norton's rise was steady, Congress remained an uphill climb for her, not much easier than it had been for Jeannette Rankin, the first elected congresswoman. She faced both subtle and not-so-subtle prejudice. When she accepted the chair of the District of Columbia Committee, Rep. Frank Bowman, a committee member, declared, "This is the first time in my life I have been controlled by a woman." Norton responded, "It's the first time I've had the privilege of presiding over a body of men, and I rather like the prospect."[40]

The citizens of Washington, D.C., grew to admire the capable woman who governed them, and she came to be called the "mayor of Washington." She conscientiously worked to fund a new tuberculosis hospital and to clean up slum areas.[41] Norton got no votes from the District of Columbia citizens, and she earned no points with her own New Jersey constituents for this work; she did it out of compassion and conscience, eventually achieving passage of legislation that merged the two District street railway companies, provided a sewage disposal plant and new municipal building, and legalized boxing and liquor. Most important, she attempted to give the city self-government, since the District of Columbia had remained a stepchild of Congress from the founding of the Republic and had no home rule.

In 1934 Norton became the first woman to chair a major political party in any state, the New Jersey State Committee (1932–1935 and again during 1940–1944). She played a part in every major Democratic Party Convention for the next two decades, becoming the first co-chair of the national party platform committee in 1944 and, in 1948, chair of the Credentials Committee. At the convention in 1932 she had the opportunity to second the nomination of Al Smith, the first Roman Catholic to be nominated for the presidency, and simultaneously turned down a nomination for vice president herself. Although Hague and Norton had actively supported Smith's candidacy, Hague immediately switched his support to Roosevelt when it became apparent that his chances were bleak, and Norton concurred.

After Franklin Roosevelt took office as the president of the United States in 1932, Norton worked hard to gain passage of his New Deal legislation to lead the nation out of the Great Depression. She supported measures to stem the effects of the depression—the National Recovery Act, the Home Owner's Loan Corporation, the Mortgage Moratorium, the Reconstruction Finance Corporation, the Works Progress Administration, the Home Loan Bank, the Glass-Steagall Banking Act, and the creation of the Securities and Exchange Commission. Although she worked hard to pass labor legislation, characteristically she credited Rep. Bill Connery Jr., D-Mass., with having done more than she had done to pass the landmark National Labor Relations Act of 1935.

During Roosevelt's first term Norton's husband—who had remained at their New Jersey residence—became ill. His health deteriorated after a heart condition made worse by the anxiety of the depression. To care for him while she was away, Norton hired a housekeeper and a nurse. The Nortons spent their savings for nursing care. Thus, her work became essential to hold the household together. Mary Norton returned home to nurse her husband during his last three weeks of life. When he died, she was fifty-nine years of age. In Washington, she continued to live with her unmarried sister, Anne, who had been staying with her since her first term in 1925.[42]

Later, in 1941, she helped usher through the extension of the draft law (which passed by a single vote, 203-202). She notes in her autobiography that bills vital to America's defense often just scraped through Congress and that had this bill gone down to defeat the story of World War II might have been different. Her vote subjected her to verbal abuse, some calling her a murderess. During World War II she voted for all defense measures. But her most important work was done when she became chair of the Labor Committee, during one of the busiest eras in the committee's history—the second term of Roosevelt's New Deal. She later wrote, "During my first years in Congress, under a Republican Administration, I cannot recall a single law passed in the interest of the working men and women of this country."[43]

Norton chaired the Labor Committee from 1937 to 1946. She accepted the position when she was sixty-two years old; at an age "when most women contemplate devoting their remaining days to a leisurely household routine and the enjoyment of their grandchildren, I ... entered the most turbulent period of my career."[44] As chair of this committee, Norton was always considered pro-labor, a stance occasionally but vehemently opposite that of Frank Hague, her political "chief," as she referred to him. Hague had tried to drive the Congress of Industrial Organizations (CIO) out of Jersey City in 1937 because it was testing the constitutionality of a local ordinance forbidding the distribution of circulars without a permit. Hague was heard to say, "I am the law," and he appreciated no tampering with the internal workings of Jersey City.[45] Nevertheless, although she was deeply indebted to Hague for her start in politics, Norton was not inclined to take orders from anyone. The American Federation of Labor was opposing the legislation, as did Hague, while the CIO, along with Norton, was supporting it.

Later, when she had become Labor Committee chair, Norton protested when the Naval Affairs Committee infringed on her turf by passing a labor bill that should have come through her committee. She was not shy about expressing her belief that the reason for the incident was that a woman headed the Labor Committee.[46] She had no way to recover jurisdiction over that bill, and the episode reinforced her belief that women had a long way to go to win equality with men. "Those who really know our social system know that women have never had very much opportunity.... Women are going to be pushed in a corner, and very soon at that." She also predicted that there will not be "a dozen women in Congress in our day because women don't vote for women."[47] Even in her autobiography, she regretted that she had not been able to transfer her lifetime of experience to other women who were groping and unsure of themselves.

Still, during those years, Norton helped to create the first body of labor law for the United States. Unfortunately, she then had to watch it teeter in the late 1940s at the close of her career. As she describes it,

For ten years, I was destined to occupy a position in the center of a prolonged and relentless struggle between two gigantic forces in the economic life of this nation. On one side millions of American working men and women battled to gain new rights and privileges ... on the other side, diehards in industry, who resented and feared this new giant, fought back with every resource of power and money they could command, yielding ground inch by inch.[48]

Norton was determined to put a bill before Congress that would "place a floor under wages and a ceiling over hours for some twenty million unorganized, exploited, and heretofore defenseless American workers."[49]

Her most outstanding legislative achievement during this period was the passage of the wages and hours bill, known officially as the Fair Labor Standards Act of 1938. This bill established a minimum wage of twenty-five cents an hour and a maximum work week of forty hours, provided for time-and-a-half pay for overtime, and prohibited child labor, backed by strong enforcement provisions.[50] Clearly, this bill was a pivotal part of Roosevelt's legislative program, and it was also considered a major victory for organized labor, still a fledgling movement.

Passing the wages and hours bill took twelve months of Mary Norton's life. She devoted all her time and energy to this legislation, skipping her vacation to read testimony. In order to get the bill through the House, Norton first had to push it through the House Rules Committee. This proved to be quite a task because both Republicans and southern Democrats opposed this pro-labor legislation. She recounted, "Wages had always been lower in the South than in the North, and now textile plants and shoe factories in New England were closing down as Northern capital, lured by the promise of cheap labor, moved down South."[51] She went on national radio to urge the voters to pressure their representatives for passage.[52] Finally, Norton had to resort to a parliamentary device, the discharge petition, to bring the bill out of the committee. She collected the requisite 218 signatures on the petition, a process that took seventeen days, and brought the bill to a vote on the floor.

Debate on the floor of the House centered on wage differences between North and South, which had been written into the bill. Debate went on for five days before a vote was taken. By a vote of 216-198, the bill was sent back to committee, even though Norton had tried to accommodate the opposition by drawing a line across the nation and establishing a different set of wages on each side. The failure of this bill was the greatest disappointment of her career because she had wanted to outlaw sweatshops, starvation wages, and child labor. The day after the vote, Norton's telephone rang with a call from President Roosevelt. "Sorry about the bill," he said. "What are you going to do now?" Norton replied immediately, "Give you another bill, Mr. President, one that I hope we'll get through."[53] The bill was rewritten without the offending wage differences, but again, a discharge petition was necessary to bring it to a vote. Norton gathered 218 signatures a second time, although this time the process took her only 212 minutes.[54]

As she would do so many times in her political life, Norton put a human face on the reason for proposed legislation. On the wages and hours bill, she recalled,

A woman who worked in a toy factory told me she was obliged to report for work every day even though she was paid by the piece and frequently the work would be held up by material shortages, which would mean that she got no work that day—and no pay. She would have to stay there just the same, she said, sometimes all day and into the evening. There was no overtime law then. One week her pay envelope contained $3.45 for six days' work![55]

When the bill came to a vote the second time, and after considerable assistance from the Roosevelt White House, it was passed. Norton herself said of this bill, "I am prouder of getting that bill through the House than anything else I've ever done in my life."[56]

World War II, and the stresses and emotions of serving in high elected office during a period of grave uncertainty, complicated Norton's later career. She called the period one of "unadulterated misery." On a Sunday afternoon in December 1941, at age sixty-six and ill with a 103-degree fever brought on by the "grippe" (influenza), she learned that she would have to assemble with her colleagues in full session at the Capitol to receive the president of the United States. As she describes Roosevelt's speech in her autobiography:

The president looked grim, not the smiling, confident man we had welcomed so many times to the Capitol since 1933, a serious, determined President, intent on the responsibility that had come to him as Commander-in-Chief of the Army and Navy of the United States. He told us how the Japanese had pulled their sneak attack on Pearl Harbor, even while their envoys were here deceiving us with talk of peace. He ended his address with these unforgettable words: "There is no blinking at the fact that our people, our territory, and our interests are in grave danger. With confidence in our armed forces, with the unbounded determination of our people, we will attain the inevitable triumph—so help us God."

He then asked Congress to declare a state of war between the United States and the Japanese Empire. There were not many dry eyes in the House Chamber, and I know my own were moist. I was weak from my illness and fearful that emotion would conquer my determination not to show any emotion.... Thirty minutes after the President had finished speaking, both Houses of Congress had passed a resolution declaring "a state of war exists between the United States and Japan."[57]

When Franklin Roosevelt died in 1945, Mary Norton was one of the select members of Congress who rode in the funeral cortege to Hyde Park. She wrote in her autobiography that Roosevelt's accomplishments rivaled Lincoln's, and then she recalled the memorial service:

The Episcopal burial service was read. Soldiers fired a volley across the grave. There was the sound of taps—and little Fala (Roosevelt's dog) barking sharply. Someone removed the flag from the casket, folded it, and handed it to Mrs. Roosevelt. And the body of Franklin Delano Roosevelt was lowered into the grave. His soul, I knew, was with the God he had served so well.[58]

Although she generally had supported the Democratic Party leadership and gradually had risen through the ranks, Norton remained close to the interests of her Jersey City constituents. She introduced and got passed many pieces of legislation that would help them, including authorization for a veterans' hospital for the state. She especially wanted to help the poor and working-class women, and she devoted much of her life to founding or enlarging institutions to serve them. The Queen's Daughters Day Nursery, the Red Cross Employment Center, the county maternity hospital—all were directed at improving the plight of working-class women in industrial New Jersey. As chair of the District of Columbia Committee, she had shepherded bills through Congress to allow women police in the District and to grant women the right to serve on juries. As chair of the Labor Committee, she enlarged pension equity for women through collective bargaining along with the old-age pension system. She once wrote, "I think that women should first of all be interested in other women, interested in other women's projects, their dreams, and their ambitions. It's up to women to stand for each other."[59]

Nevertheless, Norton occasionally did things that seemed counterproductive to advancing the cause of women. In 1932, she refused to allow her name to be placed in nomination for vice president at the Democratic National Convention. "Women deluged me with letters criticizing me for what they regarded as a betrayal of the cause of women," she said, but added that the nomination would have been only "a grand gesture" because John Nance Garner had already been chosen by a majority of delegates as the nominee.[60] Norton insisted that she be "considered as a worker and a person rather than as a woman" and "that she had no desire to receive concessions because of her sex," although "she did not anticipate giving any concessions" either.[61] This attitude is characteristic of many women pioneers in Congress; Sen. Margaret Chase Smith also firmly stated that she "never apologized for being a woman."[62]

Norton served in Congress, in large part, during an era when women members still represented the entire female sex, as Jeannette Rankin had when she was elected. Thus, her legislative priorities in each of her committee assignments reflect her belief that women should "stand for women." On the District of Columbia Committee, for example, Norton fostered a bill that called for equal training and treatment for policewomen in the District of Columbia and another bill that won women in the District the right to serve on juries.[63] In her first term, she sponsored a bill that allowed American women who married foreigners to retain their U.S. citizenship, as men did when they married foreigners.[64]

In 1941, Norton organized bipartisan support of eight of the nine women in the House and by enlisting the help of Clarence Cannon, the chair of the Appropriations Committee, was able to pass $6 million in appropriations to support federal nursery schools to care for the children of mothers working in war industries. In time, the amount rose to $75 million. Her road was never easy. Southern members, such as Carl Vinson, D-Ga., tried to undercut labor legislation during World War II on the grounds that the war effort required setting aside established law—like the forty-hour work week—to increase productivity and reduce absenteeism. Norton's hearings on the matter revealed that the reason for the high rates of absenteeism was that the women working in war plants whose husbands were in service had no way to care for their children while at work. Thus, her successful efforts to obtain support for federal nursery schools advanced women while preserving her newly won labor law victories.

As chair of the Labor Committee, Norton took on still more issues affecting women across the nation. Equal pay for women fell under the jurisdiction of the committee, and in 1947 she co-authored a law "declaring it a national legislative policy to make no distinctions on the basis of sex," a sort of forerunner to the proposed Equal Rights Amendment to the U.S. Constitution.[65] Protective legislation covering women workers also came under the committee's scope. Both Norton and Eleanor Roosevelt initially opposed the Equal Rights Amendment, fearing that it would undermine their work to protect women in industrial occupations. Another controversial issue that faced Norton as a woman and a Catholic was birth control; she opposed removing birth control from the obscenity laws that forbade shipping information about it through the mail. She explained, "the fine womanhood of America ... consider ... the pressure of a baby face against their own the highest form of earthly happiness."[66] Norton's perspective was certainly influenced by the loss of her only child in 1910 and by her mother's loss of three of her seven children.

In *Past and Promise* (1990), the Women's Project of New Jersey selected Norton as a significant role model for women in politics. Yet, as a Roman Catholic, she had opposed the birth control movement of Margaret Sanger in the 1920s (in contrast to Jeannette Rankin) and in 1931 had voted against the Gillett bill, which allowed federal funds to be used to dispense birth control information. Still, her writings and her legislative achievements demonstrate that she "adeptly analyzed [such] problems of working women as maternity leave, child care, myth of 'pin money,' job training programs, latch key children, displaced homemakers, and equal pay for equal work."[67]

When she was sixty-nine, Norton mounted her second biggest fight in Congress in an attempt to pass a bill authorizing a permanent Fair Employment Practices Commission. She failed on several attempts, but her spunk and candor reveal "Battling Mary" at her best. Her objective was to remove any vestige of discrimination based on race or color that would block a person from earning a living wage. During this period, she again found great comfort and support from the Church, through advisers such as Monsignor Francis Haas, who counseled her during her later years, much as her brother had done in her early years. The National Catholic Welfare Conference provided the intellectual grounding for her efforts.

As Frederick C. Othman reported in the *Washington Times Herald*, her appearance before the Rules Committee on this bill was illustrative of the type of blocking that committee had done to her bills for more than a decade. She sought the committee's clearance of her bill, which made it illegal for anyone to refuse a black person employment because of color:

"There are certain groups who have been greatly discriminated against," Mrs. Norton began.
"Who?" demanded bushy-haired Gene Cox of Georgia.
"You can't be serious!" exclaimed Mrs. Norton, "The Negro, of course."
"Where?" Cox asked.
"Everywhere," snapped Mrs. Norton....
"Wait a minute, Mr. Chairman," Cox yelled.

"Wait a minute, yourself, Mr. Cox," said Mrs. Norton...."Aside from your prejudices on some questions, I am very fond of you."

"Thank you, ma'am, " Representative Cox said. "But this bill is against our Jim Crow laws."

"The sooner you get rid of them, the better off the South will be," she retorted. Representative Charles Halleck of Indiana took up the questioning with the remark that he was not trying to embarrass her.

"I am not easily embarrassed," said Mrs. Norton.... "Why are you gentlemen so determined to be unfair?"

"Are you speaking of the committee collectively?" asked Representative Clarence J. Brown of Ohio.

"Individually some of you are fine," conceded Mrs. Norton. "I'm not the smartest person in the world, but I am sincere. Collectively, I think you fall short of that."

The gentlemen of the Committee gulped. Representative William M. Colmer of Mississippi ... said, "I don't think your law will work."

"If it won't, we'd better stay home from San Francisco," she retorted. (This was shortly before the United Nations charter meeting in San Francisco.)

"In my section, we feel kindly toward the Negro," Colmer added.

"What have you done for him in over 200 years?" Mrs. Norton cried.

"Fed him when he was hungry and clothed him when he was naked," Colmer said.

"Humph!" said Mrs. Norton.

"I quit," said Colmer. He did, too.

"Mrs. Norton, I give you round one, hands down."[68]

Norton did not succeed in gaining passage of that legislation, but a decade later civil rights and equal employment opportunity legislation swept through Congress during the presidency of Lyndon B. Johnson.

At age seventy-one, Norton was selected by President Harry S. Truman to travel to war-ravaged Europe to attend the International Labor Organization conference in Paris. The sight of rubble-strewn Europe with its hungry and cold refugees deeply moved her, and she even shared her soap and extra hosiery with those she met. Norton contracted a serious infection on that trip that severely hampered her activities throughout 1945 and 1946.

Meanwhile, the Republicans regained control of Congress in 1946 for the first time in seventeen years and began undoing many of the labor reforms she had spent a lifetime enacting. The Taft-Hartley Act, named for its sponsors, Sen. Robert Taft, R-Ohio, and Rep. Fred Hartley, R-N.J., amended the National Labor Relations Act of 1935, which had given labor the right to bargain collectively and to organize. The Taft-Hartley Act limited the ability of unions to strike and weakened national labor standards by delegating to individual states the power to limit workplace labor organizing. Although companies heralded the act as "balancing" the power between union and management, unions saw it as a move to control working men and women and to limit their rights to fair treatment. It also lessened the pressure on the states of the South to ratchet up their working standards and wages to levels similar to those in the North.

When, in 1948, the Democrats regained the helm of Congress, Norton became chair of the House Administration Committee, a less taxing position than the others she had held. Near the end of her career, she observed dryly,

Too few women have the courage and the stubbornness to battle the men who are strongly entrenched in political leadership. It will probably take another generation to make women realize their own power and the importance of using that power to get the things they want in government. It's still a man's game after 31 years.[69]

The Administration Committee involved many managerial tasks related to the operations of the House as well as election laws. Norton introduced— and successfully passed in the House as her last bill—an anti–poll tax law, a progressive attempt to expand voting rights to all persons regardless of race. This legislation had languished in Congress for decades; it was filibustered to death in the Senate during that session of Congress and would not be passed for another decade and a half. Some of the momentum for this law had arisen from the raucous Democratic National Convention of 1948, which split along racial lines. During that convention she chaired the Democratic Party's Credentials Committee, as southern Democrats, like Strom Thurmond (later, Republican senator from South Carolina), broke with the party and ran on a separate "states' rights" ticket.

By the end of the 1940s, the Hague machine had passed its prime. In 1947, at age seventy-two, Frank Hague retired as mayor of Jersey City. Republicans swept local elections, defeating his handpicked successor in 1949.[70] Hague's state foothold crumbled as his candidates lost to Republicans.[71] Norton decided to run for Congress again and to announce her decision on March 7, 1950, her seventy-fifth birthday. But in early March she was stricken with pneumonia, and during her hospital stay she changed her mind.[72] Her service spanned twenty-five years; it covered seven presidential elections, the post–World War I period, the Great Depression, and World War II. In fact, her life embraced the industrial advance of urban America.

In 1950, before finishing out her final year, she was surprised one day when she walked onto the floor of Congress and Rep. Reva Bosone, D-Utah, Rep. Edna Kelly, D-N.Y., and Rep. Frances Bolton, R-Ohio, presented her with a gold bracelet, each of the links engraved with the autograph of one of the eight female members of the House of Representatives with whom she had been serving in her final term: Frances Payne Bolton, Reva Beck Bosone, Helen Douglas of California, Cecil M. Harden of Indiana, Edna Kelly, Edith Nourse Rogers of Massachusetts, Katharine St. George of New York, Chase Woodhouse of Connecticut. Hanging from the bracelet was a round gold disk bearing the signature of Sen. Margaret Chase Smith of Maine, who had taken her seat in 1949, the first woman to be elected to the U.S. Senate in her own right. When Norton first arrived on Capitol Hill in 1925, she was the sixth woman in history to be elected to Congress. During her years in the House she watched more than two dozen women follow.[73]

Eight years later, at the age of eighty-four, Norton—this woman of great heart—died of a heart attack at her sister's home in Greenwich, Connecticut. She is buried in Holy Name Cemetery in Jersey City. She is the only congresswoman to have chaired three major committees and ushered through social legislation of such sweeping impact.

NOTES

1. Gary Mitchell, "Women Standing for Women: The Early Political Life of Mary T. Norton," *New Jersey History* 96 (spring-summer 1978): 27.
2. Mary T. Norton, Autobiographical manuscript (hereafter, "Autobiography"), Jersey City Public Library, Jersey City, N.J., 3.
3. Ibid., 5.
4. Ibid., 6.
5. Joan Lovero, "Life of Mary Norton," Jersey City Public Library, Jersey City, N.J., 2.
6. Norton, "Autobiography," 8.
7. Lovero, "Life of Mary Norton," 1.
8. *Encyclopedia Americana,* international ed., 1994, s.v. "Hague, Frank."
9. Norton, "Autobiography," 60.
10. Ibid., 13–14.
11. Lovero, "Life of Mary Norton," 3.
12. Ibid.
13. Ibid.
14. Norton, "Autobiography," 18.
15. Ibid., 24.
16. Frances Parkinson Keyes, "Truly Democratic," *Delineator,* March 1933, 39.
17. Lovero, "Life of Mary Norton," 4.
18. Norton, "Autobiography," 30.
19. Ibid.
20. Keyes, "Truly Democratic," 39.
21. Ibid., 22.
22. Keyes, "Truly Democratic," 39.
23. Lovero, "Life of Mary Norton," 6.
24. Norton, "Autobiography," 11.
25. Ibid., 29–30.
26. Joan Lovero, "New Jersey City's Mary Norton Blazed a Path for Women in Washington," *Hudson County Magazine,* Spring 1991, 28.
27. Norton, "Autobiography," 98.
28. Ibid.
29. Ibid., 50.
30. Lovero, "Life of Mary Norton," 8.
31. Norton, "Autobiography," 46.
32. Norton, "Autobiography," 39–44.
33. Maureen Rees, "Mary Norton: 'A Grand Girl,'" *Journal of the Rutgers University Libraries* 47 (December 1985): 59.
34. Hope Chamberlin, *A Minority of Members: Women in the United States Congress* (New York: Praeger, 1973), 53.
35. "Politician: A Congresswoman Who Learned from a Master," *Newsweek,* June 26, 1937, 18.

36. Norton, "Autobiography," 57.
37. Ibid.
38. Chamberlin, *A Minority of Members,* 54.
39. Norton, "Autobiography," 85.
40. Chamberlin, *A Minority of Members,* 54.
41. Rees, "Mary Norton," 65–66.
42. Norton, "Autobiography," 127–129.
43. Ibid., 125.
44. Lovero, "Life of Mary Norton," 12.
45. "Hague at Twilight," *New York Times,* April 25, 1952, 14.
46. *Current Biography 1944* s.v. "Norton, Mary T.," 502.
47. Ibid.
48. Norton, "Autobiography," 139.
49. Ibid.
50. Rees, "Mary Norton," 66–67.
51. Norton, "Autobiography," 141.
52. Mary T. Norton, "Wage and Hour Legislation: 'The Object' of the Law," radio broadcast over Mutual Broadcasting System, May 15, 1938, *Vital Speeches of the Day,* June 1, 1938, 485.
53. Lovero, "Life of Mary Norton," 13.
54. Norton, "Autobiography," 156.
55. Ibid., 158.
56. Ibid., 159.
57. Ibid., 181–182.
58. Ibid., 209.
59. "Have You Heard?" *Erie (Pa.) Daily Times,* May 13, 1935, in Scrap Books, Mary Norton Papers, Rutgers University Library.
60. Rees, "Mary Norton," 68.
61. Mitchell, "Women Standing for Women," 31–32.
62. Margaret Chase Smith, interviewed by the author, Skowhegan, Maine, July 13, 1993.
63. Mitchell, "Women Standing for Women," 33–34.
64. Ibid., 36.
65. Rees, "Mary Norton," 72.
66. *Current Biography 1944,* 501.
67. The Women's Project of New Jersey, *Past and Promise: Lives of New Jersey Women* (Metuchen, N.J.: Scarecrow Press, 1990).
68. Norton, "Autobiography," 219–220.
69. Ibid., 47–48.
70. "Frank Hague Dies at Age 81," *Washington Star,* January 2, 1956, 22.
71. "Hague at Twilight," *New York Times,* April 25, 1952, 14.
72. Lovero, "Life of Mary Norton," 18.
73. Norton, "Autobiography," 264.

Edith Nourse Rogers
Republican–Massachusetts (1925–1960)
Longest-Serving Congresswoman

The essential qualities of a Congresswoman are the abilities to fight hard, fight fair, and persevere—all of which a woman can do as well as a man.
Edith Nourse Rogers, quoted in the *Boston Globe*, July 25, 1925

The first congresswoman from New England, and the longest serving, Edith Nourse Rogers—elected to the House of Representatives at age forty-four—worked tirelessly for veterans and for Massachusetts. In 1929 she became the first woman to gavel the House to order. As a member and later the chair of the Veterans' Affairs Committee, she advocated war preparedness and played a prominent part in drafting the GI Bill of Rights and the Korean Veterans' Bill of Rights. In addition, she drafted a bill establishing a Nurses' Corps within the Veterans Administration and became the first woman in Congress to have her name attached to a major bill—that establishing the Women's Army Corps in 1942. She also achieved enactment in 1938 of her bill establishing the National Cancer Institute. She was heavily involved in tariff and trade issues that were essential to the survival of New England's shoe and textile industries, which faced import competition from low-wage nations. Rogers's international travel prior to her election gave her a world view that prompted her speeches in 1933 against the rise of Adolf Hitler in Germany and his brutal treatment of Jewish people.

Edith Nourse Rogers was born in Saco, Maine, on March 19, 1881, the daughter and namesake of Edith (Riversmith) Nourse and her husband, Franklin Nourse, a wealthy textile mill executive. She had one brother, Benjamin. Although her father never ran for office, he was well-connected politically and an active Republican, counting many Republican Party leaders among his friends.[1] The textile business—particularly cotton—was an industry sensitive to import and tariff laws, and it demanded political involvement by the executives in charge. As a child, Edith was exposed to political discussions at home. In her early years she was taught by a governess and later attended Grove Hall, a private school for which her father was a trustee.

In 1895, when Edith was fourteen, her family moved from Saco, Maine, to Lowell, Massachusetts, on the Merrimack River. The original settlers of Lowell traced their roots back to England and the Puritans. She was a direct descendant of Priscilla Mullins Alden, a passenger on the *Mayflower* and one of the first Puritans to be married in this country.[2] The names of the towns and counties of Rogers's youth sounded interchangeable with those of her Anglo-Saxon ancestors in England—Andover, Tewksbury, Chelmsford, Middlesex County, Essex County. Life in Lowell, much as in Lancashire, England, was molded by the booming textile industry. Although it was first settled in 1653 as a farming community, it was incorporated as a town in the early 1800s and named for Francis Cabot Lowell, an early textile manufacturer. The mill town of Lowell typified the textile industry's history in America at its zenith and nadir.

Although Rogers was brought up in affluence, her world revolved around her father's mill yard, located near the Nourse home in Lowell. She played there with her friends, some of them probably the children of mill workers. From her father, she learned about the textile industry and the life of mill owners. Meanwhile, her family ensured that she was properly educated by sending her to Rogers Hall School in Lowell and supplying her with tutors, both in the United States and in Europe. After her graduation, "[s]he was sent to an aunt in France to study music, having a fine soprano voice" and was enrolled in Madame Julien's school in Paris.[3] During these years she corresponded with her childhood friend, John Jacob Rogers, a young man from a wealthy and prominent Lowell family who was a student at Harvard University and then Harvard law school. Their desire for companionship led her to abandon her musical career one year after she began professional study.

Shortly after her return to Lowell, Edith Nourse was presented to society, and in 1907, when she was twenty-six, she married John Rogers, now a Harvard-educated lawyer. John Rogers was elected to Congress in 1912, just before the outbreak of World War I, and he served seven terms. His wife accompanied him to Washington, D.C., and abroad, assisting him in his duties and serving as his hostess. Their home on Sixteenth Street in Washington became a mecca for parties and entertaining. The *New York Times* later commented, "The couple toured through Europe on their honeymoon and it never ended."[4]

When her husband was elected to Congress, Edith Rogers, one news article commented, "shared her husband's responsibilities, studied political situations and sought such information as she thought requisite for the wife of a man in public life."[5] She denied that she had an overt hand in her husband's political affairs, preferring to say that any influence she had was "in a wife's obscure way."[6] This demure and unthreatening behavior later helped her advance politically beyond the limits of most women's experiences at that time.

During World War I, John Rogers enlisted as a private in the army and concurrently became one of the members of a congressional delegation sent abroad. Edith accompanied him to Europe. In 1917, she volunteered, through the Women's Overseas Service and, in conjunction with the YMCA and Red Cross, visited army field hospitals in France.[7] Because she had nursed patients on the Continent and in London and he had a deep and abiding interest in European affairs, the couple developed a reputation and friendship among their European colleagues. When Edith and John Rogers traveled on congressional delegations to Europe during the war, only they were invited by the French to tour near the front lines: "the other Congressmen were not permitted to do so, much less be accompanied by their wives."[8] Edith Rogers was also exposed to air raids, both in France and in England, and pronounced them "more exciting than dangerous."[9]

These experiences were to change her life. Once stateside, she continued her work with the Red Cross, and she served at the Walter Reed Hospital from 1918 to 1922. According to the *New York Times,* "She could be seen each morning leaving her Washington house, wearing the Red Cross uniform, on her way to Walter Reed Hospital, while her husband departed in the opposite direction for the Capitol. She often returned to her house later than Mr. Rogers."[10] Her volunteer work with disabled veterans at the hospital earned her the title of "Angel of Walter Reed."

In March 1925, John Jacob Rogers suddenly died in office after an operation. Local political leaders and her friends persuaded a reluctant Edith, then forty-four, to run in a special election to complete his term.[11] Her campaign was described as "almost silent," with the public's knowledge of her abilities sufficing to gain her election.[12] A local writer commented, "The sheer power of her personality and her known capabilities accumulated the vote," no doubt acknowledging the family's social position as well as her own nursing reputation with veterans and broad acquaintanceships through the Red Cross, YMCA, and her husband's political network.[13] In fact, she described the campaign as a blessing in disguise, helping her to overcome the grief at her husband's death.

Edith Rogers need not have worried about her chances, it seems; she won a larger percentage of the vote than her husband had in 1924, beating her opponent by a 3 to 1 margin on a vote of 23,497 to 9,144. She became the sixth woman in U.S. history to be elected to the House of Representatives, one of three widows to achieve election. A writer noted at the time, "She is rare, rounded reserve that enobles. She is mentally superior to a season of nothing but teas."[14] Another observed that Rogers was a woman officeholder coming from a new venue—"the home"—as one of a new class of politicians who had, through close association with her husband's activities, gained the knowledge to take up his public burdens where he dropped them.[15] John Rogers's widow would go on to serve Massachusetts for thirty-five years, making her the longest-serving female member of Congress. She, like several other widows of representatives, became a much more prominent politician than her husband had been.

In some ways, it seemed highly unlikely that this particular region of northeastern Massachusetts would elect a woman to Congress. Just twelve miles separated Lowell from the historically infamous town of Salem, Massachusetts, notorious for the witchcraft trials held in the late 1600s, when more than a dozen people, mainly women, were charged with witchcraft and put to death in the public square. In fact, one of Edith Rogers's ancestors had been burned as a witch.[16] Salem became the locus of Nathaniel Hawthorne's *The Scarlet Letter*, written in 1850, in which Hester Prynne, the main female character, is publicly condemned for adultery. This Puritan region would seem to be less than welcoming for any woman assuming a new cultural role. And yet northeastern Massachusetts was the first area in New England—and one of the first few in the country—to send a woman to Congress. Upon her election, the *New York Times* reported, "Another New England tradition has been shattered by Mrs. Edith Nourse Rogers of Lowell ... to represent the Fifth District of Massachusetts in Congress. Heretofore, New England has frowned upon the aspirations of women who wanted a seat in Congress, and few have had the temerity to offer themselves as candidates for national honors."[17] Thus Rogers's early emphasis on carrying on the work of her husband and not threatening woman's traditional role in the home proved acceptable to her constituents.

Most politicians thought Rogers would not want to serve more than her husband's unexpired term. Even on election night she went to extra lengths to assure her constituents, and probably herself, that she intended to carry on the policies of her husband and those of President Calvin Coolidge:

This was her message of thanks to the men and women who had stirred up the voters in the mill section and pulled the door bells at the homes of New Englanders who pride themselves on their traditions. One of these traditions is that the place for a woman is in the home and she ought not to devote herself to public matters beyond church and school affairs.[18]

Although on the morning after her election she was surrounded by her "Woman's Campaign Committee," neither she nor her husband were suffragists.[19] But Rogers was well educated, and worldly, and had been transformed by her travels. As the popular song at the time reminded, "How you going to keep them down on the farm, after they've seen Paree."

In her first weeks in office, Rogers vowed to go straight to work, saying, "When I'm here [in Washington], I'll be at the office every day. There will be a time when I shall steal off to the cottage Mother has by the sea. It will not be for long. I can't be away for long. I shall be able to visit with her weekends and then I shall rest."[20] It was her mother who helped Rogers over her tragic loss as well as the illness and death of her father two years earlier. "Mother took a deep interest in my campaigning.... Mother is happy when her children are in service for other people."[21] She admitted that running for office was never something she had planned to do, even saying that the idea of holding office had not appealed to her before her husband's death. But she

finally consented to run because his friends thought I could carry on his work better than any one else at this time. I hope that everybody will forget as soon as possible that I am a woman. I have told my constituents that they may expect just the same service they obtained from my husband. I shall try to give my personal attention to every call on my office, and when I vote I shall try to represent them as accurately as my conscience will let me.[22]

Rogers thus became noted as a member of Congress who worked extremely hard in office. She allowed herself only ten minutes to eat lunch while at her desk. She was an effective worker as well, knowledgeable about the stuff of politics from her years at her husband's side, and with "a talent for bobbing up aggressively and speaking her mind."[23] What seemed to motivate her most was her feelings of patriotism, steeled by years of study abroad and travel with her husband as well as her year of volunteer nursing service in Europe during World War I.

This patriotism led her to be a firm advocate of war preparedness and a devoted fighter for veterans. Veterans' issues became Rogers's prevailing interest, and she dedicated her congressional career to helping veterans like the ones she had met in her years working with the Red Cross. Before her election to Congress, President Harding had appointed her to be his personal representative for disabled veterans' issues. Presidents Coolidge and Hoover followed his lead.[24] Rogers's strength and devotion to veterans had taken her into the battlefield hospitals on the front lines in Europe and the wards of Walter Reed Hospital in Washington. Wherever she went, her efforts inspired love and admiration among the veterans who lay sick or disabled. It was these efforts that earned her the nickname of "Mother of Veterans."

The one committee on which Rogers served throughout her career was, fittingly, the Veterans' Affairs Committee. After twenty-two years of service, she became its chair in 1947, one of the first women to chair a legislative committee. In order to stay on the Veterans' Affairs Committee, however, she had to relinquish her seat on the Foreign Affairs Committee, because the number of committee assignments allowed to a member was reduced in 1947.[25]

Early in World War II, Rogers sponsored the bill creating the Women's Army Auxiliary Corps, or WAAC (a year later, the word *Auxiliary* was dropped from the name and the acronym became WAC).[26] She was one of the first women in Congress to sponsor such an important piece of legislation. In stark contrast to the antiwar efforts of the first woman in Congress, Jeannette Rankin, Rogers wrote, "in introducing my bill ... my thought was that such service would give thousands of our women an opportunity to do their part in winning our war.... I felt there should be [an organization] which would be recognized by the War Department and which would be authorized to serve with the Army."[27] The bill, which was passed in 1942, permitted WAACs to wear a uniform, receive the same pay as members of the regular army, and live in barracks. Rogers's motivation in introducing this bill seems to have been more in the interest of preparedness than in equity for women; she writes that there are "many jobs which men are glad to get away from and which women perform with enthusiasm. For example, men don't like to be telephone operators—and we know men prefer women's voices on the telephone."[28]

Rogers's later photographs reveal a motherly appearance, certainly as she advanced in years, and she was known, as one member described, for her "gaiety and vivacity."[29] However, she was no lightweight on the House floor. She reputedly loved floor fights, and as one reporter said,

Once on the floor, despite her effervescing femininity, she conducts herself like a man. She doesn't get on her mark, get set, and then recite her speech in a schoolgirl fashion. Bouncing out of her seat, she shoots a question in a high-pitched Boston accent and leaps in where other gentlewomen fear to tread. [30]

Unlike many women members of Congress, Rogers was "a comparatively frequent speaker, and one who [spoke] her mind vigorously and clearly."[31] Her forthright, assertive manner probably accounts for the relative success Rogers had in passing legislation. If one bill stands out as her most enduring achievement, it is the GI Bill of Rights.

War veterans already loved Rogers for her personal ministrations and her crusades to build more veterans' hospitals, but one can only imagine their pleasure at her role in the 1944 GI Bill of Rights, which gave returning veterans such benefits as funding for a college education and low-interest home loans. Rogers was so instrumental in drafting the bill that when President Franklin D. Roosevelt signed it into law in 1944, he presented her with the pen he had used to sign his name.[32] Other veterans' bills in which Rogers played an important part were the Korean Veterans' Benefits Bill and a bill establishing a Nurses' Corps within the Veterans Administration.[33] Without question, the GI and Korean Veterans' bills were responsible for giving form to post–World War II America as millions of veterans obtained an education and a mortgage on their first home. Suburban tracts blossomed across the nation and the "baby boom" era dawned.

In addition to working for veterans, Rogers also ministered assiduously to her own New England constituency. Throughout her career, her efforts to aid the struggling shoe and textile industries took the form of initiatives both for the owners and for the workers. Because of its high labor-intensive nature, the textile industry and her cotton mill constituents were among the first to become embroiled in the trade disputes that arose with global competition. She opposed imports from Japan because they were of inferior quality and from Czechoslovakia because they would be harmful to the shoe industry of her district.[34] Rogers introduced bills to keep Japanese goods out of the country and to change cotton tariff laws.[35] She castigated U.S. secretary of state Cordell Hull for his trade treaty with pre-Hitlerite Czechoslovakia, which directly affected her shoemaking district.[36] In 1935, President Roosevelt ordered an investigation of bleached cotton cloth imports from Japan, largely because of protests from New England members of Congress, including Rogers. Debate on the issue apparently became quite heated. Rogers attempted to gain permission to speak for ten minutes about the effects that imports, and a cotton processing tax, were having on New England textile manufacturers. The chair of the Ways and Means Committee, objecting, foiled her attempt to speak. Rogers then resorted to a request for a point of personal privilege, a parliamentary maneuver that allows members to respond when their names have been impugned by others. She claimed that the secretary of state had accused her of deliberately misleading the public. The Speaker of the House answered that the secretary had not mentioned her by name and that therefore she was not entitled to a point of personal privilege. Angry at this response, a fellow Republican from Massachusetts rose to object that a quorum of members did not appear to be present; the clerk began to call the roll, a process that took far more than the ten minutes Rogers had requested.

Often speaking on the floor, Rogers was known to bring along some props to demonstrate her point. While speaking about the damage done to American business by Japanese imports, she displayed an array of one hundred imported items, everything "from tennis shoes and hot water bottles to fish nets and casseroles."[37] Each product sat next to a domestically manufactured version, with all prices labeled. Each import cost significantly less than the American version, even after import duties, but the Japanese articles appeared to be poorly made.[38]

Rogers had excellent political instincts and a flair for performance. With less fanfare, she also procured funds from the Department of Commerce to improve textile manufacturing in Massachusetts and develop foreign markets for American goods. She became entwined in international trade disputes as she worked hard to protect U.S. jobs and fought to ensure fair treatment of her constituents in trade initiatives. She opposed the imposition of tariffs on imported cottons because it would result in higher costs to her manufacturers.[39]

Rogers's conscience impelled her to work on several other issues during her terms in Congress. She called for a popular vote on Prohibition in 1932, when the country had become polarized between the "wets" and the "drys." Rogers wrote, "personally I am dry; all my votes have been dry votes." But she conceded that the matter should go to the public, saying, "This is a free country and people have the right to express their feelings. They cannot and will not be thwarted. Congress has no right to prevent it. It is the people's problem."[40]

The same instincts that led Rogers to the cause of the veterans led her to speak out against Hitler before many were aware of his brutality. In 1933, she spoke out on the House floor to protest his actions in Germany, reminding Americans, "When we recall the early history of our own nation we must expect the eyes of the less fortunate to be turned toward us for help."[41] Historians later would acknowledge those prescient Americans who recognized early on the evil that was brewing in postwar Germany. Rogers's European travels and sense of history developed in her a unique awareness worthy of expression in Congress. She opposed U.S. neutrality in World War II, voted for the Selective Service Act and all defense appropriations through 1945, and endorsed strengthening the U.S. foreign service. She originally supported the formation of the United Nations, but in the event Communist China were admitted to membership she advocated moving the UN headquarters outside the United States.[42]

Few members of Congress had the warmth of Edith Nourse Rogers. Her lengthy service in the House meant that she witnessed many members come and go, including many women members. Gracie Pfost of Idaho remembered meeting Rogers in 1953, when Pfost was a new member of Congress. Although they were of different parties, Rogers was a source of advice and encouragement.[43] Other women recalled her playing a similar role as mentor; Leonor Sullivan of Missouri described her as "a tower of strength to all of the women in the House ... helping us to become better acquainted with the legislative realities."[44]

Seldom did Rogers anger her colleagues, and when she did they usually forgave her quickly, as when she would invite the constituents of other Massachusetts members to have lunch with her.[45] Rogers did not build a career on overly dramatic speeches nor defend controversial causes. Rather, she epitomized graciousness, cheer, and charm, as symbolized by the fresh flower she always wore pinned to her lapel, a trademark that Margaret Chase Smith admired and later, when she became senator, adopted.[46] Throughout her career, Rogers remained "ebullient, a gifted bargainer, and utterly beguiling."[47]

At age seventy-nine, after thirty-five years of service, and two days before the 1960 Massachusetts primary, in which she was running unopposed for a nineteenth term, Rogers died quietly at Massachusetts General Hospital, in Boston. Her death was as unassuming as it could be; she had checked in to the hospital under a different name three weeks before. The perseverance, courage, and strength that had carried her around the world and into the hearts of millions girded her for her final journey.

NOTES

1. Corinne Danforth, "First New England Congresswoman to Fight Hard and Fight Fair," *Boston Globe*, July 5, 1925.
2. Hope Chamberlin, *A Minority of Members: Women in the United States Congress* (New York: Praeger, 1973), 57.
3. "A New Congresswoman: 'The Lady from Massachusetts,'" *New York Times*, July 5, 1925.
4. Ibid.
5. "Women Office Holders Are Now Coming from the Home," *New York Times*, July 12, 1925.
6. Danforth, "First New England Congresswoman."
7. *Current Biography 1942*, s.v. "Rogers, Edith Nourse," 698.
8. Danforth, "First New England Congresswoman."
9. Ibid.
10. "A New Congresswoman."
11. Chamberlin, *A Minority of Members*, 58.
12. Danforth, "First New England Congresswoman."
13. Ibid.
14. Ibid.
15. "Women Office Holders."
16. U.S. Congress, House, *Memorial Services Held in the House of Representatives and Senate of the United States, Together with Remarks Presented in Eulogy of Edith Nourse Rogers, Late a Representative from Massachusetts*, 86th Cong., 2d sess. (Washington, D.C.: U.S. Government Printing Office, 1961), 22.
17. "A New Congresswoman."
18. Ibid.
19. Ibid.
20. Danforth, "First New England Congresswoman."
21. Ibid.
22. "A New Congresswoman."
23. *Current Biography 1942*, 698.
24. "Veterans' Voice in Congress," *U.S. News and World Report*, February 28, 1947, 70.

25. House, *Memorial Services*, 11.
26. *Current Biography 1942*, 699.
27. Edith Nourse Rogers, "A Women's Army?" *Independent Woman*, February 1942, 38.
28. Edith Nourse Rogers, as told to Alfred Toombs, "The Time Is Now," *Ladies' Home Companion*, August 1943.
29. House, *Memorial Services*, 70.
30. Chamberlin, *A Minority of Members*, 59.
31. "Veterans' Voice in Congress."
32. Chamberlin, "A Minority of Members," 59.
33. U.S. Congress, House, Office of the Historian, *Women in Congress, 1917–1990* (Washington, D.C.: U.S. Government Printing Office, 1991), 220.
34. "Japanese Textiles Put under Inquiry"; *Current Biography*, 699.
35. *Current Biography 1942*, 699.
36. Ibid.
37. "Japanese Textiles Put under Inquiry," *New York Times*, April 18, 1935.
38. Ibid.
39. "Hits McNary-Haugen Bill," *New York Times*, April 30, 1928.
40. "Mrs. Rogers Favors Vote on Prohibition," *New York Times*, March 16, 1932.
41. Edith Nourse Rogers, "A Protest in the House for the Jews of Germany," *New York Times*, May 21, 1933.
42. Chamberlin, *A Minority of Members*, 60.
43. House, *Memorial Services*, 30.
44. Ibid., 64.
45. Chamberlin, *A Minority of Members*, 60.
46. House, *Memorial Services*, 70.
47. Chamberlin, *A Minority of Members*, 58.

Part 2: The Greening Years
World War II through the 1960s

The Greening Years
Overview

During the greening years (1940–1970), the number of women in Congress slowly began to rise. Until 1941, there were never as many as ten women in Congress at the same time. The high-water mark of women serving during this period was 1961–1963, the Eighty-seventh Congress, when twenty women served in the two houses. A total of fifty women took the oath of office in these years. Their average age at election was close to fifty, as it had been in the earlier era. Their average length of service rose to eight years, similar to that of their male colleagues. The rate at which women served inched up from 1.3 women per year in the period between 1920 and 1940 to 1.67 per year between 1940 and 1970.

In January 1955, the midpoint of this era, seventeen women, the highest number in history till then, were sworn into the Eighty-fourth Congress—sixteen members of the House of Representatives and one senator. Of the twelve incumbent women who were reelected, six had succeeded their husbands; six had not. Four of the five freshmen women elected to the House that year did not fill a husband's seat, departing somewhat from the usual entry path of women to congressional service. The four were Iris Faircloth Blitch, a Democrat from Georgia, who was elected at age forty-two and served eight years; Edith Starrett Green, a Democrat from Oregon, who was elected at age forty-four and served twenty years; Coya Gjesdal Knutson, a Democrat from Minnesota, who was elected at age forty-two and served four years; and Martha W. Griffiths, a Democrat from Michigan, who was elected at age forty-two and served twenty years.

On the day they were sworn in, Griffiths sat next to a male member of Congress who glumly remarked: "At this rate, it won't be any time before you ladies have a majority here."[1] As one of her first official acts, Griffiths asked the Library of Congress to calculate how long it would take at the then present rate of entry for women to gain the majority in the House. The answer that came back was 432 years.[2]

Martha Griffiths was to blossom as a member, in part because of the unwavering support of her attorney husband, Hicks Griffiths. Coya Knutson was not as lucky. She began an illustrious congressional career in the House by defeating an incumbent male Republican and then becoming the first woman to win assignment to the Committee on Agriculture. Having risen through the ranks of Minnesota politics by way of the Democratic Farm Labor Party, she immediately became a strong voice for farmers. She won election again in 1956, but as she prepared to kick off her next campaign for reelection, her husband undermined her career. He publicly released a letter announcing that her career had "devastated his home life" and accusing her of involvement with a younger man on her staff.[3] Although her husband was a known alcoholic, his actions completely upset her chances, and she lost her seat in Congress, the only incumbent Democrat to do so in 1958.[4] Subsequently, she asked the House Administration Subcommittee on Elections to investigate. It found that the letter had, in fact, caused her defeat and that the charges were false. Her marriage ended in divorce. She attempted to gain reelection in 1960 and again in 1977 to no avail.

During this middle era, women became more outspoken, more active legislatively, and more prominent, partly because of the advent of television and partly because by World War II more women were able to take advantage of a higher education, which had been denied to most of them earlier. One ultimately would run for the presidency of the United States (Margaret Chase Smith); another would become the first woman in history to gain election to the Ways and Means Committee (Martha W. Griffiths). The progress of women was glacial but steady.

After Oberlin College in northern Ohio became the first college in the nation to award degrees to women in 1841, other barriers slowly began to be lowered. For example, in 1869, Iowa licensed the first woman attorney, although it was not until 1920 that states permitted women to practice law under the same provisions as men.[5]

In the earlier era, those rare women who rose to federal office had achieved an education quite advanced in comparison with other women of the time. Rankin's college education set her apart from most women; Rogers's family wealth afforded her private tutors and foreign travel; and Norton attained secretarial and business skills as the oldest daughter of Irish immigrants who, denied of it themselves, valued education for their eldest child. In the post–World War II period, women's increased educational attainment and their legal status as full persons had readied a new generation for office.

Of the fifty women who served in Congress during this period, seventeen served ten years or longer. The longest-serving woman of this era was Margaret Chase Smith, a Republican from Maine, who ended her congressional career after thirty-two and one-half years. She was first elected as a member of the House in 1940, succeeding her husband, then achieved election to the Senate in 1948. Other women whose service was lengthy and notable were Frances Payne Bolton, a Republican from Ohio, who served twenty-nine years as a member of the House; Leonor Kretzer Sullivan, a Democrat from Missouri, who served twenty-four years; and Edna Flannery Kelly, a Democrat from New York, who served twenty years. Each one of these women was a widow whose education was better than average and who had worked outside the home. As they rose to congressional prominence, Mary Teresa Norton and Edith Nourse Rogers, both of whom first took their seats in 1925, were completing their service, Norton in 1951 and Rogers in 1960.

Some other women who were elected to Congress in these greening years deserve mention. Women like Clare Boothe Luce, a Republican from Connecticut, wife of the publisher Henry Luce, received extensive publicity, much of it self-generated, but did not serve long—in Luce's case, only from 1943 to 1947. Others, many of whom served longer periods, were almost unknown. Katharine Price Collier St. George, who served from 1947 to 1965, was a first cousin to Franklin D. Roosevelt. Born into a wealthy family, St. George lived in Tuxedo Park, New York. A Republican, she demonstrated a commitment to equal rights for women. She proposed a bill to strengthen the mandate for the Women's Army Corps by expanding Veterans' Administration laws to cover WAC personnel. In 1950, she tried, but failed, to have a proposed Equal Rights Amendment brought to the House floor. Her proposal to outlaw wage discrimination met with more success and was passed as the Equal Pay Act of 1963.[6] St. George was defeated for reelection in 1964.

Marguerite Stitt Church, a Republican from Illinois, served twelve years in Congress, from 1951 to 1963. She entered the House initially as a widow elected to fill her husband's seat and served until she retired at age seventy. Her husband had died while sitting at a House committee hearing, but she accepted a seat on this same committee, the Committee on Expenditures in the Executive Department. In the next Congress, she moved to the Government Operations Committee and the Foreign Affairs Committee. The Foreign Affairs assignment led to extensive foreign travel, particularly to Asia. During her dozen years in the House, Church focused her domestic concerns on making government more efficient, including work to pass the act that put the federal government budget on an annual basis.[7]

Maude Elizabeth Kee, a Democrat, took her husband's seat in the House in the West Virginia delegation and served from 1951 to 1965. She is the only woman who has ever been elected to Congress from West Virginia. Kee served on the Veterans' Affairs Committee during all of her years in the House and eventually became one of the few women in history to chair a House subcommittee—the Veteran Affairs Committee's Subcommittee on Hospitals and Health Care. Her son James Kee took her seat in Congress when she retired.

Known as "Hell's Belle" for her spirited attempts to gain the federal, rather than private, development of the Hell's Canyon branch of the Snake River, the Democrat Gracie Bowers Pfost was a staunch supporter of her native Idaho, which elected her to Congress in 1952. During her ten years in Congress, Pfost served on a committee whose mandate was to investigate philanthropic organizations to ensure that federal funds were not being used for Communist activities. In the midst of McCarthyism and anti-Communist hysteria, Pfost took a stand for truth. On May 24, 1954, she and Rep. Wayne L. Hays of Ohio walked out of a committee hearing, accusing the committee of allowing unsubstantiated testimony against employees of foundations. The committee then voted in July to end its hearings, but Pfost still found it necessary to dissent from the final report, which determined that some of the foundations had unintentionally funded un-American activities. Instead of running for a sixth House term, she entered the 1962 Senate contest but was defeated in the November election.[8]

Florence Price Dwyer, a Republican, began her political career as a lobbyist in New Jersey; in 1950, she won election to the state assembly. In 1956, she ran successfully for Congress, where she served until she retired in 1973. Like Leonor Sullivan, Dwyer concentrated on consumer issues, sponsoring legislation to create the Consumer Protection Agency and to outlaw discrimination in lending. She was a leader of a Republican move to change the House rules that had allowed southern Democrats to wield disproportional influence. Because southern Democrats opposed much civil rights legislation, the future of the civil rights bills of the 1960s hinged on such a change.

As the first woman in Congress from Washington State, the Republican Catherine Dean May devoted her congressional career to working for her agricultural constituency. Before running for Congress, she worked as a radio broadcaster and served six years in the state legislature. She served on the Agriculture Committee during her twelve years in the House, from 1959 to 1971. Beet sugar was an important commodity produced in her district, and May did all she could to protect her producers from sugar imports from low-wage nations, favoring a fee on imported sugar and reserving a higher share of the U.S. market for domestic sugar production. In 1970, she sponsored a proposal of Richard Nixon's administration to provide extremely disadvantaged families with free food stamps. May lost her attempt at reelection in 1970.

The Democrat Julia Butler Hansen was elected to Congress in 1960 from a Washington State congressional district that bordered on Rep. Edith Green's district, just across the Columbia River. Her lengthy political career included eight years on the city council of Cathlamet, Washington; twenty-one years in the state house; and, finally, fourteen years in the U.S. House of Representatives. She was the second woman in history to serve on the House Appropriations Committee and the only woman in history to chair one of its subcommittees, Interior and Related Agencies. Had she chosen to serve fewer years in the state house and to run for Congress earlier, her intensive background could have moved her into top-level positions in Congress. Among the bills Julia Hansen introduced were acts that would establish a national traffic safety board and the Federal Maritime Administration.[9] In her last House term, at the behest of the Speaker of the House, Hansen chaired the influential Democratic Committee on Organization, Study, and Review. She resigned her seat in the House in 1974.

Patsy Takemoto Mink's career in Congress spans the end of the greening years and the modern era. A Democrat, and a versatile and effective legislator, she became the first woman of color to be elected to Congress. An Asian American of Japanese ancestry, Mink first ran for Congress in 1959 in Hawaii's first elections after it had become a state, but she lost that nomination. In 1964, however, she won one of Hawaii's two seats in the House of Representatives. Like Edith Green, she managed to get a committee assignment—Education and Labor—that matched her previous expertise and interest in social issues, particularly children and education. Her achievements have been significant. In the House, she introduced the first child care bill, as well as bills to set up bilingual education, student loans, special education, and Head Start. She also served on the Interior and Insular Affairs Committee to support her lifelong commitment to the development of the Pacific region. As early as 1965 she was successful in gaining passage of legislation to support construction of schools in all the U.S. Pacific territories. In 1976, Mink lost a bid for the Senate against fellow Democrat Spark Matsunaga. Subsequently, she served as president for Americans for Democratic Action and returned to elective office on the Honolulu City Council. In 1990, this determined and able woman returned to the House in a special election held to fill a vacancy in Hawaii's Second District, left open by the resignation of Rep. Daniel Akaka, who was appointed to the U.S. Senate. She remains in the House today, having served a total of eighteen years to date. Her committee assignments again include Education and Labor, but also Budget. Her philosophy of service revolves around the idea that she serves to "enlarge the horizons of children, since our whole purpose of being here in the Congress is for the future."[10] In 1995 Mink established a Democratic women's caucus in Congress and serves as its first chair.

NOTES

1. Peggy Hanson, *Few Are Chosen* (Boston: Houghton Mifflin, 1968), 87.
2. Ibid.
3. U.S. Congress, House, Office of the Historian, *Women in Congress, 1917–1990* (Washington, D.C.: U.S. Government Printing Office, 1991), 134.
4. Ibid.
5. Ibid.
6. Ibid., 228.
7. Ibid., 46.
8. Ibid., 199–200.
9. Ibid., 94.
10. Patsy Takemoto Mink, interview by author, Washington, D.C., August 3, 1995.

Frances Payne Bolton
Republican–Ohio (1940–1969)
Richest Congresswoman

I have heard chivalrous members of the male sex … express unalterable opposition to any measure which would require their daughters, their sisters, or just women in general, to serve in the armed forces. I am afraid such gallantry is sadly out of date.

Frances Payne Bolton, "Women Should Be Drafted,"
America Magazine, 1949

Born to wealth and privilege and once the wealthiest woman in the country, Frances Payne Bolton nevertheless worked relentlessly for the twenty-nine years she was a member of Congress.[1] She sponsored the Bolton Act of 1943, which created the U.S. Cadet Nurse Corps; she worked for legislation that permitted men to join the Army Nurse Corps; and as a member and later chair of the Foreign Affairs Committee she contributed immensely to its work because of her extensive study of and travel to foreign countries, especially in the Near East. Her interests were wide, and her vast philanthropy encompassed most of them. She was responsible for the founding in 1923 of the Frances P. Bolton School of Nursing at Western Reserve University, the inauguration of the first college-level nursing program in the United States, and the purchase of 485 acres across from Mount Vernon, George Washington's home in Virginia, so the vista of this national monument would never be impaired. Bolton lived with "steam engine energy" throughout her life and admirably bore extensive personal and family adversity that would have broken a person of lesser spirit.

Frances Payne Bingham Bolton was born into the aristocratic world of Euclid Avenue in Cleveland, Ohio, on March 29, 1885. The fourth of five children of

Charles Bingham and Mary "Molly" Payne Bingham, she and her brothers and sister—Oliver, William, Elizabeth, Frances, and Henry—were the ninth generation of the family in America, both sides of English heritage. She was named after a maiden cousin, Frances "Fanny" Payne, who had been banished to Cleveland from New York City by her father for reading books regarded as "unsuitable for ladies," in this instance the poetry of Ralph Waldo Emerson.[2]

The Paynes, her mother's family, were descended from a signer of the Declaration of Independence, Robert Treat Paine. Her uncle Oliver Payne was the partner of John D. Rockefeller. Her maternal grandfather, Henry B. Payne, served as a Democratic member of the U.S. House of Representatives (1875–1877) before being elected senator from Ohio (1885–1891). Henry Payne was a Democrat and a classmate of Stephen Douglas, renowned for his debates with Abraham Lincoln on the issue of slavery. In fact, Payne helped the young Stephen Douglas establish himself as a lawyer in Cleveland before Douglas moved to Illinois, where he also was elected a representative and senator. Douglas argued there for popular sovereignty, or states' rights, in allowing states the option of determining the status of slaves within their borders. In 1860, when Douglas became the Democratic candidate for president and Abraham Lincoln won the Republican nomination—and the presidency—the Paynes actively supported Douglas.

Bolton's grandfather on her father's side, William Bingham, served in the Ohio legislature as a Republican. Her father pursued business interests rather than politics. He instilled in his children a thirst for knowledge and a sense of noblesse oblige, the notion that the fortunate owed something to those born with less. His academic pursuits were constant, and he was insatiably curious. Charles Bingham made his fortune as a prominent and creative business leader who established the U.S. machine tool industry. He brought German toolmakers to Cleveland and held his production to the highest standards in the craft.

Ohio—the Buckeye State—is situated within reach of a majority of the nation's population. The opening of the Erie Canal in 1825, which linked the entire Great Lakes with the Atlantic Ocean's world trade routes, unleashed a powerhouse of economic activity in the state. Carved out of the Northwest Territory in the early 1800s, Ohio draws its name from Iroquois words meaning "something great." It is a diverse land, both urban and rural. Even today, Ohio boasts more urban centers than any other state in the Union—Cleveland (the largest), along with Akron, Cincinnati, Columbus, Dayton, Steubenville, Toledo, and Youngstown. Still, agriculture and food processing are Ohio's biggest businesses. Ohio is one of just a dozen states in U.S. history that have managed to elect at least five women to serve in the U.S. Congress. The first was Frances Payne Bolton.

About the middle of the nineteenth century, the role of women in society, beyond the home, was slowly broadening. In the 1840s Oberlin College, in northern Ohio, became the first institution of higher education in the nation to admit women for advanced degrees. Only a few years earlier, it had become the first coeducational institution in the Union. Just east of Oberlin, in the far northeastern quadrant of the state, perched on the rising bluff of Lake Erie, sits Cleveland, Ohio's premier industrial center. It would not be surprising for such a region of America to elect a woman to Congress. But a woman would not be elected for one hundred years.

During the last quarter of the nineteenth century, the Standard Oil Company, which was founded in Cleveland in 1870, pieced together refineries and distribution networks. Within two decades, this gargantuan firm, under the grip of John D. Rockefeller, controlled the world's oil trade. Folklore in Ohio still recalls the tale of Rockefeller handing out dimes to needy children along Cleveland's downtown streets. In 1892, in the famous antitrust case, the Ohio Supreme Court dissolved the Standard Oil Trust, forcing it to divide its assets. Frances Bolton became an heir to this enormous fortune.

As historian David Loth recounts of that time in his biography of Bolton:

Cleveland was typical of the rising might of the Midwest ... throwing off the tutelage of New England. The Payne and Rockefeller refineries, the coal and iron interests of William Bingham and Company, and Rhodes and Company (in which young Mark Hanna recently had become a partner by marrying a Rhodes), the big wholesale firms of which the Hanna grocery business was a good example, the crowded Great Lakes shipping—all these and a stream of immigrants to work the mills and build homes and docks and factories, were producing an authentic boom.[3]

The Bingham family's sense of patriotism and power that had been derived from business success led Bolton's father to help found the Case Institute of Technology and to donate money to the Cleveland Library and the Cleveland Museum. The connections of the Payne and Bingham families reached not just to the state capitol but to Washington, D.C., New York, and international financial centers, and the families appeared destined for political legend. But an unusual set of misfortunes entwined with the exploits of an ambitious family that valued its business and political involvements. Frances Bolton's childhood memories were overcast by her parents' worry about the health of her older brother Oliver, who had inflammation of the heart, endocarditis, that followed a bout with scarlet fever. His illness enveloped the family in a frantic search for healing. Molly Bingham was propelled relentlessly to seek more favorable climates to aid her son's recovery. She sought refuge for him in Florida, Bermuda, California, then in Europe, dragging her other children with her on long train rides or ocean-sailing vessels. Oliver's illness subjected Bolton and her siblings to isolation and loneliness. In Cleveland, she attended the exclusive Hathaway-Brown School, but when she was traveling with her mother and Oliver, she was torn apart from her friends at the school and continued her education with tutors in Palm Beach.

Bolton's spirit was "bruised ... by what seemed to her indifference or contempt" by her own parents. Her older sister, Betty, was regarded as the pretty one, and the clothing that she outgrew was often handed down to the stocky Frances. The most pleasant moments of her childhood were spent in the company of her maternal grandparents, to whom she was sent many times while her parents were absent.[4] In her grandparents' home, she found comfort in a loving, nurturing, and stable environment. She was immeasurably influenced by the politics of her grandfather Henry, who was the apple of her eye, and by exposure to his world. Men customarily at that time excluded women from their discussions of politics or public life, but as a child at her grandfather's knee, Bolton overheard the conversations between the men and became a good listener.[5] She also listened, captivated, to the fascinating stories told by her grandmother, which awakened in her a love of adventure and the exotic and helped pass the time without her mother. Her biographer writes:

[Bolton] saw that men seemed to do all the interesting things in the world. When a woman had to earn a living she was a servant or a teacher, or more rarely started a genteel little business like Ella Grant Wilson who came twice a week with flowers and sometimes helped to arrange them.... Mostly the world outside the home was regarded as beyond feminine comprehension.[6]

Frequently throughout Bolton's young years, her schooling was interrupted not only by the trips taken in pursuit of her older brother's health but also by family expeditions to such faraway places as Turkey. These travels led to a broad but uneven education. Nonetheless, Bolton became well read and deeply interested in a wide range of subjects, much like her father. In the Bingham household, girls were not allowed to read certain types of books; but Bolton was intrigued by the forbidden and, like her namesake cousin Fanny, read them secretly as she sat in her father's library. She would always be interested in the philosophy and theology books she came upon there. In the loveless environment fostered by her mother, whose attention was absorbed by her eldest son, and her father, who was not affectionate but strict, righteous, and intellectual, she found a means of escape in scholarship and reading. She liked to be alone, and a lifelong habit of intense reading grew from these secluded hours.

When she was eleven years old, in 1896, Bolton viewed William McKinley's parade for president as it moved past her house. That same year, she lost her beloved grandfather Henry Payne, and then, in January 1898, her mother died. Molly Bingham was only forty-four, but her total dedication to the welfare of her children, especially Oliver, and her husband had exhausted her. In late 1899, less than two years after their mother's death,

Bolton's brother Oliver died in Palm Beach. Bolton was devastated. The lingering illness of her older brother had preoccupied her early years, and his death at age twenty-one no doubt shaped her deep interest in the profession of nursing.

Immediately after these losses, her father, characteristically, packed up his two daughters along with a governess and booked them on a sailing ship to Europe on a journey that lasted two years. He did not accompany them. While in Europe, Frances attended an international private school for girls, the Dieudonne, at Bornel, France. The trip—which also included sojourns to England, Scotland, Paris, Berlin, and other sites in Europe—was an overwhelming experience for a young girl, but Bolton's grief and confusion could not be suppressed. In a search for solace and explanation, she spent much time alone, and she embarked on a reading program that included German philosophers like Schopenhauer and Kant.[7]

After her return to the United States, her father enrolled her in Miss Spence's School for girls in New York City. Bolton was seventeen. Back home in Cleveland two years later, in 1904, she joined a debutante club, the Brownies. According to tradition in Cleveland society, the members of such clubs were expected to take on a service or charity project. Other clubs had already adopted more socially acceptable tasks, such as assisting visiting nurses by rolling bandages, which at that time were not commercially available. Bolton suggested that the Brownies help the nurses by going with them into the tenements to hold bandages and extra supplies. Knowing that her father would forbid her to take part in such a project, she neglected to tell him where she was going. The project exposed her to the field of nursing as women tended to infected children, drug-addicted women, and the poor and sick in Cleveland's urban slums. Finally, when questioned by her father, she admitted what she had been doing, saying that she knew he would not have allowed her to go. Charles Bingham replied, "You're right," but added that he was glad that she had seen how many people lived.[8] Thus, Bolton helped to broaden the sphere of public life for herself and other affluent young women.

From this early, enlightening experience grew a lifetime of work on behalf of the nursing profession. Upper-class women were not expected to work outside the home at all, much less to risk the dirt and disease of nursing in the tenements. But Bolton was inspired by the good works performed by nurses, and she had learned from her family the notion that she owed something to those who were less fortunate. She became one of the few women of her era to use the advantages of her class and education to break through convention and act on her deep interests, especially nursing, taking them into the political realm.

In 1907, at age twenty-two, she married Chester Bolton, a lawyer and successful businessman. A Brahmin like herself, he built a fortune in the steel industry. Frances spent the next ten years raising their three sons—Charles, Kenyon, and Oliver—in Cleveland. In 1917, when Chester, because of his knowledge of industry as well as his political connections, was asked to serve with the War Industries Board, the Boltons packed up and moved to Washington, D.C. It was Frances who located a large house for the family. They left behind a half-completed house and stored their furniture. Before she left Cleveland, however, Frances made what could be considered her first political appearance. In addition to other philanthropic work, she served on the board of directors of Cleveland's Lakeside Hospital. A speech she made about the lack of qualified nurses in the armed forces, as well as her access to political circles, laid the groundwork for persuading the secretary of war to establish an Army School of Nursing.[9]

The year the Boltons moved to Washington, Frances, then thirty-two, was bequeathed the trust fund that her bachelor uncle Oliver Payne had set up in her name. She instantly became one of the wealthiest women in the world, some say one of the six wealthiest. But she was so concerned that the size of the bequest would diminish her husband's image of himself that she gave him the largest share. Through the fund, which she named the Payne Fund, she contributed generously to support work in her broad-ranging interests; these included education, children's literature and literacy, public health and nursing, radio communication, the negative effect of movies on children, and even parapsychology.

Like other women whose husbands were in public life, Frances Bolton spent the years during World War I volunteering for the war effort. While her husband served on the War Industries Board and worked his way up in Republican circles, she helped coordinate groups of nurses to support the war effort.[10] Foreshadowing one of her major initiatives in Congress, she campaigned to have trained nurses, rather than nurses' aides, sent to Europe. Her energy was so noticeable that the other women on the ad hoc lobbying committee, formed by the National Association of Nursing Education and including the American Nurses Association and the National Organization of Public Health Nurses, asked her to be the chair. But her political instincts cautioned her to refuse, for the committee was lobbying her husband's superiors at the War Department, and Frances knew it would look improper for her to spearhead the effort.[11] Although her access to influence was obvious, her political views and opinions seem to have come less from her husband and his position than from her family and from her reading.

Chester Bolton initially was more taken with military challenges than with business, political, or philanthropic pursuits. At age thirty-six, after having served as an aide to the assistant secretary of war in charge of munitions, he was appointed to the Army War College for officers' field training and was promoted to the rank of lieutenant colonel, becoming assistant chief of staff for the 101st Division. He was struck with Spanish influenza, however, and that illness along with the armistice ended his military career. He returned home to Cleveland in 1918.[12]

The following year, the death of the couple's newborn daughter prompted Frances Bolton's own illness, and she almost died of influenzal pneumonia, complicated by neuritis, which lasted for several years. A kidney operation finally afforded her some relief. When she was told she had only five years to live, she fought back with classic response, somewhat exotically—she began practicing yoga after learning about it at a ladies' club meeting.

She traveled to New York to learn Buddhist and other Far Eastern exercises (Gatustha Yoga), healing techniques, and philosophy. She explains:

The Buddhist chants were designed to help control the emotions because they dictate certain patterns of breathing which contribute to or reduce certain inner feelings. Once one has learned to breathe in this sense of the word, one finds new self-control. For example, if you take a low breath and push it out strongly against the abdominal muscles, you can suppress the outward expression of any emotion. Signs of fear can be prevented from showing in the face or manner; I have done it often. And of course, when you avoid the display of fear, the very feeling of it passes too. This is the benefit to you, but also you can sometimes convey your courage, or seeming courage, to others through your own calm.[13]

Several times in her life, she had to draw from this inner spiritual well to be strong for others. She painstakingly nursed her oldest son, Charles, when he was paralyzed in a diving accident at age eighteen. Much later in her career, in 1952, she saw her third son, Oliver, win a seat in Congress only to have to leave at the end of his second term because of ill health. He won election again in 1963, but a heart attack prevented him from seeking reelection. To this day, the Boltons remain the only mother and son team to have served simultaneously in Congress.

Chester Bolton slowly, and no doubt as a result of Frances's encouragement, became a rising star in the Republican Party. He won election to the Ohio Senate in 1922, and then, in 1928, was elected to the first of his two terms as a member of the U.S. House. Frances became a Washington hostess for her husband's political gatherings and aided him throughout his career.

Because of the couple's wealth, social connections, and political interests, Chester Bolton seemed destined for a national presidential ticket. In 1935 he was selected as chair of the Republican Congressional Campaign Committee. But when he lost his bid for reelection in 1936, partly because he had spent so much of the campaign working on Alf Landon's campaign for president, the Boltons moved back to Ohio. That departure from Congress gave the Boltons a needed respite, but Chester developed a heart ailment, which contributed to his decision not to seek the Republican national chairmanship. Frances meanwhile became active in the State Republican Central

Committee. After much hard work to regain his foothold, Chester was returned to Congress in 1938. One year later, at age fifty-seven, he died of heart disease.

Republican Party leaders, much out of sympathy, agreed on his widow, Frances Payne Bolton, as the nominee to fill the vacancy. At the special election, held in February 1940, she won more votes than her husband had. There was opposition, of the kind she had seen as a child, to a woman in a public position. One party leader said, "We don't want that woman in Congress," but she was determined to go, and she was confident that she was the right person for the job. She argued, "I had worked so closely with my husband that when I was asked to run for election to fill his unexpired term, I did not hesitate to do so, certain that I could fulfill that year more nearly as he would have done than could anyone else."[14] Yet she had not worked so closely with her husband as she claimed; when he came home at night, he was tired of talking about politics. Chester had never given her much important information. He had not confided in her or told her who liked and disliked whom or who had which pet projects. He had not told her what kind of work went on from day to day in committee, on the House floor, or in the congressional office.[15]

When it came time to assume office, the fifty-four-year-old Bolton faced a triple burden. In the eyes of many, because she was a widow, she was not to be taken seriously; because she was a woman, she was weak, emotional, and unstable; and because she was wealthy, she could not be expected to understand the problems of the common people.[16] By the close of her career, Frances Payne Bolton would come to surpass her husband's accomplishments in Congress, both in time served and in legislation passed. Her biographer recounts that one of the reasons for her success was that "for all her overflowing vitality, she gave an impression of self-effacement. When her ideas or desires encountered opposition, she was more likely to drop them, or at least keep them to herself, than to press for them."[17] This knack for knowing when to push and when to hold ground was also characteristic of one of the other long-serving female members of Congress, Mary Norton.

Party leaders had supported her nomination as a "graceful gesture which would do them no harm since they were sure I would get tired of politics in a few months and flit on to something else," she remembered. The following November, 1940, Bolton surprised and annoyed the leaders by declaring that she would run for a full term of her own. As she put it, "the men so much wanted to get me out, that I determined they would have to put up with me." She served for another twenty-eight years.[18]

Bolton entered Congress during one of the most chaotic periods in the twentieth century—World War II. Initially, she was assigned to several minor committees, but in 1941, as America girded for war, she resigned from all of them to accept a seat on the Committee on Foreign Affairs, where she served for the remainder of her years in the House.[19] Somewhat surprisingly because of her background, she had been an isolationist before World War II began. She was a staunch critic of President Franklin D. Roosevelt's New Deal programs and voted against both the lend-lease program of aid to the European war effort and the creation of the selective service system. Once the war began, however, she supported the nation's cause and concentrated mainly on nursing, introducing and shepherding through Congress the Bolton Act of 1943, which created the U.S. Cadet Nurse Corps and appropriated 5 million dollars to pay for it.[20] The bill provided for proper training for army and government nurses, who previously had gone to work at battlefield hospitals with a minimal course in nursing.[21] Bolton did not merely legislate for army nurses; she donned her nurse's uniform and traveled to England and other places to witness the conditions in which nurses worked during World War II. She also helped pass legislation to permit men to join the Army Nurse Corps.

Bolton's assignment to the Foreign Affairs Committee gave her a good reason to go abroad, and she became one of the most knowledgeable members of the committee as a result of her travels and her extensive study. She became a nationally known expert on the Near East, an area of the world that had interested her since she had traveled with her family to Cairo, Palestine, and Turkey when she was nineteen. Like the sights she had seen in the tenements with the visiting nurses, the poverty she saw in Egypt and Turkey had a strong effect on her. Bolton's quest for knowledge about the Near East brought her to the Library of Congress, where she sat for many weeks reading everything she could find about that region.[22] Because she used her own money to finance her trips, the taxpayers were not charged even though she traveled as a member of the committee.

When the Republicans swept Congress in 1946, Bolton continued her work on the Foreign Affairs Committee. She focused on documenting "the strategy and tactics of world Communism," railing against the policies of Harry S. Truman and Roosevelt before him, which she regarded as abject appeasement of Soviet Russia and its aims in Asia.[23] Her organizational abilities were evidenced in her efforts to reorganize the Foreign Affairs Committee into geographic subcommittees, herself serving on the Subcommittee on Eastern Europe, the Balkans, and the Middle East.

Shortly after World War II she had communicated with the Soviet ambassador Andrei Gromyko and successfully arranged a visit to the Soviet Union with a small group of members of Congress. When the trip took place, in 1947, she became the first woman to lead a congressional excursion abroad and the first member of the Foreign Affairs Committee to journey to the Soviet Union. Her adventuresome nature held true. During that trip, which included a tour of Europe and the Near East, she managed to visit twenty different nations.

Her travels put her in sympathy with the plight of countries directly affected by World War II, and she became a voice of moderate internationalism in her own party. She was the only Republican in the House to support postwar loans to Britain and was only one of two to support aid to Turkey and Greece during a period when other Republicans, like Rep. Joseph McCarthy, R-Wis., were ranting against most foreign involvement and accusing innocent citizens of being Communists.

Despite her supposed independence, however, Bolton adhered faithfully to Republican Party lines in her votes. She opposed the Roosevelt national programs so contrary to the states' rights and federated republic views traditional in her family. She supported the Taft-Hartley Act, which weakened labor's right to organize. Yet she also supported the right of labor unions to strike, although she did worry about labor's power to dominate rather than to be an equal force with business.

No one could accuse Frances Payne Bolton of laziness. For her, an average work week was sixty to seventy hours.[24] Perhaps her childhood experiences led to her belief that "all women—especially in Congress—had to work twice as hard as men for everything they accomplished."[25] Bolton stood out as a member who was conscientious about being on the floor during long nighttime sessions, always looking neat and alert.[26] As a young child, she had been belittled by her older sister, who had made her feel she could do nothing right, so perhaps her diligence was partly motivated by a yearning for the praise she had never received.

Although by most accounts Bolton was a fairly conservative member of Congress, she proved to be ahead of her time during the 1940s by speaking out against segregation in the military. A few years later President Truman issued an executive order to integrate the armed forces, amid protests that the move would be bad for morale. Later, in the 1950s, Bolton advocated a women's draft, recounting how she had

heard chivalrous members of the male sex—including some of my esteemed Congressional colleagues—express unalterable opposition to any measure which would require their daughters, their sisters, or just women in general, to serve in the armed forces. I am afraid such gallantry is sadly out of date, and as a woman I find it rather stupid. Why should we imply that American women are not as ready as American men to serve their country? ... Woman's place includes defending the home.[27]

A leading proponent of war preparedness, Bolton argued that the draft laws should be changed during peacetime so that the best possible army could be drafted in case of war. She noted that "[a]t the beginning of the war, the Army decided that women could be useful in 4 jobs: clerk, telephone operator, driver, and cook. Before the end of the war, women were doing more than 200 different kinds of jobs in the Army, and filling some 450 different billets in the Navy."[28] Still, she never went so far as to suggest that women serve in combat positions. This idea is one whose time still has not come, although women have been given wider roles in battle. Nevertheless, there are no provisions to draft them.

In 1953 President Dwight D. Eisenhower appointed Bolton as the first female congressional delegate to the United Nations. She brought to this endeavor diplomatic skills that had been honed by years as helpmate to her husband at Washington parties and by her own extensive global travels. In 1954 she delivered a historic speech before the United Nations, speaking about South Africa and its policy of apartheid. She said,

Negro Americans in the U.S. are truly Americans who would not change their heritage if they could.... We are learning that as we rub shoulders we gain experience which can be gained only when we come together ... [Y]ou will find that cooperation between peoples, not segregation and separation, slow and difficult as the process may be, is the way to salvation [and that] prejudice [must be put down] wherever it raises its head, whether we are the victims or not ... an attack on any group endangers everyone's freedom.[29]

During the 1960s, Bolton built a strong civil rights record, fighting for equal rights for male nurses and for including women in the federal Civil Rights Act. Her Payne Fund had consistently supported scholarships for young people of all races. Her support for civil rights won her accolades from black groups, who noted that a major section of the Bolton Act, which established the U.S. Cadet Nurse Corps, required that funding be spent without regard to the race, color, or creed of corps members.[30] Bolton's inheritance made it possible for her to contribute to many different charities and causes, and among them were the National Association for the Advancement of Colored People and the National Urban League.

In 1955, at age seventy, she journeyed to East Africa as chair of the Near East and Africa Subcommittee. During this trip, which lasted nearly three months, she visited twenty-four countries. Her biographer writes:

She had climbed mountains afoot, fled in a Jeep from a charging wild elephant, embraced a Nigerian mother who had a son studying in America on a Payne Fund scholarship.... But mostly she had seen how people lived and worked. She had spent most of her time analyzing their struggles for education and health and development of their land. She had walked about where malnutrition and disease stalked so that the smooth little bodies of children turned a rough, red-brown and their hair gray. She had reviewed the armies of defense against these enemies—the hospitals, doctors, and nurses. Missionaries and miners, businessmen and lawyers, foreign agents and national political leaders, tribal chiefs and city workers, all told their stories to the visitor.... For ninety-nine days, Frances kept up a pace which tired her companions.[31]

She left with impressions of "[m]alnutrition, disease, the majesty of the country, a continent of new life … new hope." She felt the potential in this land of contrasts. Still, she believed that the experience was "unfinished and needing fulfillment." She had a sense, born of her mystic, Buddhist philosophical leanings, that "somewhere in her long past Africa had played a part." She believed that "you and I are part and parcel of the stream of universal life—as water drops are part of the Great Sea."[32]

Bolton's social class could have shielded her from the crueler aspects of the world, but instead she "addressed herself to the realization of the American ideal" and "believe[d] passionately in the equality of people."[33] It was said that her money allowed her to be independent of interests that might try to influence her, but her wealth certainly did not corrupt her. She judiciously did not overspend on congressional election campaigns, sometimes following in the footsteps of her husband, who spent all of $120.94 in his last campaign.[34] But, facing some diligent opponents, she possessed the wherewithal to wage a hard-fought race and to hire extra congressional staff above and beyond what an average member was able to afford.

Bolton always campaigned energetically, speaking at church meetings and union halls, meeting people at Parent-Teacher Association meetings, shaking hands at local Grange gatherings. In her last campaign, in 1968, none of these tactics mattered. Her district had been redrawn, and a fellow Democratic representative, Charles Vanik, challenged her and was able to claim victory.

Frances Payne Bolton was a remarkable woman who could have lived an extremely comfortable and affluent life without ever holding a paying job, much less working six dozen hours a week to fight for constituents, for nurses, for the disadvantaged, for a better way of life for people in remote corners of the world. She yearned for greater fulfillment, for more knowledge and work, and, no doubt, for affection. It is true that she had material comforts beyond the imagination of most citizens. She owned three homes, in Cleveland, Palm Beach, and Washington, D.C. Her Washington home became the Republican Club (now know as the Capitol Hill Club) and is used by Republicans for their political and business meetings.[35] She had a special love for West Palm Beach—its beauty, the surf and the birds, and childhood memories. She remembered the Native Americans who had paddled their canoes in the rivers nearby. As a member of Congress, she entertained world dignitaries there, including Saudi princes, who would pilot their boats to her dock, adjacent to the mansion of her neighbor, Merriweather Post, the richest woman in America.[36] Yet even with her wealth, life always seemed to force her to be strong for others, especially for ill family members.

Rep. Joseph Martin, House majority leader and, later, Speaker of the House (1947–1949 and 1953–1955), summed up her public persona: "Representative Bolton is loved and respected by her every colleague, regardless of the side of the aisle on which he sits."[37] Perhaps the finest compliment came from her hometown upon the news of her appointment in 1953 as a delegate to the United Nations. One Cleveland newspaper declared, "All of Cleveland knows that Mrs. Bolton will measure up."[38]

As a woman, pushing at the edge of human advancement at home and abroad, Frances Payne Bolton was extraordinary for her perseverance and spirit. Her zest for life and her vast wealth allowed her to exert her influence to ease the path for other women. She rose above personal grief, and although she never considered herself a crusader strictly for women's rights, her fortitude directed her to pursuits she found more absorbing. Her life's work of rearing a family and serving twenty-nine years in Congress, her philanthropy and travel, and the advances she managed to gain for the nursing profession moved women into a new realm. Bolton expressed her philosophy in an interview with the journalist Edward R. Murrow:

I believe that what we call a life span is but one of our endless numbers of lifetimes during which, bit by bit, we shall experience all things. I believe that we are responsible for our thoughts and actions from the moment the soul asks, "What am I?" I am not dismayed by the darkness into which mankind has betrayed itself, for I know as only women can that all new life comes out of darkness through the gateway of agony and anguish into the light.[39]

After her defeat for reelection, Bolton returned to Ohio, where she lived quietly in Lyndhurst, a suburb of Cleveland, and pursued her philanthropic interests. She died there on March 9, 1977, a few weeks short of her ninety-second birthday.

NOTES

1. Virginia Roller Batdorff, "Hard Work—She Likes It," *Independent Woman*, December 1953, 441–442.
2. David Loth, *A Long Way Forward: The Biography of Congresswoman Frances Payne Bolton* (New York: Longmans, Green, 1957), 1.
3. Ibid., 15.
4. Ibid., 23.
5. Ibid., 37.
6. Ibid.
7. Ibid., 76–77.
8. Ibid., 65.
9. Hope Chamberlin, *A Minority of Members: Women in the United States Congress* (New York: Praeger, 1973), 130.
10. U.S. Congress, House, Office of the Historian, *Women in Congress, 1917–1990* (Washington, D.C.: U.S. Government Printing Office, 1991), 22.
11. Loth, *A Long Way Forward*, 105.
12. Ibid., 111–114.
13. Ibid., 117.
14. Ibid., 193.
15. Ibid.
16. Ibid., 197.

17. Ibid., 80.
18. Ibid., 193, 203.
19. House, *Women in Congress, 1917–1990*, 22.
20. Ibid.
21. Annabel Paxton, *Women in Congress* (Richmond, Va.: Dietz Press, 1945), 67.
22. Batdorff, "Hard Work," 441–442.
23. Ibid., 441.
24. Ibid.
25. Chamberlin, *A Minority of Members*, 136.
26. Loth, *A Long Way Forward*, 198.
27. Frances Payne Bolton, "Women Should Be Drafted," *American Magazine,* June 1949, 47.
28. Ibid.
29. "The Lady Congressman from Ohio," *Negro History Bulletin,* April 1954, 156.
30. Ibid., 155.
31. Frances Payne Bolton, quoted in Loth, *A Long Way Forward,* 289–290.
32. Ibid.
33. Ibid., 155.
34. *Current Biography 1940,* s.v. "Bolton, Frances P(ayne Bingham)," 96.
35. Charles B. Holstein, administrative assistant to Rep. Leonor Sullivan, to author, October 27, 1994, 7.
36. Rep. Charles Vanik, interview by author, Washington, D.C., June 1994.
37. Batdorff, "Hard Work," 442.
38. Ibid.
39. Loth, *A Long Way Forward,* 267–268.

Margaret Chase Smith
Republican–Maine (1940–1973)
First Woman to Serve in Both Houses of Congress

> *I don't want to see the Republican Party ride to political victory on the four horsemen of calumny—fear, ignorance, bigotry, and smear ... surely we Republicans aren't that desperate for victory.*
>
> Margaret Chase Smith, quoted in *Newsweek*, June 12, 1950

Like Jeannette Rankin—the first woman elected to Congress—Margaret Chase Smith attained summits until then unconquered by any woman. Throughout her quest she remained keenly aware of the original nature of her undertaking. Proper but not stiff, unflappable, and tenacious, Smith was the first woman in U.S. history to be elected to both houses of Congress. She was the first woman to be elected to the U.S. Senate in her own right, serving from 1949 to 1973, longer than any other woman even today. She was the first woman to have her name placed in nomination for the presidency of the United States, the first person to chair a televised Senate committee hearing, and the first woman to chair the Senate Republican Conference, the caucus of all Republicans in that body. She founded the first library devoted to the papers and memorabilia of a female senator, the Margaret Chase Smith Library at Northwood Institute in Skowhegan, Maine.

Skowhegan, where Smith was born on December 14, 1897, is an aging mill town along the Kennebec River, called "a place to watch" by Native Americans. It had a population of approximately 5,000 when Smith was first elected. In a state whose population did not reach one million during Smith's years of public service, she became well positioned to run for Senate once she had established congressional credentials. The summer day I drove to Skowhegan from Bangor to interview her, farmers' roadside stands were selling orange tiger lilies and strawberries, although several blueberry outlets were boarded up, awaiting harvest season. Her house, white with red shutters, sat on top of a hill. A brand new Cadillac, with the license plate "Maine 1," graced her front yard.

Smith's beginnings were humble. She was the eldest of six children, two of whom died in childhood. Her father, George Emery Chase, of English descent, was the town barber. His shop was attached to their five-room frame home. Everyone in town knew the Chase family. Mr. Chase often took ill with severe headaches. Legend has it, although she denied it, that Margaret would take over the shop and give the customers a shave and a haircut. As she later said:

I was always ambitious in wanting to try new things; and at the time there was a good deal of talk about women barbers and about beauty parlors and so on, so I thought my father should teach me the business. He did. He taught me how to give a shave and I got so I could do a fairly good job when I could find anybody who would let me try.[1]

After he retired, George Chase worked as a caretaker in a local woolen mill.

Her mother, Carrie Matilda (Murray) Chase, who had nearly completed high school, was descended from Canadians who had immigrated from England and then moved to the United States. Carrie Chase had a strong influence on her four surviving children—Margaret, Wilbur, Evelyn, and Laura.[2] "She was strong minded and ... taught us to appreciate everything we had, to work hard, and obey her and Papa."[3] Smith recalled that both her parents worked hard. "We were a family that worked together and played together. I remember the first automobile my father had. We would go on picnics. We always went on picnics. We made our own fun. It was real family living."[4] But she attributed her reputation for hard work and stalwartness to her mother. She seemed flabbergasted that her mother could work and simultaneously raise six children. "My mother worked, she always worked. She, in the early days, waited tables [at the Coburn Hotel] ... she also worked in a five-and-ten-cent store [Green Brothers] in her spare time. She worked in the shoe factory. She was a fancy stitcher."[5] The family pinched pennies. "Mother always got my clothes too big, so I would grow into them.... how well I remember that."[6] Her advice to women was "Work your way up instead of expecting to start at the top."[7]

At age thirteen, following in her mother's footsteps, Smith became a clerk at the Green Brothers five-and-dime, working after school for ten cents per hour. Then, still in high school, she filled in as a night switchboard operator at the local telephone company. After graduating from high school, where she had taken commercial courses—shorthand, typing, bookkeeping—Smith

could not afford college. This perhaps explains her later penchant for tabu-
lating all honorary degrees she had been awarded in her life, a total of nine-
ty-five. She taught briefly in the one-room Pitts primary school after high
school for $8.50 per week, of which she spent $5.00 for room and board, and
then moved on to become a telephone operator. "One of her frequent callers,
who usually wanted to know the correct time, was Clyde H. Smith, Skowhegan's first selectman (akin to Mayor)," and Margaret's future husband. "He
had the most fascinating voice," she would later recall.[8]

In 1919, Margaret was hired for eighteen dollars a week as jill-of-all-trades
(circulation, advertising, editorial) by the Skowhegan *Independent Reporter,* a
publication co-owned by Clyde Smith. In the following eight years, she
helped build the paper to seventh place among country weeklies.[9] During
this period, she also became active in Maine's Business and Professional
Women's Club. She organized the Skowhegan chapter in 1922 and in the following year was named president of its statewide affiliate. In 1928, she
became office manager for the Daniel E. Cummings Company woolen mill,
being paid the "unheard of sum of fifty dollars per week."[10] Two years later,
after a long courtship, she married Clyde, a divorcé twenty-one years her
senior. She was thirty-three. He was wealthy (he owned a thirty-room mansion) and was politically connected (he served as chair of the State Highway
Commission).[11]

In 1936, Clyde Smith was elected to the U.S. House of Representatives,
and Margaret became his secretary at a salary of $3,000 per year, a sizable
sum for a woman.[12] She was elected treasurer of the Congressional Women's
Club, an organization made up of the spouses of members. Called a "satura-
tion point politician" by *Time* magazine, Clyde had been elected to his first
office at age nineteen and then ran for office forty-eight times in his life without a single defeat.[13] "He was ultraliberal for his times, pushed hard for labor
and pension legislation" in a state noted for harsh economic circumstances.
In addition, "he was known in every nook and cranny in this state, and well
known, and could carry almost any kind of weight in any campaign."[14]

Four years after his election to Congress, Clyde became ill. To keep his
place in the primary to be held in June 1940, Margaret agreed to file to run.
She withdrew when he recovered, but fate dealt another hand. Shortly afterward, Clyde Smith died of a heart attack, and Margaret Chase Smith became
a widow at age forty-three.[15] The couple had had no children.

A press statement by Clyde Smith had been released earlier, saying that he
was seriously ill and if he did not recover, "his wife and partner in public life
would run."[16] Margaret braced herself for the road ahead:

I was sad, but I was so busy … I didn't have time for anything because … I had to be
a candidate. Three of the men who had worked for him so hard through the years,
came to me immediately, and said they had someone, a young man, they were groom-

ing in a case like this, but he was not ready. Would I be willing to run for the unexpired term? They would do the work, the hard work, if I would do it.[17]

In order to win the remainder of her husband's term and a full term of her
own in the House, Smith had to win a special primary, a regular primary,
and two general elections, all within five months. She won her first general
election handily with a margin of 25,000 votes. "I'd been taught by my husband not to do it halfway."[18] Her first office was in the Cannon Building,
Room 231.

Smith had acquired a political education while she traversed the state with
her husband in their big black Maxwell, from Caribou to Kittery. She had
often driven the car in the 1930s, a period when women drivers were still
rare. Maine was not much larger than a single congressional district, and thus
a highly motivated but underfunded candidate could make political inroads.
She recollected:

We could do twice as much, you see, with me driving. I was the first woman in the
state, of course, that did anything of the kind. It was an interesting life, a very interesting life.... We worked on the campaigns. I'd drive part of the time. I used to needlepoint when I was waiting for him to go in to some place. I used to carry it around in
the back seat of the car because he'd say, "I'll only be gone fifteen minutes." I knew
that meant fifteen hours, so I would do that while I was waiting for him, and people
would visit with me while I was waiting, while we were at the Statehouse.[19]

Smith's needlepoint now adorns the chairs, furniture, and walls of the Margaret Chase Smith Library in Skowhegan.

Her composure and appearance worked to her benefit. Reporters noted
Smith was "attractive but not glossy," possessing the kind of beauty that "wins
the admiration of men without arousing the antagonism of women."[20]

The new congresswoman seemed matter-of-fact about what she wanted
to do almost from the moment she stepped into office. Her career was focused
on the Naval Affairs Committee and, later, the Armed Services Committee,
because, she explained, "Maine has such a long coastline, and so much ship-
building."[21] She recounted how she went about requesting her first House
committee assignment:

When I asked for a committee, I asked for Appropriations, knowing that I would not
get it.... I asked for it, because that was the thing to do in those days. You didn't expect
to get what you asked for, so you would ask for something that was impossible. And
then, practically in tears, go down a step. So when I asked for Appropriations, I said,
well, I suppose I can't take Naval Affairs. And Naval Affairs was what I wanted; I did-
n't want Appropriations.... I think I was smart.[22]

Smith's career spanned almost thirty-three years in the House and the
Senate. She far outdistanced her husband in her prominence and achievements as a legislator and stateswoman. She became an expert on many issues,

rising to the position of lead Republican on the Senate Armed Services Committee. During the eight years she served in the House of Representatives, one of her most important legislative involvements—as it was of other women members—was the 1945 legislation that gave permanent status to the WAVES (Women Accepted for Volunteer Emergency Service, a navy program). Smith found herself in a protracted struggle with the navy over this initiative, which she had championed. The navy was not yet ready to offer women permanent standing, preferring instead a peacetime reserve. Smith opposed this solution, saying, "[E]ither the armed services have a permanent need of women officers and enlisted women or they do not."[23] However, her proposal was omitted from the House bill, and essentially she was defeated by default in the full House vote. She then turned her attention to ensuring that the House-Senate conference committee (in which members of the Armed Services Committees from both chambers work out differences between their respective bills) would include it when they agreed on a final bill. She wrote directly to the secretary of defense, enlisting his support. Defense Secretary James V. Forrestal then instructed the conferees that the "National Military Establishment felt it imperative that women be granted permanent Regular status in the Armed Services."[24] The House conferees receded to the Senate position. She had won.

Two years later, the Naval Affairs Committee and Military Affairs Committee were merged into a single Armed Services Committee. Smith became the chair of one of its subcommittees and in 1947 arranged for her committee to make a postwar inspection of Europe, the Near East, and the Far East. During this trip she appeared before the Iranian legislature, the first time a woman had done so.

As described in the *Guide* to her library, Smith was "more hawk than sparrow," even though it sometimes meant going against the Republican Party.[25] She invested her life in the Armed Services and National Aeronautics and Space Administration committees of the Congress. She considered her greatest House achievement obtaining permanent status for women in the military. And former NASA director James E. Webb said, "If it were not for a woman, Margaret Chase Smith, we never would have placed a man on the moon."[26]

She maintained a wide streak of Maine independence. Early in her House career, she broke with the majority of her party to vote for the Lend-Lease Act requested by President Franklin D. Roosevelt. This plan was developed by the United States during World War II to transfer equipment, food, and weapons to nations fighting against Nazism and Communism. She also broke with her party in supporting the Selective Training and Service Act for mandatory draft registration. And in 1947, she supported the Armed Services

Unification Act, which combined the separate branches of the military into a Department of Defense.

While a member of the House, she voted against her party's legislation that attempted to increase the power of the Committee on Un-American Activities by changing it from a special to a standing committee. And though in 1945 she cosponsored the Equal Rights Amendment (ERA), she preferred that women seek positions based on their abilities, not because they were women. Much later she acknowledged, "I was not a great women's woman. Women were always apologizing: 'I know I'm a woman, but....' I thought women were people. I didn't think I should be called 'Mrs.' It was OK, but I was a representative and then a senator." Until her death, she maintained that too many women "think just because they are women, they ought to have special consideration. I didn't think so."[27] She devoted little time to the ERA; it is not mentioned in the index to her book, *Declaration of Conscience*.

In early 1947, Maine's senior senator, Wallace White, indicated his desire to retire. On June 1, 1947, after seven years in the House, Smith announced her candidacy for the seat. Her campaign slogan became "Don't Trade a Record for a Promise." And, indeed, her record of hard work, honesty, and forthrightness stood her in good stead. One of her constituents said of her: "She's as straight as a yard of pump water."[28] Her campaign depended heavily on volunteers, friends she had made through the Maine Business and Professional Women's Club network, and her telephone operator friends throughout the state. She had little cash; her strength was rooted in personal friendships and personal loyalty. She also possessed endless energy and determination. During the campaign, she flew back to Portland from Washington, D.C., picked up her car, and "took to the icy roads, the snowdrifts, the sub-zero temperatures as she covered the state of Maine, reaching even the remotest spots where occasionally she had to put up for the night at a farmhouse." At one point she slipped on the ice and fractured her arm; after being rushed to a hospital in Bangor by ambulance, she kept a speaking engagement two hours later in Rockland, sixty miles away.[29] The campaign was not absent innuendo and mud slinging. Her Senate campaign opponents started a rumor that Smith had caused her husband's divorce from his first wife, even though the divorce occurred three years before they met. And a photograph of Smith in Europe revealed beer cans on a table in the background.[30]

Nonetheless, on June 21, 1948, her intense campaigning paid off; she beat three Republican men in the primary race, logging more votes herself than the sum of all their tallies. Her narrow plurality was 4,765 votes. Because Maine was largely a Republican state in the late 1940s, her opponent in the general election was token. Thus, she became the first woman in U.S. history to be elected to the U.S. Senate in her own right.

Technically, she ran her own campaigns, although the vigilance of Major General William C. Lewis Jr., her longtime friend and personal assistant, is well noted in the records of the time, as well as in her autobiography. The *Maine Sunday Telegram* recounted: "William Lewis was the master strategist behind every campaign and the moving force behind Mrs. Smith's remarkable career."[31] And *Time* magazine explained: "Senator Smith shuns the Washington social whirl and lives quietly in a 3-apartment building in suburban Silver Spring, Maryland. The other apartments are occupied by Bill Lewis, her ubiquitous administrative assistant, and his parents."[32] In 1972, Lewis wrote in the Editor's Preface to her autobiography: "The author herein is the Quiet Woman. Her deeds and speeches are the heart, brain, and backbone of this book. The editor and annotator has merely filled in, adding flesh to the body of the book."[33] It appears that Lewis had painstakingly assembled the chapters of what would become Margaret Chase Smith's only published volume on her extensive career. He remained in the background but his handiwork was evident. Writers of the time wondered why they never married.[34] Their lives and careers, as the book demonstrates, were inseparable:

Always with her, though often remaining in the background, is William C. Lewis, her fifty-five year old administrative assistant, whose association with the Senator dates from the days when she was on the House Naval Affairs Committee ... and he was on the Committee staff. An attorney, he was the son of two lawyers and credited with influencing the Senator, some would say "a Svengali-like" influence over her, making her more suspicious and petty; her warm down-to-earth nature becoming unforgiving, vindictive, and thin-skinned. One analytical account criticizes her legislative accomplishments as not encompassing new legislation to benefit Maine though she has staunchly protected what others have created.[35]

When Smith first arrived in the Senate, there were no facilities for women senators. She was forced to use visitors' restrooms, and the barbershop or gym were then open only to men. She proclaimed, "I am proud that I cost the American taxpayer less money than any of the other Senators." As the lone woman, she entertained guests in the Senate dining room.[36]

Although she nearly always voted along Republican Party lines, she gained a reputation as an independent, and often a maverick, for her highly publicized votes on singularly controversial and dramatic issues. These were the votes on which Margaret Chase Smith voted her conscience, votes on which she did not conform to her party's line or to her friends' advice. In fact, her moral pronouncements became her trademark. When asked what she viewed as her major accomplishments, she stated, "I had a variety of interests. I was a generalist ... I never made a speech just to make a speech."[37]

Nonetheless, she singled out and is probably best remembered for her "Declaration of Conscience" speech, made on June 1, 1950. Without referring to him by name, she attacked a fellow Republican, Sen. Joseph McCarthy, for his tactics of accusing other citizens of being Communist sympathizers. McCarthy's accusatory tirades labeling citizens as Communists with no real evidence created an environment of suspicion between Americans in Washington and in the nation as a whole. (McCarthy's congressional immunity protected him from charges of slander and defamation.) This particular moment in Smith's long congressional career, when she stood strongly for the politics of a higher order, was a watershed. *Declaration of Conscience,* the only book that bears her name as author, painstakingly retraces these moments of history.

Smith had been contemplating making such a speech for quite a while before she actually did so. On February 9, 1950, Senator McCarthy had delivered his accusatory remarks in West Virginia: "I have here in my hand a list of 205 [men in the State Department] who are known to be members of the Communist Party."[38] At first Smith took him at his word, assuming the list he held was backed by hard evidence. But as the weeks progressed, and she had the opportunity to probe the nature of his research and proofs, she concluded that he was unable to document his charges. She spent the Memorial Day weekend at her home in Maine preparing a rebuttal. Lewis "asked me what I was doing, [and] I told him I was making notes.... I had a notepad making notes all the time." Exactly how the speech was written is not clear; she says "we wrote the draft of a full speech.... No one else participated in the drafting." Yet she insists, "That's the one thing Mr. Lewis would never do for me. He would never write my speeches."[39]

On June 1, she headed for the Senate to give her speech. She would be the first Republican to openly criticize a highly publicized member of her own party, and she had been in the Senate only one year. As she was about to board the train that runs to the Capitol from the Senate Office Buildings, Smith encountered Senator McCarthy. He said to her, "Margaret, you look very serious. Are you going to make a speech?" and she responded, "Yes, and you will not like it." McCarthy asked, "Is it about me?" Smith answered, "Yes, but I'm not going to mention your name."[40]

She kept a close hold on advance copies of the speech, explaining that "I didn't want anyone to know I was going to do it, [because] the Senate rules would cut short debate." Instead, press releases were prepared and entrusted to Lewis. She told Lewis "to let me talk a few minutes; I didn't know if I would have the courage to go through with it. He said, 'You know what's on your mind, and you have a speech.' I told him let me be on my feet two minutes.... Golly, I was nervous.... He [Lewis] went up and asked the Presiding Officer to recognize me first."[41]

When Smith was recognized to speak in the Senate, she rose and began speaking, and "after just two minutes, Mr. Lewis walked out the door to give the releases to the press. I said to myself, 'Here I am. I'm on my own.' "[42] She spoke with determination:

I would like to speak briefly and simply about a serious national condition. It is a national feeling of fear and frustration that could result in national suicide and the end of everything that we Americans hold dear.... I speak as a Republican. I speak as a woman. I speak as a United States Senator. I speak as an American.... Those of us who shout the loudest about Americanism in making character assassinations are all too frequently those who, by our own words and acts, ignore some of the basic principles of Americanism:
    The right to criticize;
    The right to hold unpopular beliefs;
    The right to protest;
    The right of independent thought.
    The exercise of these rights should not cost one single American citizen his reputation or his right to a livelihood nor should he be in danger of losing his reputation or livelihood merely because he happens to know someone who holds unpopular beliefs.[43]

When Smith came to the end of her speech, she expected McCarthy to have some response. She recalls, "I waited for McCarthy to ask me questions."[44] Instead, a page came up to her and relayed to her the ominous message, "The Senator from Wisconsin has left the floor." He had chosen not to answer her nor to refute her claims. Smith had anticipated this moment with trepidation because of her junior status as well as her laconic nature. For her to challenge an icon of the Senate was indeed courageous.

Holding unpopular beliefs was a burden Smith learned to shoulder, and she was soon to discover the cost of expressing those beliefs. Seven months after her speech, McCarthy, who chaired the Senate's Committee on Executive Expenditures, which made Republican assignments on the subcommittees, removed her from the Permanent Investigations Subcommittee and replaced her with Sen. Richard Nixon, her junior in seniority. When she protested the move, McCarthy told her that he wanted Nixon on this committee because of his investigative experience on the House Un-American Activities Committee. Smith responded that she had been on investigative committees for four years before either McCarthy or Nixon had been elected to Congress.[45] McCarthy refused to budge, however, and she had no recourse.

The enmity was to play out in the succeeding Maine Senate race in 1954. Smith had concluded her remarks by offering a resolution in the Senate named after the title of her speech, "Declaration of Conscience." She denounced elements of the Republican Party who had "hopes of riding the Republican Party to victory through the selfish political exploitation of fear, bigotry, ignorance, and intolerance."[46] She and the other Republican senators who had joined her cause of condemnation were "sneeringly referred to by McCarthy as 'Snow White and the Six Dwarfs.'"[47] He entered a candidate against her in the 1954 Republican primary race, Robert L. Jones, who had been a staff member on McCarthy's Congressional Committee on Investigations. She beat Jones by a whopping 5-1 margin. Her real election fight that year came from the Democratic candidate, Paul Fullam, a member of a resurgent Democratic Party. The Republican Party had controlled Maine for years, but in that year a popular Democrat, Edmund Muskie, would be elected governor, and his election caused voters to switch to the Democratic column on their ballots. Although Smith beat Fullam by 40,000 votes, his vote count was the best showing of any of her opponents until her defeat in 1972.[48] Her margin was 58.6 percent, down from 71.3 percent in 1948.

The Declaration of Conscience speech was certainly the zenith of Margaret Chase Smith's nearly thirty-three years in Congress. One week after the speech she appeared on the cover of *Newsweek,* and talk began about her possible vice-presidential bid. Her meteoric rise in attention from the press sprang from the Senate confrontation that the media declared a rise above partisanship in the national interest. "Literally, she had 'twisted the elephant trunk.'" At the Republican National Convention in 1948, she had suggested that it might be a good idea to choose a woman as a vice-presidential candidate. Then, in 1949, she declared that although she had no interest in the office herself, "the party that nominates a woman will win the 1952 election." In fact, her wit shone through when a radio commentator asked her what she would do if she woke up in the White House. "She twanged right back: 'I'd go straight to Mrs. Truman and apologize. Then I'd go home.'"[49]

Those who answer only to appeals of conscience are not always well liked, and such was the case with Margaret Chase Smith. In 1961 she made another well-publicized speech criticizing President John F. Kennedy for a lack of fortitude in his relations with Nikita Khrushchev, the Soviet premier. On the Senate floor she stated, "we have the nuclear capability, but not the nuclear credibility."[50] Kennedy's failure to follow through on the ultimatum he had delivered to the Soviet Union ordering it to remove Communist troops from Laos triggered Smith's speech. Neither Kennedy nor Khrushchev seemed terribly pleased with what she said, and both responded publicly. An article in *Look* magazine described the president as angry and said that he had called Smith "ignorant."[51] Khrushchev, in a letter to the British House of Commons, described her as "the devil in a disguise of a woman" outdoing "all records of savagery," and even Mrs. Khrushchev joined in to call her a warmonger. Smith dismissed Khrushchev's comments, saying, "Khrushchev isn't really mad at me. I'm not that important. He is angry because American officials have grown more firm since my speech." Her response concerning Mrs. Khrushchev's remark was that if she "really wanted peace and sane survival then she should have a heart-to-heart talk with her husband."[52] A year later, Smith made a second speech on the same theme. Only one month after that speech, in October 1962, President Kennedy described the offensive missile buildup in Cuba and announced the naval and air quarantine of the island, which led to the Cuban missile crisis.

On September 24, 1963, an important vote came up in the Senate: the vote to ratify the nuclear test ban treaty. In writing about this vote, Smith herself brought up the question that faces every senator, namely, whether senators should vote according to the interests of their particular state and constituency or according to the national interest and their own consciences.[53] She had deep concerns about the test ban treaty's effect on the national security of the United States and raised these concerns in a speech asking sixteen questions of the president. Her concerns ranged from the feasibility of detecting violations to the definition of environments in which testing would be forbidden.[54] That Smith devoted so much time and energy to questioning the wisdom of this treaty indicates her conscientiousness, for the treaty's ratification was never at issue. She cast a "very troubled vote" against ratification, a vote that was based on her convictions and her conscience and went against both her party and progressives.[55] The vote, as had been expected, was overwhelmingly in favor of ratification. At the White House, President Kennedy was handed a note by his secretary, Evelyn Lincoln, "Vote 80-19. Mrs. Smith went wrong."[56]

In several election contests during her career, Smith blazed new territory. Her 1960 reelection to the Senate was one of these times: it marked the first time two women ran against one another for a Senate seat. Her opponent was Lucia Cormier, and their faceoff, although it seems to have been rather cordial by today's standards, attracted a great deal of publicity. Cormier was described as "an ex schoolteacher . . . a Roman Catholic of French Canadian descent, effective minority leader of the state legislature, and the darling of Maine's resurgent Democrats."[57] In this race, Cormier was chosen to run against Smith because of her gender. Smith initially felt uncomfortable about running against a woman she considered a friend, but she soon found herself engaged in the campaign. She became angry when her Senate colleague Edmund Muskie made appearances in Maine for Cormier, and she refused to debate Cormier until the end of the campaign, saying such an event would only increase publicity for the challenger.[58] In the end, Smith won the election, by the largest vote in Maine's history and the highest winning percentage of all Republican senatorial candidates: she took 62 percent of the vote.[59]

Smith's run for the presidency in 1964 was historic. She was the first woman to seek her party's presidential nomination. When asked what motivated her to run for president, she answered:

Nothing motivated me. I had a telephone call from a group of Young Matrons of Illinois who did not want to vote for the likely Republican nominee—Barry Goldwater or Nelson Rockefeller. Then a call came to me from a young Illinois legislator who said he wanted to visit from Illinois and he asked me to think about making an announcement. I said I'd think about it and spoke to Mr. Lewis on my staff. He said he knew I couldn't win but actually had nothing to lose. So I went to Illinois since I had been invited to speak at a hospital lunch there. I really didn't travel around the U.S. campaigning.[60]

Her formal announcement that she would enter the New Hampshire presidential primary came at a speech to the Women's National Press Club in January 1964, in which she listed all of the reasons why she should not run: lack of money, no organization, little time, and the great odds against victory. Then she announced, "because of all the impelling reasons against my running, I have decided I *shall.*"[61] Smith then went on to campaign in New Hampshire, where she was photographed in snowshoes when the temperature failed to reach twenty degrees Fahrenheit. Her feminine image was accentuated by her practice of handing out recipes and homemade muffins along the campaign trail and posing for photos while cooking.[62] In fact, her muffins got so much publicity, Nelson Rockefeller countered by distributing his fudge recipe.[63]

Smith received 205,690 votes nationally and logged primary votes in Illinois, Massachusetts, New Hampshire, Oregon, and Texas. She spent $25 on her New Hampshire campaign and $85 on the Illinois campaign. In Illinois, she received 26 percent of the vote to Barry Goldwater's 63 percent.[64] At the Republican National Convention in San Francisco on July 12, 1964, she won twenty-seven delegates.

Not long after this expected defeat, she campaigned to have the rose designated as the national flower. She ran headlong into her fellow Republican Everett Dirksen, who favored the marigold and deadlocked the bill. Not until October 1987 did the rose become the national flower through the unflagging efforts of her friend and colleague Rep. Lindy Boggs, a Democrat from Louisiana. Even at the end of her life, Smith's eyes sparkled when she recalled how hard Boggs had worked on the rose bill. Smith symbolically used the red rose often in her career—she wore a fresh one daily in her lapel. When the Senate eulogized the assassinated president John F. Kennedy, her tribute took the form of silently unpinning her rose from her dress, walking across the aisle to the desk the president had occupied when he was a senator, and laying down her single red rose. The rose adorns the cover of her book, *Declaration of Conscience.* When I interviewed her for this book, she wore a pink rose, and a fresh peace rose in a vase adorned a side table beside a picture of William Lewis.

At times, Smith verged on being quirky. From June 1955 until September 1968, when she had hip surgery, she was present for 2,941 consecutive roll calls in the Senate.[65] Smith believed that she would be derelict in her duty if she allowed herself to disregard votes in order to campaign or to conduct other personal business. Consequently, she traveled home to Maine only when no votes were scheduled. Her compulsion to be present for roll call votes illustrates her concern for principled representation, and for many years she was called the "conscience of the Senate."[66] Nevertheless, she was criticized, mainly near the end of her tenure, for this record because many of those roll calls came on ceremonial occasions, which many legislators consider too unimportant to take precedence over committee hearings, travel back home, or other significant matters.[67] The idea that she neglected her home state later in her career was apparently a delicate subject with her, and she insisted defensively that "we kept the house here [in Maine]. My home here was never closed, even all the years that we were in Washington; we could walk into the house. We had the heat on and the people busy."[68]

The lengths to which Smith went to ensure that her voting record went unbroken are apparent in a story she tells in her autobiography. The hip surgery that caused her to break her string of votes took place on August 6, 1968, while the Senate was on recess for the national party conventions. Lewis was able to ascertain that the Senate would next vote on September 6 at about 1:30 or 2:00 o'clock in the afternoon. Smith was scheduled to fly back from New York City, where the surgery had been performed, that morning and arrive almost four hours before the votes began. Fog delayed the flight for three hours, but Lewis still predicted that she could arrive at the Senate an hour before the vote. When Smith's plane landed at Andrews Air Force Base at 12:30, Lewis telephoned ahead to check on the status of the voting. Only then did he discover that in order to permit senators to leave earlier in the day the voting time had been changed and the votes had already been cast, at 12:15.[69]

As the years progressed, Smith's voting record proved more conservative than moderate:

Though she voted with the Democrats against the Smith-Connally antistrike bill, for broadening Social Security, and raising federal salaries, as no doubt her husband would have done, yet she remained an unswerving hawk on the Vietnam War, and received a 22% rating from the liberal Americans for Democratic Action (Muskie got 91 percent). She voted against the ABM missile because she felt it wouldn't work, not because she wanted to reduce defense spending. She opposed President Nixon's nominations of Clement Haynsworth and Harold Carswell not because they were conservatives, but because she felt they were unqualified for the Supreme Court.[70]

On June 1, 1970, the twentieth anniversary of her "Declaration of Conscience" speech, Margaret Chase Smith made a second declaration of conscience. This time, the evil she saw came not from any member of the U.S. Senate but from the dangers of student unrest on the nation's college campuses related to the undeclared war in Vietnam and the repressive measures the Nixon administration was taking to combat it.[71] With certitude about the rightness of U.S. involvement, she said,

[T]he campus has been made a rendezvous for obscenity, for trespass, for violence, for arson, and for killing.... The excessiveness of overreactions on both sides is a clear and present danger to American democracy.... As was the case twenty years ago when the Senate was silenced and politically intimidated by one of its members, so today many Americans are intimidated and made mute by the emotional violence of the extreme left.[72]

Her formal remarks as highest-ranking Republican on the Armed Services Committee revealed little understanding of the tidal wave of war opposition that was building around the nation, especially among young voters, and she underestimated the impact it would have on the elections of the 1970s. The *New York Times* reported in 1972 about "the Colby affair," a tense political situation Smith inspired at Colby College in Waterville, Maine, two years earlier, right after the bombing of Cambodia and the shootings of students at Kent State University in Ohio. She tried to defend the Nixon administration's policies to a crowd of angry, antiwar, striking students from sixteen schools. When one of them asked her how her mail on Cambodia had been running, she

asked audibly of her aide William Lewis, "Bill, how has the mail been running on Cambodia? (6 to 1 against the invasion)." The students gasped.

... Then another student asked how he could trust a President who lied to the American people about the presence of U.S. troops in Laos. Smith insisted there were no U.S. troops in Laos. Whereupon a Bowdoin student named "Brownie" Carson ... got up and told how he had been wounded and half his platoon wiped out in Laos the year before.[73]

Smith later would describe that afternoon as the most unpleasant experience of her entire career.

In 1972, rumors flew that Smith would retire and leave the Senate. Her trusted assistant, William Lewis, was not well, and she was seventy-four years old. Her loyalty to Lewis was so great that "when he suffered a heart attack [in December 1971], she quietly left the Senate—and the roll call votes—for two weeks to be by his bedside at the hospital."[74] Lewis recovered somewhat, and Smith ran for reelection, for what would be her last time. Her Democratic opponent, William Hathaway, charged that she was out of touch with the needs of her state, that her practice of traveling back home only when there were no Senate votes was unfair to her constituents, and that a change in leadership was necessary to boost Maine's declining economy.

Some people also said that Smith had grown ineffective as a legislator in recent years, introducing few bills; others found her stands on defense and her frequent scoldings of other senators to be annoying traits.[75] She appeared unaware of certain key national debates of the era, especially the civil rights struggle. One Senate aide commented on a reason for her ebbing effectiveness in the Senate:

She encourages only the most formal exchanges of views. She sees the role of the Senator as judge, rather than as one who argues, questions, and persuades. Her rigid morality becomes a barrier to communication. It undercuts the open persuasive give and take that is part of the legislative process.[76]

Even her practice of holding out on announcing her position on important votes, which she did throughout her career, came under fire. A former Senate aide said, "[A]ll she's holding out is her own vote.... If she'd announce her position earlier, and if she really had influence, she might swing some other votes with hers. That's power."[77]

Critics multiplied. Some charged that in 1957 she had used her considerable power to hold up the nomination of the well-known actor Jimmy Stewart for promotion to brigadier general in the Air Force Reserve because Lewis had not been promoted to a similar position. She argued that Stewart lacked proper training and the promotion was inappropriate to his skills and experience. Eventually, the Senate committee rejected his request on a vote of 13-0.[78]

In her 1972 primary election, she did not keep pace with modern campaign practices and spent only $10,000. She stayed in Washington to vote and attend to Lewis, as her opponents—first other Republicans and then the ultimately victorious Democrat—crisscrossed the state. In a year when the nation was divided by war and youthful uprising, Senator Smith lost her first election at age seventy-four.

For nearly thirty-three years she had expended an enormous amount of personal effort and good will, honestly serving the people of her state and nation. Whatever her critics may have charged, Smith's place in history is secure. Her battle, as a woman without a college education, to gain ascendancy in an all-male world was a monumental achievement. Her reliance on both her husband and later her administrative assistant to help guide her through the channels where no women had passed is commendable. She needed shepherds and they needed her.

Her legacy remains her electoral achievements as a woman of "firsts" coupled with moral conviction, her years of dedicated and thoughtful service on the Armed Services and Appropriations Committees, and her commitment to a strong national defense in which women are afforded an equal opportunity to participate. Her example proved to future generations of women that they too could run for office. Beginning in the mid-1950s, she also proposed legislation to expand research at the National Institutes of Health and to construct an NIH medical facility. Although the legislation never passed under her name, because Congress was under Democratic control, NIH received a series of increases beginning in 1956 that by 1967 had risen to $1.3 billion annually, a sixteen-fold expansion. Her congressional committee service spanned a broad horizon, which included the Armed Services, Appropriations, Elections, War Claims, Revision of the Laws, Invalid Pensions, Education, Post Office and Post Roads, District of Columbia, Expenditures in the Executive Departments, Rules and Administration, Government Operations, and Aeronautical and Space Committees. At the apex of her career, she held the top GOP slot on the Armed Services Committee and the number two position on Appropriations, which was responsible for the bulk of federal spending.

Her presence on national television, as the age of "the tube" dawned in the early 1950s, including as the first chair of Senate Armed Services Committee televised hearings, indelibly influenced the nation's image of itself. She captured the imagination of young women across America, who thenceforth saw nothing unusual about a woman in charge. Although her moral intonations wore thin, she as much as acknowledged this in her library's most recent compilation of political memorabilia and cartoons from her years in office. "Women were and are seen as stern moralists and people were not ready for that in a President in 1964, nor in 1993."[79] Her "Declaration of Conscience" speech shines as a singular act of heroism against the worst political terrorism of the era.

After her defeat, Smith retired to her house in Skowhegan, Maine, and devoted herself to founding and, later, furthering the academic reach of the Margaret Chase Smith Library. In 1990 she was honored by the dedication of the Margaret Chase Smith Center for Public Policy at the University of Maine.[80] In 1992 she endowed a professorship of business administration at the home of her library, Northwood Institute, in memory of William Lewis. As reported by the library itself, "General Lewis [was] a major force in bringing the Senator and Northwood Institute together to make the Library a reality."[81] In 1989 Smith received the presidential Medal of Freedom—the highest civilian award in recognition of individual achievement—from President George Bush at a White House ceremony.

Margaret Chase Smith died on May 29, 1995, at age ninety-seven. She had served in federal office for nearly thirty-three years, twenty-four of them in the U.S. Senate, a record at that time. No formal funeral service was held. However, a memorial service, attended by nearly nine hundred people was held on June 16 of that year on the back property of her home and library. So many people attended that shuttle buses were run by the Boy Scouts from nearby parking areas. Her body was cremated, and the ashes are resting in her home on the bookshelf in the living room. Her husband, Clyde, was buried in Heartland, Maine. According to Angie Stockwell, a secretary at the Smith Library, her adjoining headstone had been vandalized and thrown into a nearby river many years earlier. Her longtime assistant, William Lewis, is buried in Arlington Cemetery.

NOTES

1. Peggy Hanson, *Few Are Chosen* (Boston: Houghton Mifflin, 1968), 7–8.
2. Alberta Gould, *First Lady of the Senate: A Life of Margaret Chase Smith* (Mount Desert, Me.: Windswept House, 1990).
3. Ibid., 8.
4. Margaret Chase Smith, interview by author, Skowhegan, Maine, July 13, 1993.
5. Ibid.
6. "Women," *Time,* September 5, 1960, 15.
7. Hope Chamberlin, *A Minority of Members: Women in the United States Congress* (New York: Praeger, 1973), 145.
8. "Women," 15.
9. "The Lady from Maine," *Newsweek,* June 12, 1950, 25.
10. Ibid.
11. Ibid.
12. Hanson, *Few Are Chosen,* 9.
13. "Women," 15.
14. Smith, interview.
15. Ibid.
16. Gould, *First Lady of the Senate,* 34.
17. Smith, interview.
18. "Women," 15.
19. Smith, interview.
20. Chamberlin, *A Minority of Members,* 144.
21. Smith, interview.
22. Ibid.
23. Margaret Chase Smith, *Declaration of Conscience,* edited by William C. Lewis Jr. (Garden City, N.Y.: Doubleday, 1972), 92.
24. Ibid., 97.
25. *Guide to the Archives of the Margaret Chase Smith Library* (Skowhegan, Me.: Northwood Institute, 1991), 2.
26. Ibid., 3.
27. Smith, interview.
28. Eleanor Roosevelt and Lorena Hickok, *Ladies of Courage* (New York: Putnam's, 1954), 183.
29. Hanson, *Few Are Chosen,* 13.
30. Alice Fleming, *The Senator from Maine: Margaret Chase Smith* (New York: Thomas Y. Crowell, 1969), 59.
31. Ibid., 149.
32. "Women," 18.
33. Smith, *Declaration of Conscience,* 3.
34. Berkeley Rice, "Is the Great Lady from Maine Out of Touch?" *New York Times Magazine,* June 11, 1972, 40.
35. Hanson, *Few Are Chosen,* 27.
36. Frank Graham Jr., *Margaret Chase Smith: Woman of Courage* (New York: John Day, 1964), 66–67.
37. Smith, interview.
38. Hanson, *Few Are Chosen,* 15.
39. Smith, *Declaration of Conscience,* 11.
40. Ibid., 11–12.
41. Smith, interview.

42. Ibid.
43. Smith, *Declaration of Conscience*, 13–14.
44. Smith, interview.
45. Smith, *Declaration of Conscience*, 23.
46. "The Lady from Maine," *Newsweek*, 24.
47. Ibid.
48. Hanson, *Few Are Chosen*, 23.
49. "The Lady from Maine," 24, 25; "Women," 15.
50. Hanson, *Few Are Chosen*, 270.
51. Ibid., 273.
52. Ibid., 274.
53. Ibid., 313.
54. Ibid., 316–317.
55. Graham, *Margaret Chase Smith*, 13–14.
56. Hanson, *Few Are Chosen*, 3.
57. "As Maine Goes . . ." *Time*, September 5, 1960, 13.
58. Smith, *Declaration of Conscience*, 242.
59. Ibid., 254.
60. Smith, interview.
61. *Never Underestimate … The Life and Career of Margaret Chase Smith: Through the Eyes of the Political Cartoonist* (Waterville, Me.: Northwood University, Margaret Chase Smith Library, 1993), 85.
62. Ibid., 113.
63. Ibid., 122.
64. Ibid., 133.
65. U.S. Congress, House, Office of the Historian, *Women in Congress, 1917–1990* (Washington, D.C.: U.S. Government Printing Office, 1991), 238.
66. Rice, "Is the Great Lady from Maine Out of Touch?" 39.
67. Ibid., 40.
68. Smith, interview.
69. Smith, *Declaration of Conscience*, 197–198.
70. Rice, "Is the Great Lady from Maine Out of Touch?" 39.
71. House, *Women in Congress, 1917–1990*, 238.
72. Smith, *Declaration of Conscience*, 435.
73. Rice, "Is the Great Lady from Maine Out of Touch?" 40.
74. Ibid., 41.
75. Esther Stineman, *American Political Women: Contemporary and Historical Profiles* (Littleton, Colo.: Libraries Unlimited, 1980), 137.
76. Rice, "Is the Great Lady from Maine Out of Touch?" 40.
77. Ibid.
78. Smith, *Declaration of Conscience*, 137.
79. *Never Underestimate*, 113.
80. *Guide to the Archives*, 7.
81. *A Newsletter for Friends of the [Margaret Chase Smith] Library* 8 (October 1992).

Edna Flannery Kelly
Democrat–New York (1949–1969)

*First Elected Democratic Congresswoman
from New York City*

> [T]he leaders may have decided that it would be a sound thing for the Democratic party
> in Brooklyn to express its confidence in women by nominating one to run in an election
> that looked like a sure thing.
>
> Edna F. Kelly, quoted in the *New York Herald Tribune,*
> November 13, 1949

Edna F. Kelly was the first Democratic woman from New York City to win a seat in Congress and the fifth from New York State. A staunch anticommunist, she was chair of the Foreign Affairs Committee's Subcommittee on Europe.

Kelly was born in East Hampton, Long Island, New York, on August 20, 1906, one of seven daughters (two adopted) of Patrick Joseph Flannery, a horticulturist, and Mary Ellen (McCarthy) Flannery. Except for Kelly, all became teachers. At East Hampton High School she was a member of the debating team, and her participation in a debating tournament was the occasion of her first visit to Washington, D.C. Kelly kept a photograph from the trip "snapped of me as I stood on the steps of the Capitol."[1]

In 1928, soon after graduating from Hunter College in New York City with a degree in history and economics, she married Edward Leo Kelly, a young lawyer whose law office was in Brooklyn, New York. Edna Kelly settled down into her new role as housewife in Brooklyn, where the couple's two children, William and Maura, were born. While maintaining his law office, Edward Kelly became head of the Madison Democratic Club, a party organization in their Brooklyn assembly district. Early in 1942, he was appointed city court justice by the governor, but only eight months later he was killed in an automobile accident.[2]

Irish heritage and politics seemed to go hand in hand, and soon after this tragedy, Edna Kelly, a widow with two teenage children, decided to enter politics "to carry on in the Kelly family tradition."[3] Her political involvement behind the scenes while her husband was alive helped her, after his death, to find a political mentor, Irwin Steingut. Steingut, the Democratic minority leader in the New York State Assembly, was aware of her political work and credited her with "rejuvenating" the women's auxiliary of the Madison Democratic Club.[4] She had also been deeply involved in community service, including Catholic Charities, day nurseries, campaigns for the blind, and support for cancer research and the Red Cross.[5]

In 1943 she became legislative research director for the Democratic Party in the state assembly. She held that position until 1949, when she felt confident enough to run for Congress in a special election for the unexpired term of a member who had died.[6] In Brooklyn at that time, the popular perception of politics was of a male-dominated machine in which candidates were chosen in smoke-filled rooms. But a new era was dawning. Kelly's brand of politics came much more from the grass roots, as she campaigned at community meetings, group dinners, and street rallies throughout Brooklyn's neighborhoods.[7]

Kelly campaigned on a platform that included support for the United Nations, the Marshall Plan, civil rights, federal aid for education, slum clearance, and more low-cost federal housing.[8] She was opposed to the Taft-Hartley Labor Relations Act, which had been passed in 1947, and any other measure that stunted organized labor.[9] She claimed she was not nervous about running for Congress, saying,

I've been analyzing all sides of bills in the New York State Legislature and making reports on them for seven years. I never knew when I'd be called to a committee meeting to explain certain aspects of bills. It has been good training, seeing different sides of questions. All these years I have been studying what went on in Washington.[10]

She believed that her experience in Albany helped the Democratic Party leaders choose her to run for Congress. But she confidently added, "perhaps, too, the leaders may have decided that it would be a sound thing for the Democratic party in Brooklyn to express its confidence in women by nominating one to run in an election that looked like a sure thing."[11] Local party leaders apparently had been influenced by the national party's initiative in launching a "New Deal for Women."[12] This optimism ran contrary to later research about why so few women are members of Congress. A 1981 study analyzed the number of women who are nominated to run in so-called hopeless races, races in which the women have little chance for victory because of an imbalance in party registration or incumbency.[13] Despite Kelly's upbeat attitude, more often than not party leaders could appear to encourage women office seekers without much risk by nominating women for such "hopeless" candidacies. In any case, times had changed enough by 1949 that cosmopolitan New York City finally sent its first Democratic woman to Congress. (A wealthy Republican woman, Ruth Baker Pratt, had served from 1929 to 1933.)

Kelly polled twice as many votes as her nearest rival, and her victory was "in no wise diminished by the fact that she is slim, ladylike, and—thanks to Hunter College, ee-nun-ci-ates beautifully."[14] She received 48,769 votes to 24,505 for Jules Cohen (Liberal) and 15,112 for George Henry Kankuchen (Republican). She was the only woman among the forty-one-member New York delegation. Edna Kelly went to Congress at age forty-four saying that she "would like to be regarded as representing men as well as women in Washington" but urging more women to get interested and involved in politics.[15] She adopted a go-slow-and-learn attitude and admitted, "Why, I don't even know whether to call myself a congressman or congresswoman."[16]

In her nineteen years in Congress, Edna Kelly served on the Foreign Affairs Committee, to which she was appointed in her first term, and chaired its Subcommittee on Europe. She crusaded for economy in foreign aid bills. She was a strong supporter of unity for Ireland and opposed religious persecution in Eastern Europe.[17] She took early notice of the threat of communism in Eastern Europe. Her 1951 amendment to the Mutual Security Act provided for the resettlement of people dislocated because of war or persecution; as a result of this law, 1.5 million people, mainly Russians and East Europeans, eventually found new homes. Her other foreign affairs legislative work included amending a 1952 foreign aid bill to suspend aid to Communist Yugoslavia and amending a 1954 agriculture bill to ban sales of farm products to the Soviet Union and Eastern Europe. In 1955, as the chair of the Subcommittee on Europe, she traveled to Europe and Israel on a study trip; the committee report warned of possible danger from the Soviet Union. Her foreign affairs work was probably the highlight of her congressional career, later to be called "admirable."[18]

Kelly was known for her ability to debate on the floor. She found it much easier than speaking on the campaign trail, where she had to speak about herself:

I found it a lot more difficult—and awkward—making speeches about myself. But in the last few weeks of the campaign I was doing just that—four and five times a night.... I like the idea of addressing groups though, and I don't often use notes—except at a street-corner meeting. I feel better there with a few scraps of paper in my hand.[19]

In Congress Kelly felt more comfortable, perhaps because of her high school debating team experience.

In the domestic realm, Edna Kelly committed herself to civil rights work and an amendment to the Social Security Act to lower the retirement age. During the 1950s, she also proposed bills concerning rent control, tax relief for working mothers, and equal pay for equal work regardless of gender.[20] In 1955 she proposed the amendment that raised to $1.25 an hour the minimum wage in the Fair Labor Standards Act. Generally, she supported a positive role for government in advancing people's social and economic conditions.[21] Her role in passing the bill on equal pay for equal work, after a decade-long struggle, was prominent enough for President John F. Kennedy to present her with the pen he had used to sign it.[22] For a woman whose entry into politics was "almost an accident of history," who had been active in the community but only thought of going into politics after her husband's death, Edna Kelly served Brooklyn remarkably well.

Kelly's congressional career came to an end in 1968, when the district lines were redrawn after a Supreme Court ruling. In order to keep her seat she was forced to challenge a fellow representative, Emanuel Celler, in the primaries. She was unsuccessful, receiving only one-third of the vote in a three-way race.

Kelly now lives in Alexandria, Virginia.

NOTES

1. "On Her Way to Congress," *Cue*, December 3, 1949.
2. *Current Biography 1950*, s.v. "Kelly, Edna F(lannery)," 289.
3. Ibid., 290.
4. Ibid.
5. Ibid.
6. U.S. Congress, House, Office of the Historian, *Women in Congress, 1917–1990* (Washington, D.C.: U.S. Government Printing Office, 1991), 128.
7. "On Her Way to Congress."
8. *Current Biography 1950*, 290.
9. "Brooklyn Woman Sent to Congress," *New York Times*, November 9, 1949.
10. *New York World Telegram*, July 20, 1949.
11. *New York Herald Tribune*, November 13, 1949.
12. Hope Chamberlin, *A Minority of Members: Women in the United States Congress* (New York: Praeger, 1973), 213.
13. Irwin N. Gertzog and M. Michele Simard, "Women and 'Hopeless' Congressional Candidacies," *American Politics Quarterly*, October 1981.
14. "On Her Way to Congress."
15. *Current Biography 1950*, 290.
16. "On Her Way to Congress."
17. House, *Women in Congress, 1917–1990*, 128.
18. Chamberlin, *A Minority of Members*, 217.
19. "On Her Way to Congress."
20. House, *Women in Congress, 1917–1990*, 128.
21. Ibid., 127.
22. Chamberlin, *A Minority of Members*, 217.

Leonor Kretzer Sullivan
Missouri–Democrat (1953–1977)

First Elected Congresswoman from Missouri

> *ERA says you are my equal … I think I'm a whole lot better.*
> Leonor Kretzer Sullivan, quoted by Susan J. Tolchin
> in *Women in Congress, 1917–1976*

The first woman in Congress from Missouri, Leonor Alice Kretzer Sullivan became the nation's "consumer watchdog." Her pathbreaking work predated that of consumer advocate Ralph Nader, although she was never as well known. Among other legislation, she wrote the Food Stamp Act, and, as a member of the Banking and Commerce Committee, the Equal Credit Opportunity Act and the Consumer Protection Act. She also served as chair of the Merchant Marine and Fisheries Committee.

Born on August 21, 1902, in St. Louis, Missouri, Leonor Sullivan grew up in a struggling family of nine children (six girls and three boys), the daughter of Frederick William Kretzer, a tailor, and his wife, Nora (Jostrand) Kretzer. Her father, a German immigrant, was unemployable during World War I because of his German ancestry. Sullivan, therefore, was not able to afford a conventional college education.[1] Instead, she got a job at the local telephone company and attended night school at Washington University in St. Louis, studying vocational psychology to gain additional skills related to her work.[2] Eventually she was able to take her work experience with accounting machines and teach at a local business school, the Comptometer Corporation's Training School, and soon became its director. Because her family was large and not affluent, all the children, including the six girls, had to learn to support themselves at a relatively early age.

In 1941 Leonor Kretzer married Rep. John Berchmans Sullivan, and the next year she was serving as his campaign manager and congressional aide.[3] "Many wives of Members worked in their husbands' offices in those days. Lindy Boggs, Bess Truman, Elizabeth Kee, Margaret Chase Smith."[4] Leonor Sullivan, relying on her office skills, kept track of every constituent letter on three-by-five-inch cards and typed replies on a manual typewriter; a big, clattering monster of a machine accepted teletype tapes and could duplicate hundreds of similar, but individually personalized, letters.[5] At that time, moving these business skills into Congress was considered somewhat revolutionary. Helping her husband to win five primaries and general elections taught Sullivan the ins and outs of campaigning, and working in his congressional office for nine years, four of them unpaid, instructed her in the ways of congressional service as well:

She was not educated to be a politician but picked up the basics from the patient teaching of her husband.… [H]e was thoroughly trained in the law and in practical politics before he ever ran for office. He had been at the hub of Democratic power in the St. Louis City Hall as chief City Attorney in the yeasty days of the early New Deal when St. Louis pioneered in many civic achievements, particularly in bringing about smoke control when American cities were suffocating in smog and the sun was often blocked until well after noon. John Sullivan was the legal point man on this almost miraculous accomplishment.[6]

When John died, in 1951, the Democratic Party machine in St. Louis refused to nominate Leonor for his seat. Instead the party gave the nod to a man who would be defeated by a Republican, to the chagrin of all involved. Perhaps she first thought of running for office herself when the St. Louis papers referred to the husband and wife duo as a "two-for-the-price-of-one" bargain.[7] But, in any case, Leonor Sullivan did not have the financial resources to run a campaign on her own, so she took a job as administrative assistant to another Missouri representative, Theodore Irving. Although highly motivated, she had to overcome a terrible fear of public speaking before she felt ready to run for office. She registered for public-speaking classes at the Washington Young Women's Christian Association. With these classes under her belt, and some money saved from her new job, Sullivan returned to St. Louis to try again for that congressional seat.

At age forty-eight, Leonor Sullivan took on a field of seven candidates in the primary, as Mrs. John B. Sullivan, and then went on to defeat the incumbent who had been elected to fill her husband's seat. "She was helped materially by friends of her husband in the St. Louis labor movement, particularly the Machinists' Union."[8] Once again, she had no support from the Democratic Party; in fact, party leaders "hinted…that she would not be the leader needed in Congress if the Republicans won the Presidency in 1952," presumably because only a man could be a strong enough leader to stand up to the president.[9] Sullivan campaigned on her Washington experience working for her husband and claimed that voters "need[ed] someone who thought as a woman and would share ideas freely with other women."[10] As a woman, and perhaps influenced by her childhood in a house where every penny had to count, she felt that consumer issues were extremely important to women. Throughout her twelve terms in Congress, she crusaded on behalf of consumers, including the most vulnerable consumers of all—the poor. Charles B. Holstein, her administrative assistant, reports:

In 1957, she shepherded through the first Federal Poultry Products Inspection Act. She then joined Congressman Jim Delaney of New York in helping to write the extremely controversial Delaney (anti-cancer) Clause to the Food and Drug Act, in a bill which for the first time required manufacturers to prove the safety of all new ingredients added to food instead of leaving it up to the Food and Drug Administration to prove them unsafe.... She tried to get similar legislation through on cosmetics. It has not been accomplished as yet.[11]

In 1959 Leonor Sullivan wrote the Food Stamp Act, which allocated food coupons to citizens below a certain income level as an alternative to distributing surplus food to them. Congress passed her bill that year, but then Sullivan found herself locked in battle with the secretary of agriculture, who opposed ending the food distribution program. In 1960, while the secretary of agriculture withheld funds from the food stamp program, John F. Kennedy was elected president. Sullivan wrote to the new president, explaining her proposed program and its difficulties and persuading him to take action. In 1961 Kennedy inaugurated a pilot program, using New Deal legislation from 1935 as its mandate. The pilot program was much smaller in scope than what Leonor had envisioned, however, and in 1964 she introduced a new food stamp bill to expand Kennedy's pilot program to all parts of the country. Speaking on the floor about this bill, Sullivan said, "The States and localities, which now bear a heavy financial burden under the direct distribution system, would save added millions under the food stamp plan. Who loses, then, under the plan? Hunger. Only hunger loses."[12] In 1964 President Lyndon B. Johnson, as part of his administration's "War on Poverty," signed a bill establishing a permanent, national food stamp program. That bill was essentially Sullivan's bill, which she had shepherded through a knockdown battle with the House Agriculture Committee. Every Republican on the committee voted no, including Rep. Bob Dole of Kansas, who later, as senator, became a vocal supporter of the program.

Sullivan became only the third woman in congressional history to chair a major legislative committee when she took charge of the Merchant Marine and Fisheries Committee in 1973. But her most significant legislative accomplishments for consumers came as a member of the Banking and Currency Committee, of which she eventually became ranking member. When she arrived in the House, consumer issues were almost entirely overlooked; some years later, she recalled, "I remember what it was like when I arrived. Those of us interested in consumer legislation could have caucused in an elevator."[13] In 1953 she called for a permanent committee on consumer protection, but when that did not come to pass, she took another route.

Because her committee assignment was Banking and Currency, many of Sullivan's important bills are related to financial institutions. For example, in 1967 she introduced a truth-in-lending bill requiring banks and other lenders honestly and completely to divulge the interest rates that would accrue to loans. According to Holstein,

It was on her initiative that the National Commission on Finance, on which she served, and which was created by her Truth-in-Lending law, held the first-ever hearings on discrimination against women in credit. This led to her introduction of the Equal Credit Opportunity bill, which she drafted to apply not only to women but to all minority groups (race, color, religion, etc.).[14]

Her Equal Credit Opportunity bill was opposed by several women's organizations because it covered groups beyond women. But it passed the following year as she had originally drafted it. Sullivan's other significant consumer bills included the Consumer Protection Act of 1968, which widened the range of food and drug items that required federal inspection and approval. She saw this kind of consumer protection as a particularly "female" issue. She prided herself on paying particular attention to "feminine" consumer goods like lipstick and pantyhose, deploring the poor quality of stockings that ran at the first wearing.[15]

Sullivan was the first female member to call herself a congress*woman*, yet the only woman in Congress to vote against the proposed Equal Rights Amendment. Her reasoning on the ERA vote reflected her close relationship with organized labor and her concern, as had been the case with Eleanor Roosevelt, that such an act would outlaw the so-called protective labor laws dealing with the special equipment that women in the workplace might need, work that might be hazardous to them as potential mothers, and so forth. "The woman in organized labor had a far different view of this issue," Holstein explains, "than that of the Business and Professional Women ... who looked on the protective labor laws for women as handicaps to their advancement in the white collar world of corporate management."[16] As well, her concern extended to women becoming subject to the military draft. Her attitude on the amendment was "ERA says you are my equal ... I think I'm a whole lot better."[17]

At the same time, she worked for the Equal Pay Act of 1962 to ensure that men and women received equal pay for equal work. She voted to end discrimination in the workplace in the Civil Rights Act of 1964. "She organized a March on Speaker Sam Rayburn of all the Democratic women in the House in their successful effort to open the Ways and Means Committee to a Democratic woman, and they pushed Martha Griffiths of Michigan into that groundbreaking role."[18]

Leonor Sullivan's twenty-four years in Congress came to an end in 1977, when, at age seventy-five, she pronounced herself frustrated with the bureaucracy and decided not to seek reelection.[19] She announced to friends that she was going home to St. Louis to marry a millionaire and live along the bluffs of the Missouri River in a home she had acquired years earlier. She did both these things. She died on September 1, 1988.

NOTES

1. Hope Chamberlin, *A Minority of Members: Women in the United States Congress* (New York: Praeger, 1973), 236.
2. *Current Biography 1954*, s.v. "Sullivan, Leonor K(retzer)," 590.
3. U.S. Congress, House, Office of the Historian, *Women in Congress, 1917–1990* (Washington, D.C.: U.S. Government Printing Office, 1991), 249.
4. Charles B. Holstein, administrative assistant to Leonor Sullivan, to author, October 27, 1994, 2.
5. Ibid., 1.
6. Ibid.
7. Ibid.
8. Ibid., 3.
9. Chamberlin, *A Minority of Members*, 237.
10. Ibid.
11. Holstein to author, 6.
12. Leonor K. Sullivan, debate on the floor of the U.S. House of Representatives, April 4, 1964, *Vital Speeches of the Day*, June 1, 1964, 184.
13. Chamberlin, *A Minority of Members*, 238.
14. Holstein to author, 3.
15. Esther Stineman, *American Political Women: Contemporary and Historical Profiles* (Littleton, Colo.: Libraries Unlimited, 1980), 149.
16. Holstein to author, 3.
17. Susan J. Tolchin, *Women in Congress, 1917–1976* (Washington, D.C.: U.S. Government Printing Office, 1976), 107.
18. Holstein to author, 7.
19. Stineman, *American Political Women*, 150.

Edith Starrett Green
Democrat–Oregon (1955–1974)
First Congresswoman to Move Away from Her Party

> *[T]he ultra-liberals have moved so far to the left that they have distorted the position of all other liberals.*
>
> Edith Starrett Green, quoted by Norman C. Miller
> in "Rep. Edith Green, a Bareknuckle Fighter,"
> *Wall Street Journal,* December 3, 1969

E dith Starrett Green's handiwork shaped every major educational bill that moved through Congress for two decades. She became the second-ranking member on the House Education and Labor Committee and chaired its Sub-committee on Higher Education, which established the first federal assistance for undergraduate student aid.

Born on January 17, 1910, in Trent, South Dakota, Green grew up in Salem, Oregon, where her parents, James Vaughan Starrett and Julia (Hunt) Starrett, settled after living in Iowa and North Dakota. Salem, the state capital, offered more sophistication and a governmental atmosphere, compared with most towns in the northwestern United States in the early twentieth century. Both of her parents were schoolteachers, although her father had experimented with some business enterprises, all of which failed; consequently, the Starrett family moved on to a new community for a fresh start. The Starretts were not exactly poor, but Green could count on not having any money for luxuries. Her parents' education became a very valuable commodity when the family had to begin again, and Green may well have learned the importance of education from their experiences.[1] Her father was friendly with some local politicians and worked a bit on their campaigns.[2]

Green must have been an excellent student and a fine student leader. While she was in high school, she was chosen "Oregon's Outstanding High School Girl." For this honor, she traveled to Philadelphia and Washington, D.C., where a reception was held at the White House and President Calvin Coolidge presented her with a medal. She is quick to emphasize, however, that she underwent "no quick conversion, like Saul of Tarsus or anything. I did not decide then and there I was going to come to Washington."[3] Before becoming involved in politics, first she became a teacher.

Her entry into the field of education was in fact an artifact of societal stereotypes of gender. Edith Green had first wanted to be an electrical engineer and later wanted to go into law, but she was dissuaded by adults who told her, "Nursing and teaching are the two respectable professions for women."[4] She chose teaching, and it was through education that she first entered public life.

Green began teaching school in 1930, when many states did not require their teachers to have a college degree. Nevertheless, she attended Willamette University for a time, before her money ran out and she had to work double shifts at a Salem cannery to support herself. She returned to teaching and married Arthur N. Green, a businessman, in 1933. Finally, in 1939, she graduated from the University of Oregon in Eugene with a bachelor of science degree in English and Education.[5] To supplement the couple's income, she also worked during this time as a radio announcer for station KALE in Portland, a freelance script writer, and manager of a trailer court. The Greens later divorced but had two sons, James and Richard.

After teaching sixth and seventh graders for ten years, Green served for three years as the legislative chair of the Oregon Congress of Parents and Teachers.[6] This work exposed her to politics and exposed the Oregon public to her. Yet, her driving single-mindedness often rankled colleagues. One person who encountered her during these years said, "She is wonderful and has done a lot for education, if she were just not so damned cantankerous."[7] In 1949, she was involved in lobbying for an increase in school funding. She also directed education conferences across the state.[8] It was in her work with the state organization that she learned the organizing and lobbying techniques that would serve her well in later years.

Still, in 1952, she was unable to translate her statewide exposure to higher office and lost a bid to be Oregon's secretary of state.[9] She had joined a group of reformist Democrats in Oregon politics, who wanted to run new, young candidates for state offices. Apparently, she was pressured into running for the statewide office; she remembers, "My intent was to file for the Senate race.... [O]n the filing date at the deadline, I went to Salem to file—and there was quite a group of people there, who, shall we say, applied the pressure? And I filed for Secretary of State."[10]

Two years later, in 1954, she ran for Congress, campaigning on an education platform. Her career in education had already been long and distinguished, and she was viewed as an expert. At age forty-four, she won election to Congress in a district that includes Portland, Oregon, in a tough race against former governor Tom McCall.

Green exhibited incredible stamina in her campaigns and a keen interest in meeting and talking to people. She was believed to be one of the first Oregon politicians to have distributed lawn signs promoting her candidacy. In one instance, a lawn sign proclaiming that the inhabitants of the house supported Green was countered by a banner on a house across the street that read, "We don't."[11] Green once remarked, "When I entered politics, a thousand and one times in a condescending tone, I heard: 'How did it ever happen that *you* [meaning a woman] are running for office?'"[12] Although a number of women had been elected, many people still did not expect women to run for office. Green was the second woman in Oregon to serve in Congress (the first was Nan Wood Honeyman).

In her first term in the House, as a mark of her stature in education, Green was appointed to the important Committee on Education and Labor, a committee on which she served until her final term, when she left it to take a seat on the Appropriations Committee.[13] Like other women who amassed considerable seniority, Green was unable to catapult herself to the Appropriations Committee—one of Congress's three exclusive committees—until late in her career.

Unlike some early female representatives who seemed to need time before finding their legislative footing, Green was able to see her first bill succeed. Drawing upon her experience in the newly settled Northwest, she introduced a bill for a $7.5 million appropriation for library services in rural areas; the bill became law in 1956. She was able to see education extending to children at home, who needed access to books.

Still, Green developed a reputation for being difficult—a judgment that would grow in later years as her ideology began to be transformed and she opposed federal education programs she once had supported. Elected as a Democrat, Green was considered a liberal when she went to Congress, but her political affiliations underwent some changes as she served. Although many believed that she had moved away from a liberal philosophy, Green protests, "I considered myself a liberal by any standard that was applied then, and if anything I would be more liberal now by those same standards. But the ultra-liberals have moved so far to the left that they have distorted the position of all other liberals."[14] The basis of her shift, real or imagined, was the trend during the 1960s toward nationally funded and administered education programs, which she came to oppose as she witnessed the growth of the federal administrative bureaucracy.

Green's style in the House was described as "articulate and rational," appropriate for a former schoolteacher.[15] She was not a silent listener in the back of the room either; some called her an inquisitor in committee hearings. A Portland, Oregon, reporter wrote, "Edith Green gives rousing speeches. They are the kind that keep members glued to their leather chairs in the House chamber."[16] One reporter described her speech as "a rapid-fire attack that was nevertheless delivered in a well-modulated ladylike voice."[17] Indeed, it was her speaking ability that got Edith Green into politics back in high school, and into radio during World War II, when she broadcast programs for schoolchildren and information for women.[18]

Green could hardly have picked a more volatile time to go to Congress to work on education. The same year in which she was elected, 1954, also saw the momentous Supreme Court decision *Brown v. Board of Education.* Desegregation was only one of the enormous changes that the American educational establishment was undergoing during the 1950s and 1960s. In 1956, soon after she was elected, Green urged President Dwight D. Eisenhower to withhold federal funding from schools that were still segregated. About fifteen years later, however, she was supporting President Richard Nixon's proposals to stop forced busing for desegregation. In an interview for *U.S. News and World Report* in 1972, she said her views had evolved: "I don't think the evidence supports the conclusions that if we just mix youngsters so that there are so many blacks and so many whites in a schoolroom that they will get a better education."[19] Such apparent contradictions between her early and her later positions were characteristic of Edith Green's evolution as a legislator. Perhaps her early stances came from her firsthand experiences in the classroom, whereas her time in Congress shaped her views toward political realities as she saw America's classrooms become the battleground for larger societal imperatives.

In 1958, the United States listened in fear and amazement for news as a Soviet satellite called *Sputnik* passed overhead. In the early years of the cold war, many people feared that *Sputnik* was some sort of weapon or a threat to the United States. Sighs of relief broke out when the satellite passed without incident, but the nation's educational institutions went into high gear. Science education in the United States was clearly lagging if the Soviet Union could put objects into orbit. In this climate, the bill that passed the House came to be called the National Defense Education Act, and Green was instrumental in its passage. This bill served primarily to fund curriculum reform and improvement in math and science, fields in which scholars deplored the tremendous gap between the achievements of American schools and those in Europe and the Eastern bloc.

Green also broke new ground in higher education when, as chair of the Subcommittee on Higher Education, she wrote the 1963 Higher Education

Facilities Act. This act provided funding for new construction of classrooms, laboratories, and libraries at colleges and universities, the first time federal money had been allocated to help institutions expand their facilities.[20] The "Green Amendments" to the 1965 Vocational Rehabilitation Act expanded vocational training to urban youth; most important, the Higher Education Act of 1965, which she also wrote, for the first time established a federal program for financial aid to undergraduate students.[21] Edith Green had a personal interest in seeing the financial aid bill pass because of her own experience of having to leave college for lack of money. These education bills, along with the War on Poverty legislation of Lyndon B. Johnson's administration, greatly expanded educational opportunities for many students. At the same time, they increased the federal government's role in what had always been an entirely local or state-run school system.

The new climate of social legislation brought about by the federal government's commitment to civil rights required much more centralized control of some educational programs. Large initiatives, such as funding for special education programs, had to come from the national government, which had resources to support these programs. The federal government also had an interest in seeing that school systems followed the dictates of the Supreme Court's *Brown* decision. Although Green had supported Johnson's Great Society programs and helped to pass many of the War on Poverty bills during the 1960s, she sided with a coalition of southerners and Republicans in passing an amendment in the House that barred the Department of Health, Education, and Welfare from denying assistance to southern school districts that enacted "freedom of choice" student assignment plans. In essence, this amendment turned the Court's ruling upside down.[22] As an educator, she was torn over the debate:

[A] careful reading of the evidence shows that a child's education and his ability to be educated … depend more upon the environment in which he lives than on the six hours a day in which he is transported to a school outside his neighborhood. I also think it's a very patronizing way for the whites to view this—that a youngster who is black has to sit beside a youngster who is white in order to be educated.[23]

In 1965 Green again demonstrated her independent thinking when she became one of only six members to vote against funds for President Johnson's request to escalate U.S. military commitment to Vietnam.[24] In the early 1970s she again surprised many of her constituents and colleagues by changing her position and opposing expanded federal administrative responsibility for much of the same social legislation. She had come to believe that welfare programs and the Office of Economic Opportunity had failed the people they were designed to help and that the federal government had become so involved in education that programs could not be administered effectively.

Green called for the states to take on more responsibility for the educational system; at the same time she urged creation of a cabinet-level Department of Education to lend it prestige and visibility.

After the campus riots of the 1960s, she proposed denying aid to universities unless they filed plans to deal with future riots and codes of conduct for their students. She made this proposal, which she considered a "moderate" approach, because she feared that the student revolts would spark an overreaction and a call for cutting all aid. Instead, it was condemned by liberals on the Education Committee as extremely repressive.[25] Gradually, Edith Green was moving away from the Democratic Party.

Although she had delivered the seconding speech for presidential candidate Adlai Stevenson in 1956 and for John F. Kennedy four years later (and managed Kennedy's victorious upset in the primary campaign in Oregon in 1960), she became increasingly disenchanted with the direction of Democratic politics.[26] In 1974, at age sixty-four, she retired from the House after twenty years of service.

President Kennedy had offered her the position of ambassador to Canada, but she turned it down. She accepted his appointment to the Presidential Committee on the Status of Women, where she was able to continue her work for pay equity for men and women in similar government positions.[27] During her career she was awarded thirty-two honorary degrees, and upon leaving Congress she served on the executive board of Linfield College, the advisory board of the University of Oregon Health Services Center, and the boards of three corporations—the Ben Franklin Savings and Loan, Pacific Northwest Bell, and Oregon Physicians Services.[28]

In reflecting on her life, which included three decisions not to seek a U.S. Senate seat (against Mark Hatfield and Wayne Morse), Green considered her educational and pay equity legislation her major achievements—work study aid, college loans and grants, and equal pay–equal rights along with gender equity in the Jobs Corps. She valued her seniority, explaining that it was the major reason she did not seek election to the Senate, since no woman would ever have any power in Congress were it not for the seniority system. Summing up her political career, she mused, "It was plain hard work."[29] She died in Oregon on April 21, 1987.

NOTES

1. Marie C. Barovic Rosenberg, "Women in Politics: A Comparative Study of Congresswomen Edith Green and Julia Butler Hansen" (Ph.D. diss., University of Washington, 1973), 57.
2. Ibid., 8.
3. Ibid.
4. Ann Sullivan, "Edith Green, Stateswoman Extraordinaire, Still Serves," *Oregonian*, February 15, 1979.

5. U.S. Congress, House, Office of the Historian, *Women in Congress, 1917–1990* (Washington, D.C.: U.S. Government Printing Office, 1991), 86.

6. *Current Biography 1956,* s.v. "Green, Edith S(tarrett)," 226.

7. Rosenberg, "Women in Politics."

8. House, *Women in Congress, 1917–1990,* 86.

9. Ibid.

10. Rosenberg, "Women in Politics," 19.

11. Sullivan, "Edith Green."

12. Hope Chamberlin, *A Minority of Members: Women in the United States Congress* (New York: Praeger, 1973), 258.

13. House, *Women in Congress, 1917–1990,* 86.

14. Norman C. Miller, "Rep. Edith Green, a Bareknuckle Fighter," *Wall Street Journal,* December 3, 1969.

15. Chamberlin, *A Minority of Members,* 255.

16. Ibid., 256.

17. *Washington Post* and *Times Herald,* June 3, 1955.

18. Rosenberg, "Women in Politics," 13.

19. " 'Busing Has Gone Too Far,'" *US News and World Report,* April 3, 1972, 20.

20. Edith Green, "Much More Remains to Be Done," *NEA Journal,* February 1964, 16.

21. House, *Women in Congress, 1917–1990,* 86.

22. Miller, "Rep. Edith Green."

23. "Pro and Con on Busing," *U.S News and World Report,* April 3, 1972, 19.

24. Chamberlin, *A Minority of Members,* 254.

25. Ibid., 252.

26. Ibid., 256.

27. Sullivan, "Edith Green."

28. Ibid.

29. Ibid.

Martha Wright Griffiths
Democrat–Michigan (1955–1974)

First Woman to Sit on the House Ways and Means Committee

> *Being a woman in Congress is like being a fragile goldfish among the barracuda.*
> Martha Griffiths, quoted by Emily George, *Martha W. Griffiths*

An optimistic view of the odyssey of women's advancement in national politics in the post–World War II era can be found in the life of Martha Griffiths. This feisty, capable daughter of the Missouri Ozarks, and then of Michigan, had established herself as a lawyer, legislator, and judge long before she considered seeking federal office. She devoted her tenure in Congress largely to lowering the barriers that separated women and men from equal treatment under the law. The achievement that brought her the most gratification was her effort to bring the proposed Equal Rights Amendment (ERA) to a vote in the House of Representatives; however, she considered this only one of the milestones of her career.[1] She also made significant changes in the Social Security and Civil Rights acts and became the first woman to be appointed to the Ways and Means Committee.

Born on a farm in Missouri as Martha Edna Wright on January 29, 1912, Griffiths lived there until she was nine and her brother thirteen years old. When the Wright family's farmhouse was struck by lightning and burned to the ground in 1921, they moved to "town"—to Pierce City, population 1,500.

Both of her parents' families traced their roots back to the American Revolution, and to Germany before that. Her parents were rural mail carriers; her father worked full-time, but her mother, Nelle (Sullinger) Wright, was hired during World

War I as a substitute, at times driving a double team of horses in pursuit of her duties. Griffiths explains: "She took the job at nineteen, in the First World War, when they could not get men to work for $50 a month." Griffiths believes she may have been the first woman rural mail carrier in America.[2] Her mother took in boarders to help pay Martha's way through the University of Missouri.

Martha Griffiths admired the strong women in her immediate family. She recalls, "My paternal grandmother, after her husband's death as a sheriff at the hands of outlaws, took what money the family had and journeyed to St. Louis to learn the craft of tailoring, a field reserved for men. She returned home and raised her three boys on that income."[3]

The Wright family enjoyed town life. Letter carriers knew everyone. "We, my mother and dad, had a table, a dining room table that pulled out to seat eighteen people. And at least three times a week, if not every day of the week, that table was full to its length."

At the University of Missouri, Griffiths majored in English, planning to attend Southwest Teachers' College. But love struck early in the political science and economics classes at the university. She and Hicks Griffiths, whose family was from New York State, started dating in their junior year. She recounts,

Hicks and I were in the same classes and we were in the same quiz sections. And one day, a kid who sat by me in one class sat by Hicks in another, and he said to me: "I know a man who thinks you're the smartest girl in the school." And I said, "Who is he?" And he said, "See that guy right back there?" And I said, "Yes." "Well," he said, "that's the fellow." "Well," I said, "he's in the same quiz section I'm in, and we're the only two awake." At any rate, Hicks got so he walked with me, between one class and another. Finally one day, we had to go up four flights of steps to the fourth floor of Jesse Hall, and he said to me, "Would you go to the show with me on Saturday night?" I nearly fell down the four flights. I said, "Well, I'd be delighted to." So I did.

They married after their senior year. Rather than go to Harvard University Law School, where women were not admitted, Hicks persuaded Martha that they should both attend the University of Michigan Law School. This early experience with discrimination may have shaped Martha Griffiths's political interests, but the support of her husband must have given her hope that other men might share his views. The couple worked their way through law school. She earned $9.41 per week for fifty-four hours in a candy store, less than twenty cents per hour.[4] They graduated together in 1940.

Both Martha and Hicks were strong-minded and independent. Martha was the sole woman in her law school class. When asked why she hadn't simply become a homemaker, as most women of her generation had done, she said: "Well, in the first place, I wanted out. I wanted to do something. I had seen my mother work. I had seen my grandmother work. And I wanted to do something. I never thought about staying home and keeping house, nor having a big family or anything like that."

After receiving their law degrees, both Martha Griffiths and her husband served as lawyers for the American Automobile Insurance Company in Detroit. During this time the reality of discrimination against women was brought home to Hicks:

When we worked for the insurance company they paid him more than they did me. It was beginning jobs for both of us; we had the same education, practically the same grades, so he went and said to the chief counsel, "Why are we being paid differently? [He was making $7,500 a year, she $5,000.] I am paid more than Martha." "Oh," the chief counsel said, "you're the man of the house." Hicks said to me, "It saves them money, that's all, that's all it really is." He was furious.

Hicks then moved on to the Office of Price Administration, and Martha applied for a position at the Detroit U.S. Army Ordnance District as a contract negotiator. The awards general called her and said, "Now, we're going to give you this job, and we want you to do well. If you don't, we'll never hire another woman." She retorted, "Well, if I do, will you hire other women?" And he said, "Yes, we will."

So Martha Griffiths set out to prove herself again:

Within six months, I was the best goddamned purchaser in the whole goddamned army. I bought a 75-millimeter shot that Bethlehem and Crucible had made for twenty-five years. They charged $25 a shot [mortar]. I gave contracts to Chevrolet Gear and Axle, Oldsmobile, L.A. Young, Bud Wheel, and that was all. And in less than six months, Gear and Axle put that shot through a better ballistics test than the other had ever made, and we lowered the price to five dollars and a quarter.

In 1946 Martha and Hicks started their own law practice in Detroit, joined by a law school classmate, G. Mennan Williams. He had worked with Hicks at the Office of Price Administration. Martha proudly recalls: "Hicks was the only chief price attorney in the country who was never overturned." Williams, heir to the Mennan toiletries fortune, later became the governor of Michigan. And Martha soon began her political career. Their law firm was known as Griffiths, Williams, and Griffiths.

Detroit is a tough, industrial, gritty city, called the Automotive Capital of the World. One of the half dozen largest cities in America, it became, during World War II, the heart of America's "Arsenal of Democracy," as its factories churned out military hardware for the war effort. Civic sites in this city are named not for artists but for the brawn of the place, like the heavyweight boxing champion Joe Louis, its baseball team the Tigers, and the basketball team the "Motown" Pistons. A blend of Americans of African, Appalachian, Polish, German, Irish, Italian, Canadian, and English backgrounds, Detroit tops the charts as one of America's muscle cities.

No more perfect representative could it have had than Martha Griffiths. In 1946, with her husband's encouragement, she decided to run for her first office, the Michigan state legislature; she was thirty-four. Her story of how she made the decision makes clear her feeling that if it were not for Hicks, she might never have entered politics at all. She recounts:

This old lady called and said, "We want qualified women to run.".... Finally, in desperation, I said to her, "Look, Phoebe [Phoebe Moneybean, a prominent Republican and suffragist], I know that you are a Republican. I am a Democrat." She said, "I don't give a damn what you are. We need qualified women, and I will support you." I said, "I just can't do it." So I went back in the other room, and my husband said, "What did she ask you?" I said, "She asked me to run for state representative." He said, "Did you tell her you would?" And I said, "I told her I wouldn't." He said, "You go right back in there and call her up and tell her you just started running." So I didn't call her immediately, but I called her and told her I would run. My husband wanted me to.

Although Martha Griffiths lost her first race, she won the succeeding election in 1948 and by 1951 had been declared one of the top ten Michigan legislators. She then ran and narrowly lost a race for the U.S. House of Representatives in 1952 by a margin of 2.5 percent. Meanwhile, her husband had been building the Democratic Party in Michigan as its state chair.

In 1953 Martha Griffiths was appointed the first woman judge in the Detroit Recorder's Court by her friend Governor Williams. That position brought her to the front pages of the Detroit newspapers every day. She had the most celebrated case hearing of that year in any court, anywhere, as she describes it. "The Teamsters Union had been indicted in a labor rackets case." Martha became the hearing examiner. She recalls:

The first day I went, Jimmy Hoffa [infamous president of the International Brotherhood of Teamsters, later imprisoned for jury tampering and misusing union funds, believed to have been murdered by the Mafia in 1975] was sitting in the back of the court. I walked in; I was on time. I am a compulsive be-on-timer. The defendants weren't there. So I waited and waited for probably ten minutes after nine. I was there promptly at nine o'clock, ready to go.

At ten minutes after nine, they came in. So I said to the police officers, "Bring those men up here and line them up in front of me, please." "I would like to tell you, I am on time. I don't have to have these prosecutors, but they'll be here on time. You don't have to have your lawyers, but they were here on time. But you weren't. You don't care about anybody else's time. But I do. The jail is filled with people waiting for a trial, and under the Constitution of the United States, they are entitled to it. If one single one of you is half a minute late from this day on, I will cancel the bond of all of you, demand that you be brought over here by the sheriff every morning in leg irons and handcuffs with an officer walking beside you with a loaded gun, with the instructions to shoot if necessary. You are going to be here on time."

Well, I didn't have any further problem. But I was threatened. Of course, both my husband and I have spent our lives being threatened by people. I got two letters, presumably from some Teamsters, some older person, saying please be careful. And they sent some guy in, too, I presume to offer me a bribe. But I took my court recorder in with me to witness the conversation, and the Teamster said, "Do you trust her?" I said, "Absolutely. She'll remember every single word we say, and she'll be able to repeat it." He left.

It is not surprising that Martha's grounding in the law and in Michigan politics would lead her to a career in Congress that spanned twenty years, placing her among the ten longest-serving women in Congress at the time. Her successful race in 1954 was hotly contested in the primary, in which the Democratic Party and the United Auto Workers (UAW)—a powerhouse combination in Michigan—and its president, Walter Reuther, endorsed one of her opponents simply because Griffiths was not as well known in UAW circles. She beat them all, winning the general election by the margin she had lost by two years earlier, 2.5 percent. "I owe my election," she said later, "to all the girls who went out and rang doorbells and invited housewives to meet me." She had met thousands of citizens as she campaigned from a long trailer driven around the district, serving fruit juice and "having talks."[5] After winning her first election, she began looking for an apartment in Washington, but "history being what it is," she felt that "perhaps [she] had better rent a house with a basement [to rent out]" in case her luck soured.[6]

Martha Griffiths's rise in Congress, eventually to the fourth-ranking seat on the prestigious Ways and Means Committee, was due in part to her amiable personality, coupled with a keen intelligence and wit. She was an entertaining storyteller. She tells the story of a Democratic whip who ambled over to her one day and said,

"Mrs. Griffiths, I understand that you were reared in the district that Rep. Dewey Short now lives in and represents." And I said, "Yes, I was." He said, "Well, don't you think that those people would get rid of him if they knew how much he drank?" I said, "Well, you would think so, but the trouble is, they've all been drunk with him."

Initially, she was elected to the Committee on Banking and Currency, as well as the Committee on Government Operations, and then in her third term the Joint Economic Committee (a nonlegislative committee). Her first bill, in memory of her parents no doubt, raised the salaries of postal workers.[7] In her early terms in Congress, she also introduced bills to improve housing for the elderly, to distribute surplus food to the needy, and to increase congressional and judicial salaries.

Griffiths also served on the Joint Economic Committee, the last Democratic woman to have done so. As chair of that committee's Subcommittee on Fiscal Policy, she led a landmark three-year study and developed legislation introduced in 1974, the Tax Credits Allowances Act, designed to reorganize and improve national public assistance programs by providing per capita tax credits for moderate and low-income families and allowances for basic living expenses.[8] By the 1990s the concept of this legislation had taken the form of Earned Income Tax Credits, a federal tax credit for working families earning under $23,000, which was refunded annually.

In 1962, Martha Griffiths achieved a major first. During her fourth term she became the first woman ever to sit on the powerful House Ways and Means Committee, an exclusive committee in which all tax bills must begin. A member of this committee must be willing to work with the entire membership of the House and cannot serve on any other committees. Her story of how she reached this position demonstrates her clever style of working in the turf-sensitive Congress. She recalls:

When Michigan representative Ted Machrowicz ... accepted a judicial job in Detroit, of course, there was going to be a vacancy on Ways and Means, and I went immediately to Wilbur Mills [D-Ark., the chair of the Ways and Means Committee], and I said, "Wilbur, who would you like me to support for Ways and Means when Ted leaves?" He said, "Would you like to be on Ways and Means?" I said, "Well, of course I would like to be on Ways and Means, but I can't be on Ways and Means." He said, "What do you mean, you can't be on Ways and Means?" "Well," I said, "there's never been a woman." He said, "I don't care; I'll be glad to have you."

Mills also locked up the support of key leaders such as the Speaker of the House, Sam Rayburn, D-Texas, and the majority leader, John McCormack, D-Mass. Griffiths believed that Mills's dislike for the other candidates for the job was behind his eagerness to have her on the committee. He especially disliked Rep. John Dingell, D-Mich., who had designs on the seat but later went on to chair the Commerce Committee's House Energy and Power Subcommittee. "John Dingell is brutal. People are scared to death of John Dingell."

Although important, the support of Wilbur Mills and other House leaders was not enough; in order to be elected to the Ways and Means Committee, Martha Griffiths still needed the support of all her fellow Democrats. (To achieve appointment to a legislative committee, a member of Congress must be elected by the Committee on Committees, a small, powerful group that included party leaders and representatives of different regions of the country.) So she began to ask other members to support her. Rep. Mike Kirwan, D-Ohio, a member of the Appropriations Committee, which held jurisdiction over all federal spending, helped her line up votes. She had campaigned with him in his district, and with others, and had developed her own connections and friendships, at times even going around more senior members (like Dingell) of her own state delegation. Because she was from Missouri originally, she maintained bonds with many members from the South, so her reach extended beyond her region.

In the early 1960s, northern Democrats did not get along well with their southern counterparts, who were more conservative and held most of the committee chairmanships. Although she was part of the northern contingent, Martha Griffiths, a Missourian by birth, had rapport with those southerners:

One of the reasons that I did what I did in the Congress [was] I like the southerners.... The southerners were smarter than the northerners, they were graduates of better schools, they were wittier, and most of them were better-looking, and I had a good time with them and I knew how to enjoy myself with them, and I talked with them.... So the southerners all supported me. The rest of the northerners at that time, before they switched the rules, they hated the southerners, because the southerners ran everything.

Griffiths's hard work gaining early commitments of members and persuading colleagues to support her, and her ability to make and maintain personal friendships, paid off: she won the seat on the committee.

Martha Griffiths became known on the Ways and Means Committee as a fearless questioner, never afraid to challenge witnesses. Some said that to attempt to argue with her was "to walk into a buzz saw." She asked members of the wealthy Rockefeller family, when they appeared before the committee, "Why don't you pay taxes?" as if this were the most obvious question in the world. In one hearing, an airline was permitted to claim that only females could be flight attendants because of the requirements of the job. Then a case was unearthed in which a young woman had been fired after she married. This brought out the full force of Martha's anger and she raged, "You point out that you are asking a bona fide occupational exception that a stewardess be young, attractive, and single. What are you running, an airline or a whorehouse?"[9]

It was Griffiths's own experience along with the help she had received from the many women in her district during her campaigns that led her to sponsor the ERA in 1970. The bill had been locked in committee for twenty-two years; she worked to push it to a floor vote not once, but twice. In order to bring it out of committee and to the floor, she had to gather 218 signatures on a discharge petition to bypass normal procedures. Her efforts paralleled those of Rep. Mary Norton, D-N.J., who managed to push the 1938 Fair Labor Standards Act to a vote. While these two examples are not sufficient to constitute a pattern, they do indicate that women who served long enough to learn the rules and practices of the House and gained the respect of their colleagues became adept at moving legislation.

Griffiths later recalled her victory in getting the ERA onto the floor of Congress in August 1970 for the first vote in U.S. history:

I faced ignorance and bigotry. I knew damn well that there was not a white lawyer there who had any idea how the court had treated women. Black women wouldn't have gotten anything out of that amendment, because you had to name "women" [as a category]. When the Fifteenth Amendment was added to the Constitution, which said every citizen regardless of race, color, or previous condition of servitude, could vote, a Missouri woman asked to vote back in 1876. She went all the way to the Supreme Court, and the Supreme Court said, "Well, she is a citizen but your state has to give you the right to vote." Well, what the hell was the Fifteenth Amendment passed for if your state has to give *you* the right to vote? So that was great…. But the Equal Rights Amendment had been locked up in Rep. Emanuel Celler's Judiciary Committee for twenty-two years. I put a petition on the clerk's desk to discharge the committee. I got 218 required signatures on the petition [a majority].

Martha's recounting of this feat was actually quite modest. What she had done was to build a base of support, vote by vote, in the South by pointing out the bill's implications for civil rights and voting rights. And she was relentless. As one Democratic colleague from Michigan recalls:

Many northerners had not signed onto the ERA, including many of her fellow Michigan Democrats—John Dingell, Lucien Nedzi, James O'Hara, and William Ford. Well, Dingell never did. But I finally did. Who would want to sit next to Martha on our weekly, two-hour propeller flights back to Michigan and not be on her bill? She had real tenacity, a take-no-prisoners attitude.[10]

To gather the 218 signatures needed to bring the bill to the floor, Griffiths had to call in some old favors owed her, and occasionally make some deals, like the one she made with Louisiana's Hale Boggs. The story demonstrates the kind of camaraderie she had with southern Democrats: "Boggs, the Democratic whip, was opposed to the amendment. But he promised to sign as Number 200, convinced that I would never make it. You may be sure that when I had Number 199 signed up, I rushed to his office, and Hale Boggs became Number 200."[11] He agreed to help with a bill he had no intention of voting for. Griffiths also applied other tactics to get members to sign. She accompanied each male representative down to the front of the floor, "the well," as he went to vote and requested that each man sign her petition while she had him cornered. She did this with such regularity that one young visitor to the House, watching the goings-on from the gallery, asked, "Do those men have to go talk to that lady before they can vote?"[12] On August 10, 1970, the House, led by Griffiths, passed the amendment by a vote of 333 to 22, with 74 members not voting.

While the Equal Rights Amendment was the most publicized of Martha Griffiths's victories on behalf of women, she remembers other issues, like Social Security, on which she had an impact. The problem was

that women paid into Social Security the same amount that men did, but they did not draw the same benefits. If a woman died, her children and her husband didn't draw on her benefits, but if a man died, the widow and children could draw on his benefits…. I corrected that.

Someone in the Social Security office in Detroit later told her that when the new law had been explained to two men, one with eleven children and one with twelve, the men asked who was responsible for the change. When they heard it was their congresswoman, both men sat down and cried.[13]

Griffiths explained why she worked to pass this type of legislation: "Any law that came before me, I wanted to see to it that it was just"—for both men and women. The House deputy counsel at the time of the Social Security reforms, who benefited from the reforms, tells this story. When Martha found out, "she literally jumped up and down with glee.... It indicated how really deep down serious she felt about the things she was trying to do."[14]

She also achieved major social change by making certain that the 1964 Civil Rights Act included the word *sex*. As she says, "I put sex in the Civil Rights Bill."[15] The bill had been discussed and debated for four days, as members of Congress talked about how to ensure civil rights for blacks, and, Griffiths says, "There was not a single laugh." But when she stood to offer an amendment to include the word *sex* in the bill,

there was all this laughter. I said to the men, "If there is anything that could further show how little you think of women, your laughter has already proved it. We have sat here four days discussing blacks, and there has not been even a smile. Now that we are discussing your wives, your mothers, your sisters, and your daughters, you think that this is hilarious. You have broken American labor into three groups: first are white men; then black men and women; and third and last, the last to be hired, the first to be fired, will be your wives, your sisters, your mothers, and your daughters. How can you do this?"

She won.

This example indicates what one commentator meant when he described Martha Griffiths's speaking style as "a short burst of spontaneous oratory resulting from a sense of outrage."[16] She found there was a lot to be outraged about, like a 1967 rodent extermination bill, another bill that many found funny. Martha Griffiths stood up and mesmerized Congress as she began to discuss the living habits of rats, which she called

the living cargo of death. They must sharpen their teeth by gnawing constantly or their teeth will grow back into their jaws.... Their tails swish through sewers and over the food we eat.... They eat the lips off babies.... They carry the most deadly diseases, and some think it is funny.[17]

She shamed members into voting for the bill. When nutrition programs for pregnant and lactating mothers were being debated, Martha scolded the male members for their bathroom humor that belittled the program's intent.

In 1974, at age sixty-two, Martha decided not to run for reelection for an eleventh term. She retired after twenty years of service as the fourth-ranking member of the Ways and Means Committee. It would be nice to think that had she remained in Congress a few more years, she would have become the first woman to chair that committee; Rep. Al Ulman, who succeeded to the chair in 1975, was defeated in 1980. But Rep. Dan Rostenkowski of Illinois, his successor, did not leave until 1994, and the Republicans took control of Congress in 1995. By that time Griffiths was eighty-two years old.

Still, Griffiths went on, at age seventy in 1982, to become the first woman elected lieutenant governor of Michigan. The ticket was headed by former representative James Blanchard. The team was reelected in 1986. During their campaign for reelection in 1990 to a third term, however, Blanchard tried to remove Griffiths from the ticket because of her age (seventy-eight), her cantankerous nature, and, some said, her growing absent-minded behavior. But Martha Griffiths did not go quietly. She fought publicly and succeeded in remaining on the ticket. The two ultimately went down to defeat as Blanchard reeled from this bad publicity as well as from a revelation by his wife of his infidelity and likely divorce. One congressional colleague who requested anonymity revealed raw wounds, still tender several years after the representative had clashed swords with Griffiths and lost: "She is an evil woman. And her husband's no better."

Still, without question, Martha Griffiths's humor, intelligence, and perseverance moved America forward. On her own abilities, she mused, "You know that was always one of the funny things to me. When I first began to run, the real question was, Is she qualified? I never heard that question asked about a man, never. It was just assumed men were qualified."[18] Although she didn't consider herself a feminist, which she described as the "brassiere-burning types," her life's work paved a smoother road to the future for America's women.[19] And she never lost her sense of humor about it, no matter how difficult and intimidating. She recalled a story about Rep. Patricia Schroeder, D-Colo.:

Patricia Schroeder has the cutest story. She was the first woman in the first law class at Harvard that ever had women in it, and they had fifteen. I think it was in the 1960s. At any rate, the dean invited all of them to dinner. So they went, and Patricia said the meal was terrible, it was stewed chicken. So after dinner, he said, "Now, you know I didn't want you. The reason I've asked you here is I want to know why you came." So each girl had to answer, and you know, they were all shaking and quaking. Well, at any rate, he got to the last girl, and she said, "Well, I came here because I couldn't get into Yale." And he said, "You couldn't get into Yale? What do you mean, why couldn't you get into Yale?" "Well, I couldn't get into Yale because their exams are harder." "Oh, we have the hardest exams of anybody." She said, "Well, I couldn't pass Yale's, but I could pass yours." And Patricia said, "That girl taught me more in three minutes than Harvard taught me in three years."

Throughout her life, Martha Griffiths remained her own person, shaping her own path, often against incredible odds. She even bucked ideology. "I'm not an ideological person at all. I didn't arrive with an agenda. I arrived determined to work. And any law that came before me, I wanted to see to it that it was just." That she did.

NOTES

1. Martha Wright Griffiths, interview by author, Armada, Michigan, August 31, 1993. All quotations in this chapter that are not attributed to another source are from this interview.
2. Ibid.
3. Peggy Hanson, *Few Are Chosen* (Boston: Houghton Mifflin, 1968), 88.
4. Griffiths, interview.
5. "Mate's Brainstorm Starts Wife's Career," *Detroit News*, November 3, 1954, 22.
6. Emily George, *Martha W. Griffiths* (Lanham, Md.: University Press of America, 1982), 35.
7. Ibid., 45.
8. U.S. Congress, House, Office of the Historian, *Women in Congress, 1917–1990* (Washington, D.C.: U.S. Government Printing Office, 1991), 90.
9. George, *Martha W. Griffiths*, 154.
10. Rep. William Ford, interview by author, Washington, D.C., July 1994.
11. Hope Chamberlin, *A Minority of Members: Women in the United States Congress* (New York: Praeger, 1973), 259.
12. George, *Martha W. Griffiths*, 170.
13. Griffiths, interview.
14. George, *Martha W. Griffiths*, 113.
15. Chamberlin, *A Minority of Members*, 260.
16. George, *Martha W. Griffiths*, 69.
17. Ibid.
18. Ibid.
19. Ibid.

Margaret M. Heckler

Republican–Massachusetts (1967–1983)

First Elected Congresswoman from Massachusetts

> Women are the one minority group it is still considered fashionable to discriminate against.
>
> Margaret Heckler, quoted by Esther Stineman,
> *American Political Women, Contemporary and Historical Profiles*

Margaret M. Heckler was the first woman in Massachusetts to be elected to Congress in her own right, that is, not succeeding her husband. In a state noted for sending political talent to Congress that rose to the level of Speaker—in recent history, Thomas P. "Tip" O'Neill, John W. McCormack, and Joseph W. Martin—her election pitted her against the aging former Speaker Martin as she challenged and beat Massachusetts establishment politics.

She worked with vigor in behalf of women, sponsoring the Equal Credit Opportunity Act and trying to achieve passage of legislation that would give women equal rights and protect them from financial and other inequities. During her career, although she opposed federally funded abortion, she was not an antiabortion activist. In 1977 she cofounded, with Rep. Elizabeth Holtzman of New York, the Congressional Caucus for Women's Issues. After losing a race for reelection in 1982, she rose to become secretary of the largest cabinet-level department and received appointment by President Ronald Reagan as U.S. ambassador to Ireland. (She was the second former congresswoman to receive an ambassadorial appointment; the first was Clare Boothe Luce, who was appointed U.S. ambassador to Italy in 1953.)

Born in Flushing, New York, on June 21, 1931, as Margaret Mary O'Shaughnessy, Heckler was the only child of Irish Catholic immigrants. Her father, John

O'Shaughnessy, worked as a doorman at a hotel in New York City, and her mother, Bridget (McKeon) O'Shaughnessy, was a homemaker.[1]

Heckler dreamed of becoming a concert pianist, and her natural intelligence and drive ultimately won her a scholarship to Albertus Magnus College, a small Roman Catholic women's college in New Haven, Connecticut.[2] In her sophomore year she won her first election as a member of the student government there, but she wanted to move upward. A statewide organization—the Connecticut Intercollegiate Student Legislature—composed of university student government leaders was about to elect a new Speaker. No woman had ever held the post. Albertus Magnus's small size did not offer Heckler many votes for the job, forcing her to campaign at some of the other colleges in the state, such as Yale University and Trinity College. It was at one of those colleges, Fairfield University in Fairfield, Connecticut, that she met a young man named James Heckler, who managed her campaign and whom she later was to marry. It was a propitious choice, as well, for her political future, in that her campaign slogan "Massachusetts needs an O'Shaughnessy in the House" just wouldn't have had the same ring to it.[3] She mastered *Robert's Rules of Order* and won the statewide election among mostly male peers.[4]

She later commented, "Up to that time, all I had ever dreamed about was becoming a concert pianist."[5] She credited her future husband with changing her perspective. "[A]fter [John Heckler] helped me win, I knew I wanted to go into government through law."[6] She viewed the law as her form of public service. Her first race began a thirty-year partnership that included a series of successful campaigns for office but that after three decades ended in a bitter divorce.

As part of her undergraduate experience Heckler traveled to the University of Leiden in the Netherlands. She graduated from Albertus Magnus in 1953 with a bachelor of arts degree in political science. In August after graduation, she and John Heckler were married and she immediately entered Boston College Law School, as the only woman in her class. She advanced quickly, becoming the editor of the law review and, in 1956, graduated with a class rank of number six.[7] As a woman during the late 1950s, in spite of her obvious academic accomplishments, she could not find work in a Boston law firm. Thus, she and friends set up their own firm, where she practiced for ten years.[8]

Her husband worked as an investment broker and the couple lived in Wellesley, an upper-middle-class Boston suburb, where they reared three children—Belinda, Allison, and John Jr. The family had the benefit of a nanny, which helped Margaret juggle her family duties, career, and increasing volunteer activities in behalf of many Republican causes and officeholders. From 1958 to 1966 she sharpened her political spurs through service on the Wellesley Republican Town Committee.

In 1962, again with her husband's support and active involvement as her campaign manager, she sought a position as a member of the Massachusetts Governor's Council, a part-time advisory group to the state's top official. She was elected with a handsome margin as the first woman to serve on that group, was reelected in 1964, and served until 1966. Her campaign slogan, "You need a Heckler on the Governor's Council," rang a familiar theme.

Her decision to run for this position arose from an incident involving the Heckler family kitchen. The Hecklers lived in a beautiful Victorian house that needed extensive renovation. Margaret had decided to redo the kitchen. When her husband heard the decorators' estimate that it would cost $10,000, he asked her what she intended to do. The expense was fine, he said, but only if Margaret would commit herself to using the kitchen frequently. She was already thinking about running for office, and this ultimatum forced her to make up her mind. Heckler chose politics, and the kitchen stayed the way it was.[9]

Her decision to run for Congress seemed a natural outgrowth of her greening in local and state Republican politics. When some of the members of the Governor's Council became involved in scandals in which she had no connection, the council's esteem plummeted, Heckler began to seek other venues in which to apply her talents. Although party leaders thought she might make a good statewide officeholder, her ambitions became directed nationally.

When she was thirty-four, in 1966, the mother of three children age nine, seven, and six, she set her sights on the congressional race. She was a virtual unknown. And more than that, she chose a race that could not have riled party leaders more. She became involved in a bitter primary contest to unseat one of Massachusetts' Republican icons, eighty-four-year-old representative Joseph W. Martin, who had served in Congress since 1925.

Heckler used her neophyte status to her advantage in the campaign, calling herself the alternative to the smoke-filled, back-room, party-dominated brand of politics.[10] She would go out to meet people and end up shaking more than 1,000 hands a day during the campaign.[11] Although this grueling work took time away from the family, the children apparently were not shielded from what their mother was doing. One day, her son said that when he grew up, he wanted to be president. "You can't," his older sister replied, "you're a boy."[12]

Heckler won her primary race for Massachusetts's Tenth Congressional District, and in doing so brought down an era in Massachusetts politics. She defeated Martin in a squeaker election by 3,223 votes. Not surprisingly, Heck-

ler did not have the Republican Party's support in that election. Party leaders wanted Martin to have one more term, after which he was expected to
retire. Even the Massachusetts governor, John Volpe, stated publicly that he
had asked Heckler not to run. Heckler could not explicitly use her opponent's
age as an issue, because that tactic would offend some voters. But she did get
a stroke of luck as she began to campaign. An elderly man who had been the
administrative assistant to Martin's predecessor in the House, William S.
Greene, wrote her a letter telling her that Martin had run against his aging
boss back in 1925. Martin, the man revealed, had campaigned on the theme
that experience was all well and good, but a representative had to be physically and mentally able to do the job. Heckler was overjoyed at this news and
borrowed the theme for her own campaign. A congressional seat, she said,
"is a position for one in vigorous health if the people are to be adequately
served."[13]

Her general election was equally difficult, although she won by 51.1 percent of the vote. Her Democratic opponent, labor lawyer Patrick Harrington
Jr., pulled out all the stops in bringing in many well-known figures to support him—among them Vice President Hubert Humphrey and Robert
and Ted Kennedy. Heckler attributed her victory margin to the support of
women.

On her first day in Congress, at age thirty-five, she was much younger
than other congresswomen, and she heard a congressman whisper to another, "How did that secretary get onto the floor of Congress?"[14] Her relative
inexperience in politics was demonstrated when the time came for her to
request a congressional committee assignment. She forthrightly spoke up,
stating that she would like to be on the Judiciary Committee, an assignment
generally reserved for more senior members. Furthermore, the committee
had traditionally prided itself on accepting into its membership "lawyer's
lawyers," a status hard for her to claim based on her legal experience, even
though she had been admitted to practice before the Massachusetts Supreme
Court.

Instead, her first committee assignments in the House were Government
Operations and Veterans' Affairs, the latter a committee that had been
chaired for many years by another Massachusetts Republican woman, Edith
Nourse Rogers. Often, because of House tradition and regional equity, House
committee assignments were made based on former members' assignments,
rather than current members' interests. Heckler accepted the Veterans' Affairs
assignment, eventually rising to become the panel's second highest ranking
member. Among the early bills she championed was legislation providing
counseling to Vietnam War veterans.[15] Heckler's position had changed from
one of support for President Nixon's military policies in Southeast Asia to
opposition to the Vietnam War. She later supported the publication of the

Pentagon Papers on Vietnam to reveal to the public the manner in which the United States had become enmeshed in that conflict.[16] Her reelection campaign in 1970 was almost lost because of her initial support of the Nixon policies.[17] She also supported the creation of aging centers in Veterans' Administration hospitals to care for the rising number of veterans seeking care.

As though unsatisfied with the course of her years in the House, she also sought assignment to several other committees, including Agriculture, Science and Technology, Banking and Currency, and the nonlegislative Ethics and Joint Economic Committees. Her seniority and bargaining ability were weakened by these frequent moves, and she was forced most often to carry her agenda directly to the House floor. While on the Banking Committee, she, along with the Democratic congressman Ed Koch of New York, was the initial sponsor of the Equal Credit Opportunity Act, which granted equal credit access regardless of race or sex or marital status. She also worked to outlaw prejudicial behavior by banks against women applying for home mortgages.

While on the Government Operations Committee, Heckler used her legal background to investigate and pursue problems with government procurement. When she found that defective body armor was being shipped to troops in Vietnam, she alerted the Defense Department, which responded that defective body armor was better than no body armor at all. Heckler made a career of challenging leaders from her own party as well as the opposing one. Because she had been elected without party support, she felt no obligation to toe the party line. Although she was elected as a Republican, it was said that Margaret Heckler was "liberal" and "often crosses party lines."[18]

Heckler attended to the needs of her constituency and district. She consistently proposed tax credits to help Catholic parochial schools, added an amendment to an appropriation bill to protect U.S. fishermen against harassment by Russian vessels along the New England coast, and supported the elimination of foreign oil import quotas to bring cheaper fuels to the frigid New England states. And, like Edith Nourse Rogers before her, she was a strong voice for the New England textile industry.[19]

She used her independence to gain a certain clout within the Republican Party. For example, at the 1972 national convention, Heckler worked to make sure that the platform advocated federally funded day care. President Nixon had vetoed her comprehensive child care bill in 1971. One observer commented, "Peggy worked over a staggering total of 96 drafts on child care. For two hours she argued for the inclusion of a single word: quality. During the tedious wrangling, she left the impression she was willing to walk out."[20] No doubt, her own interest in day care was informed by the fact that as a woman with young children and a career, she understood how difficult it was for working families to rear their children properly.

As the women's movement for equal rights gained momentum during the 1970s, Margaret Heckler took part in it. In 1970 she said, "Women are the one minority group it is still considered fashionable to discriminate against."[21] With her colleague Rep. Elizabeth Holtzman of New York, a Democrat, she founded the Congressional Caucus for Women's Issues, a group that tracked and worked for legislation to help women who were reentering the work force, to achieve Social Security equity, to provide for women's health, to aid displaced homemakers, and to eliminate sexism in education.[22] When asked her ambition, Margaret Heckler said, "I have a daughter who is very bright.... I'd like us to be the first mother-daughter combination in Congress."[23]

In 1975, in recognition of her efforts in behalf of women, Speaker Carl Albert appointed Heckler to the National Commission on the Observance of the International Women's Year. In the same year she was named chairperson of the first delegation of congresswomen to visit the People's Republic of China. Throughout her career Heckler fought for passage of House Joint Resolution 264, the Equal Rights Amendment, guaranteeing equal rights to women. In October 1977, she cosponsored a joint resolution to extend the deadline for ratification. At the Republican National Convention in 1980, she tried valiantly but to no avail to persuade the conservative delegates to endorse the amendment in Congress. She also sponsored bills that would secure the pensions of working women on maternity leave, set up a national center for the prevention and control of rape, and provide shelters for victims of domestic violence. She offered a floor amendment to the Small Business Act creating the position of small business advocate to assist both women and men going into business.[24]

Despite Heckler's work for women, her opposition to federal funding of abortion cost her the support of most Washington-based national women's organizations, and in the 1980 election she lost the support of the National Women's Political Caucus.[25] In the following election she lost the support of the National Organization for Women as well. But *Working Women* magazine at the time put her record into context when it commented: "As for abortion, she consistently opposes the use of federal funds for it but also has opposed a constitutional amendment and never has been an anti-abortion activist."[26] Although some women's groups had abandoned her, she continued pressing in behalf of women and urged President Ronald Reagan to appoint a woman to the Supreme Court. He would make that request a part of his campaign in future years and followed through on the promise with the appointment of Associate Justice Sandra Day O'Connor, the first woman to receive such an honor.

During her congressional career, Heckler offered creative suggestions for reforming the institution of Congress itself. She proposed that committee chairs be elected by a secret ballot of the five most senior committee members, rather than the chair's position simply being given to the most senior member of the majority party. (Current procedure now allows election of committee chairs by secret ballot of all committee members.) Perhaps harking back to her own experience, to help challengers in campaigns against incumbents, she proposed that the franking privilege be suspended for the last month of the campaign (now a House rule). She also suggested that the president be elected directly by the people, instead of by the electoral college.[27]

After congressional redistricting in 1980, Heckler lost her bid for a ninth term in the election of 1982. Her newly drawn Fourth Congressional District forced her into a race with her Democratic colleague Rep. Barney Frank, who had served in Congress for one term. Prior to running for Congress he had served in the Massachusetts legislature and understood the makeup of the new district. The election year 1982 was a referendum on the Reagan presidency; two years after he had assumed office, the economy was souring and worsened as the election year progressed. Frank turned the campaign into a "ferocious attack on Reaganomics" and the president's defense budget.[28] Frank chided Heckler: "I'm the one [candidate] who did not kiss Ronald Reagan on the night of the State of the Union address."[29]

Furthermore, the redistricting resulted in the district's becoming more heavily Democratic and independent than Republican. The *New Republic* at the time described the district as having been "Barneymandered," with only 20 percent of the voters Republican.[30] Since Heckler had supported only 40 percent of the proposals President Reagan put before Congress in his first two years in office, her career up to then would classify her as a moderate Republican, but she found herself defending the Republican fort against an aggressive challenger.[31] Several accounts at the time also indicated that Heckler's campaign was poorly organized, and the decision to close the campaign with a "television advertising blitz accusing Frank of fostering prostitution and weakening rape laws" was ill-advised.[32] When Frank appealed to the voters, saying that he had been smeared, their sympathy swung to him and he carried the district with 59 percent of the vote. Heckler attributed her loss, at least in part, to the defection of feminists. She considered this defection almost a betrayal from a part of the electorate from whom "she had come to expect gratitude—as well as loyalty."[33]

Shortly after this bitter defeat in 1982, Heckler was nominated by President Reagan as secretary of Health and Human Services, the department with the largest budget in the federal government. Some at the time viewed his action as a way to reingratiate himself with women voters, who had flocked to the Democratic Party in the preceding election. But Heckler, caught up in Republican internecine and ideological policy battles between moderates and conservatives, was to remain at the department for only two years. During this time, she established new guidelines for the Social Security disability program and increased research and care for patients with Alzheimer's disease and AIDS.[34]

The next few years for Heckler were particularly embattled, professionally and personally. Her run-ins with some of the Reagan conservative appointees at the department were reported in the press. One story indicated that Heckler's authority was being checked by the undersecretary at the department, a Reagan appointee who was relegating Heckler to the role of speechmaker, while he controlled decisions with the White House on controversial policies such as family planning, abortion policy, disability, and welfare. Writers in *Ms.* magazine predicted, "If he runs the Department, Margaret Heckler will lose her base in Massachusetts, she will lose her support among women. She'll end up screwed."[35] For a woman whose star was rising and was being viewed as possible vice-presidential material in a future, more moderate Republican administration, the pressure to depart for self-preservation had to be significant.[36]

In 1985, in the midst of this rather chaotic period, the Heckler family underwent the humiliation of a well-publicized divorce. Her husband of thirty years admitted "he dallied with other women even as he masterminded his wife's career in Congress."[37] In December 1985 Reagan appointed Heckler ambassador to Ireland, where she served until October 1989. When she returned to the United States, she resumed the practice of law and currently practices in Arlington, Virginia.

NOTES

1. *Current Biography 1983*, s.v. "Heckler, Margaret M(ary O'Shaughnessy)," 182.
2. U.S. Congress, House, Office of the Historian, *Women in Congress, 1917–1990* (Washington, D.C.: U.S. Government Printing Office, 1991), 100.
3. Essie E. Lee, *Women in Congress* (New York: Julian Messner, 1979), 91.
4. *Current Biography 1983*, 183.
5. Ibid.
6. Ibid.
7. Shirley Washington, "Margaret Mary Heckler," *Outstanding Women Members of Congress* (Washington, D.C.: U.S. Capitol Historical Society, 1995), 43.
8. *Current Biography 1983*, 183.
9. Peggy Lamson, *Few Are Chosen: American Women in Political Life Today* (Boston: Houghton Mifflin, 1968), 109.
10. Ibid., 119.
11. Hope Chamberlin, *A Minority of Members: Women in the United States Congress* (New York: Praeger, 1973), 319.
12. Ibid.
13. *Current Biography 1983*, 183.
14. Lee, *Women in Congress*, 94–95.
15. House, *Women in Congress, 1917–1990*, 100.
16. Rudolf Engelbarts, *Women in the United States Congress, 1917–1972: Their Accomplishments* (Littleton, Colo.: Libraries Unlimited, 1974), 105.
17. *Current Biography 1983*, 184.
18. Esther Stineman, *American Political Women: Contemporary and Historical Profiles* (Littleton, Colo.: Libraries Unlimited, 1980), 66.

19. Engelbarts, *Women in the United States Congress, 1917–1972,* 105.
20. Chamberlin, *A Minority of Members,* 317.
21. Stineman, *American Political Women,* 66.
22. Ibid.
23. Lamson, *Few Are Chosen,* 123.
24. *Current Biography 1983,* 184.
25. Ibid.; Judith Paterson and Lavinia Edmunds, "Cabinet Member Margaret Heckler: Reagan's Answer to the Gender Gap," *Ms.,* July 1983, 65.
26. Peggy Simpson, "The New Secretaries: Margaret Heckler," *Working Woman,* April 1983, 113.
27. Chamberlin, *A Minority of Members,* 321.
28. "Building a New House: Election 82," *Newsweek,* October 18, 1982, 34.
29. "The House: Clash of Ideas and Styles: Incumbent vs. Incumbent," *Time,* September 20, 1982, 12.
30. "On the Hill: Barneymandered," *New Republic,* January 6–13, 1982, 9–10.
31. Washington, "Margaret Mary Heckler," 43.
32. Simpson, "The New Secretaries," 112–114.
33. Paterson and Edmunds, "Cabinet Member Margaret Heckler," 65.
34. House, *Women in Congress, 1917–1990,* 100.
35. Paterson and Edmunds, "Cabinet Member Margaret Heckler," 66.
36. Simpson, "The New Secretaries," 114.
37. "Washington's Margaret Heckler and Husband John Talk Bedroom Politics in Divorce Court," *People,* January 28, 1985, 93.

Jeannette Rankin, the first woman to be elected to Congress, is shown addressing a women's suffrage group in 1917. The Nineteenth Amendment to the Constitution gave women the vote in 1920.

Rebecca Felton was the first woman senator; she served for only one day in November of 1922 as a temporary appointment to fill a vacancy.

The women of the 71st Congress (1929–1931) included (front row) Pearl Oldfield, Edith Nourse Rogers, Ruth Baker Pratt, Ruth Hanna McCormick, (back row) Ruth Bryan Owen, Mary Norton, and Florence Kahn.

Left to right, Reps. Alice Robertson, Mae E. Nolan, and Winnifred M. Huck on the steps of the Capitol during the 1920s.

Margaret Chase Smith served longer than any other woman in the history of the Senate. After serving in the House, she was elected to the Senate in 1948 and remained there until 1973. (Top) Rep. Smith with President Truman in 1947 as he signs the bill establishing a permanent Army-Navy Nurse Corp. (Middle) Sen. Smith's 1950 speech "A Declaration of Conscience" was the first public denunciation of McCarthyism. (Bottom) Sen. Smith with President Kennedy in 1963.

Rep. Shirley Chisholm was the first African American woman to be elected to Congress; in 1972 she became the first African American to run for the presidential nomination of a major party.

After Rep. Margaret Heckler lost her seat in the 1982 election, President Ronald Reagan appointed her secretary of health and human services.

Rep. Geraldine Ferraro was the first woman to run for vice president of a major party. Here she talks with House Speaker Thomas P. "Tip" O'Neill after he endorsed her as Walter Mondale's running mate in 1984.

Rep. Lindy Boggs succeeded her husband, Hale Boggs, when his plane was lost over Alaska in 1972. She went on to serve nine terms.

Rep. Marge Roukema was the lead Republican sponsor of the Family and Medical Leave Act of 1993.

Rep. Cardiss Collins has been in Congress since 1973. Through seniority, she worked her way up to become chair of the Subcommittee on Commerce, Consumer Protection, and Competitiveness.

Rep. Pat Schroeder has been an outspoken advocate for women's rights.

Rep. Susan Molinari, chosen by presidential candidate Bob Dole to keynote the 1996 Republican National Convention, talks with an American soldier in the Persian Gulf in 1991.

Sen. Nancy Kassebaum chairs the Subcommittee on African Affairs. Here she is shown in Kenya in 1992.

Part 3: The Modern Era
Toward the Twenty-first Century

The Modern Era
Overview

T he turbulent 1960s ushered in an era of social change built on a revolution of rising expectations generated by the idealism of President John F. Kennedy's New Frontier. A more educated citizenry,
divisive anti–Vietnam War sentiment, and political struggle for equal rights
driven in large part by the civil rights movement brought forth a new group
of women who sought election to Congress. They were more diverse by background, outspoken, well educated, career-minded, and independent than
their predecessors. By the 1970s, all possibilities seemed open to them.

In 1964, the first woman of color, Patsy T. Mink, a Japanese American and
Democrat from Hawaii, took her seat in Congress. She later lost a Senate race
and worked her way back to the House of Representatives, becoming in the
process one of the most skilled female lawmakers. A feminist, she believes the
women's movement is not broadly enough based. "The women's movement," she says, still focuses on middle-class white women.... The 'glass ceiling' is an upper-class ceiling for those aspiring to be bank presidents and executives.... The majority of people working at minimum-wage jobs in the United States are women. That's the glass ceiling I am committed to doing something about."[1]

In 1969, Shirley Anita Chisholm, a Democrat from New York, became the
first African American woman to be elected to Congress. She served fourteen years. Chisholm's election, like that of Jeannette Rankin, put the country on notice that times were changing. She even ran for president in 1972.
Her optimism, confidence, and brilliant oratory challenged images of exclu-
sion centuries old. Barbara Jordan of Texas and Cardiss Collins of Illinois, also
women of color, soon followed her in 1973. Other strong characters arrived
in Congress in the 1970s, like Millicent Fenwick, a Republican from New Jersey, who defied convention by smoking a pipe, and hard-driving Geraldine
Ferraro, a New York Democrat, who became the first woman in history to
receive a major party's nomination for vice president.

When Ferraro arrived in Congress in 1979, only a handful of women were
serving—eleven Democrats and six Republicans. Although she served only
three terms, her legislative career included key accomplishments that reflected her national interests. In 1981, she introduced a bill to make private pensions fairer and to recognize marriage as an economic partnership. The bill
permitted all workers to begin participating in pension plans at age twenty,

instead of twenty-five, and broadened their access to continuing eligibility during job absences, including maternity leave. She introduced a bill to give tax credits to employers of homemakers who had been forced back into the workplace and one to provide individual retirement accounts (IRAs) for homemakers. These bills and her bill concerning fairer private pensions were incorporated into the Women's Equity Act, introduced by the Congressional Women's Caucus in 1983.

In 1984, Walter Mondale, the Democratic presidential candidate, selected Ferraro—then forty-eight years old—to be his vice-presidential running mate. At this announcement, her friend Rep. Barbara Mikulski, a Democrat from Maryland (later a senator), joyously proclaimed, "Don't call her baby! Call her Vice President!"[2] The campaign required her to travel more than 55,000 miles, stumping in eighty-five cities in eighty-seven days. She and her husband, John A. Zacarro, both came under intense verbal attack in efforts to discredit her. Ferraro's public service had been relatively brief. She had been an assistant district attorney in Queens County and a three-term member of Congress from Queens, and she had not run for statewide office. Thus, her family's financial and personal affairs had never been scrutinized, as they normally would have been in a race for statewide or national office. The natural women's base on which Ferraro rested her quest for the vice presidency consisted largely of East Coast, college-educated women activists, too narrow a reed on which to base a national campaign. The results of the election were predictable: the personally popular incumbent president, Ronald Reagan, and his running mate, George Bush, won by a margin of eighteen points. Nevertheless, Ferraro had distinguished herself as a rugged campaigner, and she wrote a new page for women in the history of U.S. politics.

Like Ferraro, other women elected in the 1970s and 1980s were more likely than their predecessors to be well educated, with many trying to negotiate both a family and a career. Margaret S. Roukema of New Jersey, the most senior Republican woman in Congress, was encouraged to seek office after the death of one of her three children. Her son Todd died of leukemia at age seventeen in 1976. He had been diagnosed with the disease two years before. "I never would have run if this had not happened," she said, and added, "Now you understand why I fought so hard for the Family and Medical Leave Act."[3] After Todd died Roukema became active in the Republican Club in Ridgewood, New Jersey, and served as its president in 1977 and 1978. In 1978, she ran for Congress. Under the slogan "It's time to stop fighting Republicans and start beating Democrats," Roukema won the primary election but lost the general election to the liberal Democrat Andrew Maguire by a narrow margin. In 1980, however, she beat Maguire by 51 to 49 percent of the vote. During her campaign, when asked by reporters where she stood on women's issues, she would reply, "All issues are women's issues."[4]

As a freshman congresswoman, Roukema became a member of the Committee on Education and Labor (since 1994, the Economic and Educational Opportunities Committee) and the Committee on Banking, Finance, and Urban Affairs (now the Banking and Financial Services Committee). When David Stockman, President Ronald Reagan's budget director, laid out drastic budget-cutting proposals on student loans, Roukema protested, arguing that the effect of the proposals was that "rich can go, poor can go, but middle class can't go."[5] The budget was modified to protect middle-income families. She fought hard to regulate proprietary and technical schools that were defaulting heavily on government loans. She was the lead Republican sponsor of the Family Leave and Medical Act, enacted in 1993, and worked for tougher enforcement of child support, included in the welfare reform bill passed by the House.[6] She supported the ban on assault weapons and the 1994 crime bill and voted with the Democrats against restarting the Star Wars missile defense program.[7] Roukema regards herself as a pro-choice Republican. She has voted for reductions in spending, supports the balanced budget amendment, and has become one of the most knowledgeable members in the House on housing policy.

Patricia S. Schroeder is one of the few women members of Congress who have served while rearing young children. Most others remained childless or had grown children at the time of their first election. During this modern era, women became less and less likely to succeed their husbands and more likely to be career women who had served in local political office or community agencies before coming to Congress. Ileana Ros-Lehtinen, a Republican from Florida who was first elected in 1988, is the first Hispanic woman of Cuban heritage to be elected to Congress. Nydia M. Velazquez, a Democrat from New York who was elected in 1992, is the first and only woman of Puerto Rican heritage to serve.

Although some of the women legislators began to develop the same career profiles as many of the male members (lawyers with state legislative experience being the most common), the range of women's life experiences before Congress continued to be more varied than those of men. Women went on fighting for equal rights in Congress and pressing for the same humanitarian issues of conscience and principle as their foremothers had. The legality of abortion, one of the most challenging legislative issues of the time, was pushed to the front of public debate by women of widely diverging views. But as the number of women in Congress grew, so did the extent of their legislative preoccupations—among them the environment, agriculture, trade and economics, defense, health, small business, the arts.

About 24 percent of the 111 women sworn in during this modern era (through June 1996) have served ten years or longer. This percentage is somewhat lower than in the previous era, in which 36 percent of the women served ten years or longer. However, if one subtracts the atypically large number of new women members (forty-two) elected or appointed in the 103d and 104th Congresses (1993–1997) and computes the length of service of nonfreshman women, that is, those not sworn in during the 103d or 104th Congresses, one finds that twenty-seven, or about 39 percent, of the nonfreshman women in the modern period have served ten years or longer. This number represents a slight increase in tenure and sophistication in the service of more senior women members compared with the earlier periods, but it also reflects a historically high number of newly elected freshwomen. The 1994 election resulted in a net gain of one seat for women members in both the House and Senate. Later in the 104th Congress, Juanita McDonald, a Democrat from California, was sworn in to replace another member, and Sheila Frahm, a Republican from Kansas, was sworn in to replace the retiring Senate majority leader Bob Dole. The average age at election of women serving in the 103d Congress was forty-eight years, slightly lower than in both previous periods, when fifty years was the average age.

The longest-serving woman of this era is Pat Schroeder, with twenty-three years seniority. She was elected in 1972, at age thirty-two, one of the youngest women ever elected to Congress. She announced that she would retire at the end of 1996. The most senior female senator is Nancy Landon Kassebaum, a Republican from Kansas, daughter of the former Republican presidential candidate Alf Landon. She has served seventeen years. In 1978, she became the first nonwidow successor to gain election to the Senate without having filled an unexpired congressional term of a predecessor. Two of her four children were in their late teens when she was sworn in, and two were grown. After the Republicans gained control of both houses of Congress in 1994, Senator Kassebaum rose to chair a full Senate committee, the Senate Committee on Labor and Human Resources, the first woman to do so. Like Schroeder, Kassebaum announced that she would retire at the end of 1996.

Other women who have established significant careers in Congress are Cardiss Collins, a Democrat from Illinois, the longest-serving African American woman in U.S. history, who has served more than twenty-two years (and has announced that she, too, will retire at the close of 1996); Marilyn Lloyd, a Democrat from Tennessee, who served more than twenty years; and Corinne "Lindy" Boggs, a Democrat from Louisiana, who served eighteen years. All three of these women originally won elections to fill the seats of their deceased spouses.

Of note, women serving in the 104th Congress set a record in giving birth while in office. As *Roll Call* observed: "This Congress holds the undisputed record as the most fertile in history."[8] Rep. Blanche Lambert Lincoln, a Democrat from Arkansas, gave birth to twin boys; Rep. Susan Molinari, a Republican from New York, and Rep. Enid Greene (Waldholtz), a Republican from Utah, each gave birth to a baby girl. Lincoln and Greene announced they would not seek reelection. Before the 104th Congress, only one congress-woman had ever borne a child while serving, Rep. Yvonne Brathwaite Burke, a Democrat from California; she left Congress shortly thereafter in January 1979 at the end of her third term. In announcing their departure, these young women demonstrated the continuing personal choice confronting most women seeking federal office: family versus career, a career-stymying dilemma their male counterparts rarely confront.

Molinari, who had been elected initially to fill a seat vacated by her father, was chosen by her colleagues in the 104th Congress as vice chair of the Republican Conference—a position held by a woman only once before. (Barbara Kennelly had chaired the Democratic Caucus from 1993 to 1996.) Molinari was also selected to deliver the keynote address at the 1996 Republican convention.

At the close of the twentieth century, the progress of women to the nation's highest lawmaking offices continues to be steady but slow. There are now nine women in the U.S. Senate—a record—and forty-nine women in the House of Representatives—also a record high. We can hope that citizens of the twenty-first century will benefit from the array of life experiences from which each of these women made the transition to lawmaker.

The next elections will determine the power of this twentieth-century legacy of enlarged liberties. Public opinion surveys show that women are still only half as likely as men to consider running for office. While one in five men have thought about an electoral bid, only about one in nine women have done so.[9]

If history is any measure, evolutionary change that enlarges opportunity and liberty never moves backward, only forward.

NOTES

1. Patsy Takemoto Mink, interview by author, Washington, D.C.
2. Geraldine Ferraro, *My Story* (New York: Bantam Books, 1985), 97.
3. Margaret S. Roukema, interview by author, Washington, D.C., April 18, 1996.
4. Ibid.
5. Ibid.
6. Ibid.
7. Michael Barone and Grant Ujifusa, *The Almanac of American Politics 1996* (Washington, D.C.: National Journal, 1995).
8. Jennifer Bradley, "It's a Boy ... Actually Two Boys for Lincoln," *Roll Call,* June 20, 1996, 1.
9. Amy Keller, "Year of the Woman ... Losing Elections," *Roll Call,* March 25, 1996, 15.

Shirley Anita Chisholm
Democrat–New York (1969–1983)
First Woman of Color in Congress

> *There is little place in the political scheme of things for an independent, creative
> personality or for a fighter. Anyone who takes that role must pay a price.*
> > Shirley Chisholm, *Unbought and Unbossed*

A fine orator, yet never weighing more than one hundred pounds, her crisp voice pungent as a branch snapping in the winter woods, Shirley Chisholm moved through life and politics as a singular force in her own right. Sometimes a maverick, her strong ego and challenging nature took on "establishment" politics wherever she found it—in the state assembly, in the ward clubs, in Congress. She was always testing limits. Her disciplined West Indian heritage, closely knit family, fine education, and geographic distance from the racial segregation that circumscribed the potential of other black Americans afforded her a different perspective on human achievement.

Born in Brooklyn as Shirley Anita St. Hill on November 30, 1924, Chisholm lived on a farm in Barbados during her formative years. Her parents had fled the Caribbean islands after World War I, when crop failures caused famine. From ages three to nine, she was reared, along with her two younger sisters, by her maternal grandparents. Her grandmother, Mrs. Emily Seale, had a "stentorian voice" and presence that Chisholm admired and, no doubt, copied.[1] The St. Hills, immigrants to New York, wanted to be sure they could give their children a good life before they brought them back to the United States. Because of these years in Barbados, Chisholm benefited from a British-style education, very strict but very effective. Her sense of self came partly from those years in the Caribbean.

When she was nine, she and her sisters returned to Brooklyn. In contrast to Barbados, Chisholm's neighborhood in Brooklyn was largely Caucasian and Jewish. She adapted to the changed environment, concerned more about the confusion of city life in comparison with rural Barbados than about the social milieu into which she was being thrust. Her mother, heavily influenced by British custom, reared her four daughters to become young ladies—"poised, modest, accomplished, educated, and graceful."[2]

Chisholm was precocious as a child, and also loquacious, gifted, and headstrong. She was raised in a highly disciplined household, and the neighborhoods in which the family lived kept her sheltered from racial remarks until her teens. Her mother, a seamstress, belonged to the religious group the English Brethren, a Quaker-like sect. Chisholm's West Indian heritage, by her own account, made her more "like Black Jews," and less like the southern black families that were to become so much a part of her world.[3]

Her father, a baker by trade, was an avid follower of Marcus Garvey, the Jamaican nationalist leader who advocated black separatism. Chisholm brought up his children to be strong and independent. In 1936, when Shirley was twelve, he again moved his family, this time to Bedford Stuyvesant, a neighborhood to which blacks from the South were moving to work in the Brooklyn Navy Yard. He cautioned his daughter about her playmates: "These are American kids, not island kids."[4]

In high school Chisholm was an excellent student and won scholarship offers to Vassar, among other schools. However, she chose to attend Brooklyn College, where tuition was free, so that she could live at home and save on the costs of room and board. She put herself on a course to be a teacher because the study of other professions—law, medicine, and nursing—was expensive, and social work did not admit blacks until the 1940s.[5]

After graduating in 1946, Chisholm taught at Mount Calvary Child Care Center in New York until 1952. Meanwhile, in 1949, she married Conrad Chisholm, whom she had dated for several years, and attended Columbia University, where she earned a master's degree in early childhood education in 1952. Early childhood education would continue to be Shirley Chisholm's primary interest for the rest of her career. In 1953 she became director of New York's Hamilton-Madison Child Care Center. Later, she moved on to become an educational consultant for the city's Division of Child Care. During these years, she also began her extensive involvement with Brooklyn's Democratic Party clubs. She rose to the governing board of one club, but the leadership soon ousted her because of her activism and agitation. It was from experiences like this that Chisholm formed her "present attitude toward politics as it is practiced in the United States: it is a beautiful fraud that has been imposed on the people for years, whose practitioners exchange gilded promises for the most valuable thing their victims own, their votes."[6]

A few years earlier, in her senior year of college, Chisholm had met two men who would greatly influence her political career: Louis Warsoff and Wesley M. "Mac" Holder. Warsoff, a blind political science professor, planted the idea that she should run for elected office. Holder, the head of the Bedford-Stuyvesant Political League and an activist devoted to electing black officials to represent black communities, taught her about politics:

I learned politics from him. He would explain to me what was happening in politics, what maneuvers the white politicians were making and what they meant, how the deals were being made. I absorbed his sophistication on how the system works, how some people are kept out and others kept in.[7]

In 1958, however, she ran against him for the league's top leadership post, believing that the group should focus more on community problems, and a long friendship was crushed.

In 1964, with the support of her husband, whom she describes as "a secure man in his own right," Chisholm began her career in elected office by entering the race for a seat in the New York State Assembly.[8] She ran as a Democrat. During this period in U.S. history black voters were abandoning the Republican Party for the first time since the Civil War. Also during this decade the broader movement for women's rights, growing out of the civil rights movement, began to take a prominent position in the country.

In her campaign, Chisholm encountered hostility because of her gender. One man on the campaign trail challenged her, "Young woman, what are you doing out here in the cold? Did you get your husband's breakfast this morning? Did you straighten up your house? What are you doing running for office? That is something for men."[9] Conrad Chisholm apparently did not agree; when his wife ran for the House and later for president, he left his job to drive her, research her speeches, and "see that she eats on time."[10] Shirley Chisholm won that election and was reelected in both of the following two years, when she had to campaign again because of redistricting. In the assembly she worked toward and achieved legislation that provided for unemployment insurance for domestic workers and day care centers supported by tax dollars.

Shirley Chisholm recalls that the timing of her decision to run for Congress in 1968 was influenced by a welfare mother who came to visit her. The woman brought along $9.62 in change collected from a bingo game and said that if Chisholm would run for Congress, they would raise funds for her every Friday night. Chisholm was immensely touched by this offer and decided the time was right to run. "I wanted," she wrote, "to show the machine that a little black woman was going to beat it."[11]

To campaign in the streets of Brooklyn, she organized an automobile caravan, with each car sporting a "Vote Chisholm for Congress—Unbought and

Unbossed" sign. Campaign workers handed out shopping bags with the same slogan printed on them. This turned out to be an ingenious idea: people could be spotted at markets, in subway stations, on the sidewalks, carrying bags advertising Chisholm's candidacy.[12] Her Republican opponent was James Farmer, former head of the Congress of Racial Equality (CORE), a civil rights organization. But Chisholm's campaign drew on the strength of women and Spanish speakers in the district. Her college minor in Spanish helped her appeal in Spanish to many voters.[13] She reached outside the bounds of her race to all the people in her district: black, Puerto Rican, Jewish, Polish, Ukrainian, and Italian. She won with 34,885 votes to Farmer's 13,777. (The Conservative Party's candidate received 3,771.)

In Congress, Shirley Chisholm sought appointment to the Education and Labor Committee because of her background in education. But when the assignments were announced, she found herself on the Agriculture Committee. Knowing that this committee had jurisdiction over areas like food stamps and migrant labor, she accepted the decision—until she learned of her subcommittee assignment, Forestry. "Apparently all they know of Brooklyn is that a tree grew there," she said of the subcommittee placement.[14] Chisholm went to the House Speaker, John W. McCormack, D-Mass., to protest. "I feel my committee and subcommittee assignments do not make much sense," she told him. McCormack replied, "You have to be a good soldier," meaning that once she put in her time on this committee, she would eventually get a more desirable assignment. But Chisholm responded, "All my forty-three years I have been a good soldier.... If you do not assist me, I will have to do my own thing."[15]

McCormack agreed to speak to Wilbur D. Mills, D-Ark., the chair of the Ways and Means Committee, and the two men went to the chair of the Agriculture Committee, W. R. Poage, D-Texas, to ask whether Chisholm could be given a different subcommittee assignment. When Poage refused, Chisholm decided that she would have to object when the assignments were voted on by the full caucus of Democrats. After trying unsuccessfully to be recognized, she eventually went and stood in the "well" (the area of the House chamber where members seek recognition to speak) until the Speaker recognized her. She told him that she was protesting her committee assignment because she had been elected to represent her constituents in Brooklyn, and she felt that this assignment was not in their interests. This maneuver got her a reassignment to the Veterans' Affairs Committee, still not her first choice, but better. As she remarked, "There are a lot more veterans in my district than there are trees."[16] When she had gained some seniority, she was elected to serve on the Education and Labor Committee, and in her last six years in Congress, she was elected to the prestigious Rules Committee.

In 1972, Chisholm launched the first campaign by a woman for the Democratic Party's presidential nomination. She campaigned across the United States and was on the primary ballot in twelve states. At the Democratic National Convention, she received 152 delegate votes, approximately as many as Margaret Chase Smith had garnered in her party a few years earlier.[17] She pursued her presidential aspirations independently, as she had so many other quests in her life. To the consternation of many rising black leaders and much resentment, particularly among male members of the Congressional Black Caucus, her decision came as a total surprise. "She had not taken any of us into her confidence and never discussed her plans for seeking the higher office."[18] Some of her fiercest critics were members of the Black Caucus because she had not asked their permission, chose to run as an individual rather than being sanctioned by a group, and often made alliances with nonblacks. Chisholm wanted to build a coalition of women, Hispanics, white liberals, students, and welfare recipients.[19] And she directly challenged the legitimacy of Democratic, black, male elected officials who derided her efforts as insensitive to black concerns.

In her book on the campaign, *The Good Fight,* she wrote:

I was not out to become only the black candidate. While I would have welcomed the support of these men, I did not seek it because, even if they had offered their backing (as I knew they never would do), I would have been locked into a false and limiting role. It was possible for me to be more than the black candidate, or the candidate of minorities generally. My potential support went far beyond the black community. It would come from the women's movement, from young voters, even from a growing number of older white women who had reached the end of their patience with the programs and candidates of the two major parties.[20]

Some male members of the Black Caucus went so far as to run favorite-son candidates in their respective states to channel convention delegates against her. Nonetheless, her electrifying speeches and commanding rhetoric galvanized audiences from coast to coast. Shirley Chisholm had the ability in an era of racial unrest to make audiences see beyond her color.

Chisholm served for fourteen years in the House, from 1969 to 1983. She did not see herself "as a lawmaker, an innovator in the field of legislation." America, she believed, "has the laws and the material resources it takes to insure justice for all its people. What it lacks is the heart, the humanity, the Christian love that it would take."[21] That is what she strove to supply. Her legislative strategy included cosponsoring bills that would help Brooklyn voters with education, welfare, unemployment, and housing. She championed the Office of Economic Opportunity, which assisted many of her constituents in their climb from poverty. A major focus of her office staff was helping constituents get grant money to improve the community. Her philosophy was that "it is going to be the have-nots ... who somehow arouse the conscience of the nation and thus create a conscience in the Congress." She saw her role as "help[ing] them do so, working outside of Washington, perhaps, as much as inside it."[22]

Chisholm introduced legislation to end the draft and create a volunteer armed forces, and she called for an end to British arms sales to South Africa.[23] She also predicted that women would play a major part in helping Congress to change. "Women I have known in government have seemed to me to be much more apt to act for the sake of a principle or moral purpose. They are not as likely as men to engage in deals, manipulations, and sharp tactics."[24] Sixty years before, Jeannette Rankin had gone to Congress with that same idea.

In 1982, at the age of fifty-eight, Chisholm announced she would not seek reelection. Later, in private conversation, she revealed that her beloved husband was not feeling well, and she wanted to spend time with him.[25] After a stint as a professor at Wellesley College, she was nominated in 1994 for the post of U.S. ambassador to Jamaica by President Bill Clinton. She declined because of poor health.

Against all odds, Chisholm's voice did indeed reach beyond the black community. She exhibited grace under pressure as the first Democratic woman to seek the presidency. She was beyond the control of any group. History will record Shirley Chisholm not only as a full person in her own right but as a person larger than life with a vision beyond race.

NOTES

1. Shirley Chisholm, *Unbought and Unbossed* (Boston: Houghton Mifflin, 1970), 6.
2. Ibid.
3. Ibid., 4.
4. Ibid., 6.
5. Ibid.
6. Ibid., 37.
7. Ibid., 39.
8. Esther Stineman, *American Political Women: Contemporary and Historical Profiles* (Littleton, Colo.: Libraries Unlimited, 1980), 28.
9. Chisholm, *Unbought and Unbossed,* 52–53.
10. Hope Chamberlin, *A Minority of Members: Women in the United States Congress* (New York: Praeger, 1973), 327.
11. Chisholm, *Unbought and Unbossed,* 68.
12. Ibid., 69.
13. Stineman, *American Political Women,* 29.
14. Ibid., 28.
15. Chisholm, *Unbought and Unbossed,* 82.
16. Stineman, *American Political Women,* 28.
17. Susan J. Tolchin, *Women in Congress, 1917–1976* (Washington, D.C.: U.S. Government Printing Office, 1976), 90.
18. William L. Clay, Sr., *Just Permanent Interests* (New York: Armistead Press, 1993), 222.
19. Chisholm, *Unbought and Unbossed.*
20. Shirley Chisholm, *The Good Fight* (New York: Harper and Row, 1973), 37–38.

21. Chisholm, *Unbought and Unbossed,* 70.
22. Ibid., 112.
23. U.S. Congress, House, Office of the Historian, *Women in Congress, 1917–1990* (Washington, D.C.: U.S. Government Printing Office, 1991), 44.
24. Chisholm, *Unbought and Unbossed,* 167.
25. Shirley Anita Chisholm, interview by author, Washington, D.C., April 1982.

Corinne Claiborne "Lindy" Boggs

Democrat–Louisiana (1973–1991)

First Elected Congresswoman from Louisiana

When the various people were trying to persuade me to run ... Lady Bird Johnson [wife of President Lyndon B. Johnson] ... called and talked to me for a long time about how I had an obligation and all of these things. Then when she thought maybe she had convinced me, she said, "But darling, do you think you can do it without a wife?" I've told her many times, it was very hard without a wife.

Corinne Claiborne "Lindy" Boggs, interview by author, October 15, 1993

When Corinne Claiborne "Lindy" Boggs retired from Congress in 1991 at age seventy-five, she was the only Caucasian woman serving in Congress from the Deep South (excluding Florida). Part magnolia, part Tabasco sauce, part French Quarter grande dame, she represented the maturation of a modern political miracle—a Roman Catholic, Caucasian woman elected for nine consecutive terms to the U.S. Congress from Louisiana's powerhouse of Democratic political families. Her religious training helped develop in her a rare social conscience that otherwise might have been blunted. Her family's wealth shielded her from the Great Depression era in which she grew up and which branded for life many people of her generation. Her family's social and economic position provided her with tutors and gave her the opportunity for higher education; she embodied southern charm at its polished best.

As a southern progressive congresswoman, Lindy Boggs sponsored legislation to guarantee women access to credit; to ensure women business owners access to small-business loans and federal contracts; to make educational opportunities in science, mathematics, and education more available to women; to provide early childhood education in public housing developments; and to provide assistance for victims of rape and domestic violence.[1] She once said that her greatest pride was helping to establish the Select Committee on Children, Youth, and Families, dissolved by Congress in 1993, three years after she left.[2]

Boggs was born a country girl, Marie Corinne Morrison Claiborne, on March 13, 1916, at Brunswick Plantation, 130 miles north of New Orleans in Pointe Coupee Parish. In Louisiana, counties are called parishes, harking back to the early French rule of the territory during which the Roman Catholic Church established them as administrative units. She was the only child of a wealthy sugar cane plantation owner, Roland Philemon Claiborne, an attorney from a family of fourteen siblings. Her mother was Corinne Morrison Claiborne, from a family of seven. Her nurse nicknamed her "Rolindy" because she thought Lindy resembled her father more than her mother.

After her father's death when she was two years old, she and her mother went to live in New Orleans with her maternal grandparents, the Morrisons. The home had a lively, family atmosphere. Her grandmother Morrison had a great influence on her and lived to be ninety-seven. Boggs and her two cousins Hayward and Claiborne Dameron, who were close to her in age, spent about six weeks every summer with their Claiborne grandparents in New Roads, the parish seat. New Roads, a town of about 2,000 at that time, was filled with cultured, strong-minded, well-educated people. Her grandfather Claiborne, an energetic man of many talents who lived until he was ninety-two, was a member of the state legislature, both the house and the senate at different times. He also served on the school board, as district attorney, and as district judge. In addition he founded a newspaper, the *Pointe Coupee Banner.*

Although her grandmother Claiborne was not well in the latter years of her life, she had calling hours because so many people wanted to see her. Both grandmothers were enterprising women and wonderful gardeners. Boggs tells the story of her grandmother Morrison's fondness for artichokes. At certain times of the year Solari's, one of the fancy grocers that sent supplies by boat up the Mississippi from New Orleans, did not have artichokes. Boggs's grandmother decided to experiment with raising artichokes herself. After a couple of years, she was shipping artichokes to Solari's.[3]

Lindy Boggs's world revolved around the plantations, which controlled the politics of the state. She traces her roots through her father's family to William Claiborne, who became Virginia's first secretary of state in Jamestown, in 1721. His descendant William Charles Cole Claiborne was appointed by Thomas Jefferson to be the first governor of Louisiana after it became a state. Her mother's family—the Morrisons—were deeply active in

Louisiana politics, and her grandmother Morrison's family traces its roots back to the *Mayflower*.[4] Several family members of Boggs's own generation were in public service, among them, her cousin deLesseps "Chep" Morrison, mayor of New Orleans; Rep. Herbert Claiborne Pell of New York; and Pell's son, Sen. Claiborne Pell of Rhode Island.

Her mother, whom she describes as "young, beautiful, vivacious, and fun" married again when Lindy was six; her new stepfather owned a cotton plantation:

And that's when I had my first introduction to politics. The sugar planters were very isolationist, protectionist, and they kept talking about high tariff walls. And in the country, we had constructions called "stiles," which were really steps over fences. And I kept wondering if Uncle Joe could build me a stile tall enough so I could see what was on the other side of that high tariff wall. But then on the cotton plantation, of course, the cotton people were free traders, to get rid of all that surplus cotton they had, so the conversation was entirely different. So I learned early on that families can be divided over political situations.

Her formative years as a child on a plantation were filled with an endless stream of family and friends gathered in the manor house. The plantation drew weekly outsiders from the larger world:

The women on plantations were absolutely remarkable. They had an autonomous situation. They had to do everything in the house, "in-plantation," and everything had to be done in time for a huge mid-day dinner. Then, in the afternoon, after a short rest, they created their own cultural environment. They had musicals, and they had book reviews, and they played a lot of cards, and all that sort of thing. But the plantation homes were really the centers of everything you can imagine, all the social life, all the cultural life, all the business life. It all occurred within those houses. And the women had to be very well read. They had to provide their own musical entertainment. They had to be wonderful managers.

The dining rooms were always big. They always had chairs and rocking chairs and sofas in them. So when your friends dropped in after dinner, if they had already had dinner, they sat and maybe had dessert if they wanted it, but certainly coffee, and the conversation went on. And the children were not banned from that, they were not banished from the table; you were able to stay and listen to all of it. And you learned early who was on what side, and you never crossed them. That helped me a great deal in Congress. I had members of my family who didn't see eye-to-eye politically.

Many years later, it was said of Boggs, "Lindy got along with everyone—even [Richard M.] Nixon."[5]

Until she was nine, Boggs was educated by a private tutor on the plantation. She then attended St. Joseph's Academy in nearby New Roads, run by the Sisters of St. Joseph of Medaille. The small town was home not only to her paternal grandparents but also to several aunts and uncles. She boarded at the school during the week and went home on weekends. At an early age, she traveled the byways of Louisiana and was exposed to a vast extended family and to enormously different lifestyles. She often visited three aunts, three step-aunts, and her maternal grandmother in New Orleans.

New Orleans—Louisiana's largest city with over a half million citizens and home to America's early wealthy settlers—evokes images of crayfish, red beans and rice, strong coffee, and the sound of the Creole language. The community is notched into the alluvial plain where the Mississippi River meets the Gulf of Mexico. Established by French adventurers, then ruled by the Spanish, and finally sold to the United States, it was, until the Civil War, the fourth largest city in the United States and the South's major metropolis. Foreign immigrants flocked to New Orleans more than to any other area of the South.[6] The life of the city's French Quarter, settled heavily by Catholics, became separated from what was regarded by the original settlers as the real America—the Protestants—on the other side of Canal Street. In fact, the "new downtown" of New Orleans was built east of Canal Street. "To this day, the ground between lanes of traffic is not called dividers but rather 'neutral ground,'" important code words describing the history of this ethnically, racially, and religiously complicated settlement.[7]

By contrast, New Roads is a country place that even today, with a population of 3,900, clings to the antebellum graces. The bright young people of New Roads went to Poydras High School and then on to college. The young women went away to college because there were no women's colleges in the vicinity. After graduating, most of them, men and women, returned to New Roads, vying with each other in all the professions, including politics. Boggs recalls celebrating her Uncle Ferd Claiborne's election as district attorney at his home and then going on to dine at her aunt's, whose husband was the defeated incumbent district attorney:

And that happened frequently in that volatile kind of political situation that existed in that town. But the wonderful lesson was that the women never let it disturb them. They always remained close friends through all of the political shenanigans. And they were helpful and supportive in every way, when babies were born, when people were sick, when people died. They were all in the same clubs and organizations and all still played cards together, which was very important. That's where I learned women can be a steadying influence in politics, and that you don't really have to be aggressively out to fight each other so hard that you can't kiss and make up. The best thing is not to even have to make up, not to ever veer from your personal relationships because of politics. I think that helped me a great deal in Congress.

Although Lindy Boggs rarely refers to her mother or stepfather with deep affection, her early years were filled with attachments of lasting influence. One was Aunt Hannah Hall, a black woman who had helped to rear her stepfather:

She was an enduring presence, a great philosopher.... Aunt Hannah always worried about me going to the convent during the week. She didn't think they were going to feed me enough.... So she would send me to the convent on Monday morning with ham or turkey and she would—well, I may as well say it correctly—she would steal twenty-four Mars bars or Milky Ways or something out of the commissary, and I used to trade my candy bars with some town children whose families had fruit stores, for their fruit.

At a young age, Lindy Boggs was developing the trading skills essential to moving bills through Congress.

The nuns at the convent were another great influence:

The sisters were important to me because it didn't occur to me that women couldn't do everything. The nuns were not only the principals of the schools, but they were the directors of the hospitals, and the presidents of colleges. I've often said, people in New Roads, even the men, were a little bit in awe of Father Hoes, who was our pastor, but Father Hoes was scared to death of Mother Gertrude.

Boggs matriculated at Newcomb College in New Orleans, founded in the 1880s, the first women's college in Louisiana. It was the sister college to Tulane University. After graduating in 1935, she taught American history to high school seniors in St. James Parish, world history to juniors, and English and literature to sophomores and freshmen. She also did graduate work in library science at Loyola University, served as the school librarian, and even coached the girls' basketball team.

In January 1938, at age twenty-one, she married Thomas Hale Boggs, whom she had met at college during her freshman year. Hale—tall, dark, and handsome—was a law student and editor of the Tulane University newspaper, the *Hullaballoo*. Lindy was women's editor, which, she noted, "was the highest job to which a woman could aspire at that time."

Launching forth into politics from their university connections, Hale and Lindy Boggs became part of a grass-roots political reform movement in Louisiana in the late 1930s during the tumultuous aftermath of the assassination of Huey Long. Elected governor in 1928, Long had built a remarkable political empire. With his election to the U.S. Senate in 1932, he had his sights set on the presidency. A driven, complicated man, he not only became a champion for the common people but also used violence, bribery, and bullying to get his way. His accomplishments were legendary: he built a road system for Louisiana, constructed public works such as a new state university and a new capitol, and made free textbooks available to every child. But, as the classic biography of Huey Long notes, his character "revealed all the cynicism and contempt of democracy, and all the ruthlessness of the man who seemed in the 1930s to be the first American dictator, the first great native fascist, who compared to Hitler and Mussolini commanded one of the largest mass followings" in the depths of the Great Depression.[8] Some credit Long with pushing President Franklin D. Roosevelt to enact the great social agenda of the New Deal, by challenging the aristocratic Roosevelt with his "share the wealth—make every man a king" philosophy.

Although the established Democrats tried to right the party after Long was assassinated, his cronies were imprisoned one after another, some for fraud and other crimes emanating from the state machine they had built.The governor went to the penitentiary, as did the president of the state university, several other officers of the state, and some business and financial leaders.

The Boggses quickly rose to political fame in the aftermath of the assassination. Since Long's time Louisiana politics "has often been a struggle between reformist and conservative forces on one side and roguish populists on the other."[9] The Boggs family landed firmly in the reformist camp, and in fact, shaped it.

Lindy Boggs explains the grass-roots movement for reform:

The opening for reform and change could only come from young people, who could challenge the well-established professional politicians and the firmly entrenched, powerful professionals.... It was difficult for older and well-established professional and business people to be outwardly against a very strong and firmly entrenched political system. But the young people had nothing to lose.

Thus the People's League was formed, with Hale Boggs at the head of it:

We were aided and abetted by the women. My father's eldest sister was a suffragette—Aunt Celeste Claiborne Caruth.... My uncle, who was the oldest boy in my father's family, a family with fourteen children, was a member of the state legislature, and at one time was lieutenant governor, and then district attorney. But while he was a member of the state legislature, there was this great debate because state roads were being built, and they had to get new rights-of-way.

One of the pieces of legislation to accompany the highway legislation was introduced as a "no-fence law." The highway specifications had demanded that fences be built along the properties to keep the animals from coming onto the highway. And this "no-fence" legislation was introduced because the people who owned the property didn't want to go to the expense of putting up the fences; they thought they should be compensated if they had to do that.

And so my uncle made this impassioned speech about the "poor widow women" who own the properties along this route, and how dreadful it would be for them to have to pay to build these fences. Well, his sister, my aunt, and some of her suffragette friends conducted a survey from one end of the state to the other. There was not one poor widow woman who owned a piece of property, and they defeated his legislation.

Other women helped in ways that were different but as direct:

My aunts Rowena Morrison Buffington and Maybart Morrison Blackshire, and many wonderful women ... were the mainstays of our organization. They financed us as well. They also taught us how to organize.... They were the heads of the opera guild and the community chest, and all the different organizations in town.

Clearly, even then it was Lindy's large, extended family and their wealth that added the extra wind under the wings of the Boggses' reform efforts.

The initiators of the People's League included most of Hale's law school class at Tulane (1937). Statewide elections in 1939 afforded the organization the opportunity to integrate with the followers of Sam Jones, who had been selected as the reform candidate for governor, and form a ward-precinct organization.

Huey Long had done away with the poll tax, but citizens still had to get a poll tax receipt each year if they wanted to vote. At registration, which was required yearly, they had to produce two receipts to prove they had resided in the state for two years. In addition, potential voters had to take a rigged examination before they could register. Lindy Boggs explains the reform efforts of the People's League:

One of our first, major thrusts [was] to do something about the registration laws. And then we learned too about all of the shenanigans that could go on on election day. The lights would go out. They would switch ballot boxes. They would have stuffed ballot boxes. We had poll watchers. But, oftentimes, they were disqualified.... And so for election day, we were all trained.

The reformists won the governorship, most of the statewide offices, and the majority of the House and Senate.

In the midst of this turmoil, and as spearhead of the People's League, Hale Boggs won his first election to Congress from New Orleans. He was twenty-six years old, Lindy twenty-four. Lindy was involved in every aspect of that campaign and ran all twelve of his subsequent campaigns. Publicly she said, "He didn't have a campaign manager; nobody could manage him."[10]

Boggs's recollections of her husband's first term in Congress (1941–1943) center on World War II:

Hale called me one day and—we had two babies—and said, "Lin, you have to come down to the Lend Lease hearings; you will never understand it unless you do." So, I hastily threw on some high heels and lipstick and ran down. In those days, you didn't have your picture on your driver's license or any other kind of card. I went up to the hearing room, overcrowded, and I was very young, and I said I'd like to get into the hearings, please, my husband's a member of the committee. The officer responded, "Oh, yeah, honey, sure." How was I going to get in there? Then I remembered Mrs. Alise Dougas, who was a grande dame of New Orleans. When she heard I was coming to Washington, she said: "My dear, the most becoming and sophisticated thing a woman can wear is a purple veil." So, I went home, I put on my black Davidow suit, my white kid gloves, my black velour hat, and I went down to the Palais Royale and said, "Please drape a purple veil around my hat." It was very expertly done, and I walked back to the committee hearing room and took off one glove and then the other, and I said, "I'm Mrs. Boggs; I'd like to be seated please." "Oh, yes, ma'am, come right in."[11]

Hale was defeated after his first term, by Paul Maloney, the man he had defeated, an influential member of the House Ways and Means Committee with the ability to use his position to reward powerful interests in Louisiana—

like oil and gas, sugar and cotton. At that time, the Ways and Means Committee named other House members to key committees, and Paul Maloney had several IOU's to collect, including those in the Louisiana delegation. Lindy Boggs, in her understated way, recounted: "He was really a fine man. We became good friends, Mr. Paul 'Senior,' as I called him," perhaps implying that the young Turks would pause, but not relent.

Hale returned to New Orleans after his defeat, determined to do his part in World War II by going into the military. "He felt he had voted for war and that he should volunteer. As he used to say, he went from being the youngest member of Congress to the oldest ensign in the navy." Hale was assigned as legal adviser to the Maritime Commission. Instead of going to PT boat school, he went to Washington, and Lindy and their two children joined him there. Their third child, Cokie, was born while he was in the navy. A fourth child, William, born after the war, died in infancy after a difficult birth, and Lindy learned she could have no more children.

After the war, Hale resumed his political career, gaining election in 1946 to the House of Representatives from New Orleans. After this reincarnation as a member of Congress, Hale Boggs began a steady rise in the House. In 1952, he ran unsuccessfully for governor of Louisiana against Earl Long, Huey Long's younger brother. One member of Congress, who wished to remain anonymous, recalled:

When Hale ran for governor, Earl Long started every possible rumor about him because he was viewed as more cosmopolitan, "New Orleans" in a state with an anti–New Orleans bias, a national Democrat. In Louisiana if you were labeled "left," you were called a Communist. In North Louisiana, heavily Protestant, tradition-bound, and rural, Earl would say, "They say my opponent Hale Boggs is a Communist. He can't be a Communist. He's too good a Catholic from New Orleans to be a Communist." No doubt about it, a lethal quote—mean, dirty, and brilliant.[12]

After this defeat, Hale continued to build his career in Congress, becoming whip, majority leader, and eventually Speaker of the House. Lindy managed his Capitol Hill office, and politics became the family business. She chaired numerous organizations, including John F. Kennedy's and Lyndon B. Johnson's inaugural ball committees in 1961 and 1965, respectively. She was elected president of the Women's National Democratic Club, the Democratic Wives' Forum, and the Congressional Club. She steered Lady Bird Johnson's whistle-stop campaign tour through the South. Hale and Lindy Boggs were major forces in the Democratic Party and a likely presidential family themselves in the future.

Then, in mid-October 1972, everything suddenly changed. An airplane carrying Hale Boggs and freshman congressman Nick Begich, who were on a campaign trip in Alaska, never reached its destination in Juneau. An extensive search was made until weather conditions forced its cancellation in late

November. The whole time, Lindy Boggs was confident that they were going to be found. Among the numerous supportive messages she received were many from the families of men missing in action and prisoners of war. They advised her to keep sending her husband positive thoughts, so when people suggested that she run for Hale's seat in Congress, she would say, "Oh, no, we already have a Congressman."

At that time in Louisiana, there was no way to declare a seat vacant:

We had to wait until Congress reconvened [after January 1] and they declared the seat vacant. And then the governor called an election. All in the intervening weeks, people had asked me to run, and I had not entertained the thought at all. I woke up and just found myself running one morning; I never made a conscious decision to run.

The following March, 1973, Lindy Boggs was elected to Congress, the first and only female representative ever elected from the state of Louisiana, although the wives of both Huey Long and Edwin Edwards had served briefly as senators in interim appointments. Her campaign slogan was "Let Her Continue." Lindy won her election by 75 percent in the Democratic primary and 80 percent in the special election. "I had a Republican running against me by the name of Robert E. Lee," she said. "I knew he was an impostor!"

She was Catholic in a state that had never elected a Catholic to any major state office until Edwin Edwards was elected governor in 1972; he never admitted so in his literature. In earlier times, before television and mass communications could catch a half-truth, candidates in Louisiana could cater cleverly to the state's split personality—Protestant and Anglo-Saxon in the north, more Catholic and mixed ethnically in the south. When Huey Long was campaigning for governor, he was advised by a local political boss:

"Huey, you ought to remember one thing in your speeches today. You're from north Louisiana, but now you're in south Louisiana. And we got a lot of Catholic voters down here." "I know," Huey answered. And throughout the day in every small town Long would begin by saying: "When I was a boy, I would get up at six o'clock in the morning on Sunday, and I would hitch our old horse up to the buggy and I would take my Catholic grandparents to mass. I would bring them home, and at ten o'clock I would hitch the old horse up again, and I would take my Baptist grandparents to church." The effect of the anecdote on the audiences was obvious, and on the way back to Baton Rouge that night the local leader said admiringly: "Why, Huey, you've been holding out on us. I didn't know you had any Catholic grandparents." "Don't be a damn fool," replied Huey. "We didn't even have a horse."[13]

Boggs's eventual election was a tribute to her family's legacy and her substantial political wiles. As one southern male member of Congress later confided: "Culturally, even in 1994, Caucasian women can't attain election from the South. If they're pretty, people say they've slept their way to the top. If they're not attractive, they hold them in a certain disdain."[14] The rise to power of Lindy Boggs, a genteel, well-mannered daughter of the South, wrote history anew. True, she was the widow of a power broker in Louisiana and Congress, but as one acquaintance remarked: "She was the only woman I ever knew who was a genuine political asset to her husband."[15] Once she was forced to solo, her grit spoke for itself. "Some thought she'd be a typical caretaker after Hale's death, a spouse and all, but she took over this place [Congress]!"[16]

Characteristically, Lindy minimizes the giant step she took in that campaign. As Mike Roccaforte, past president of the Uptown Democratic Association recalled:

As it turned out, Mrs. Boggs would become the first woman to ever cross the doorway in Terpsichore Street [where an all-male political dinner had been planned for Hale]. When they found out that she would try for the congressional seat ... a couple of changes were required.... I told my wife she had to go too.... [T]he only restroom facility over at that place was an outhouse, and I just told my wife she had to go to that dinner so that if Lindy needed to use the restroom, she could go with her! Well Lindy went, and so did Roccaforte's wife, and another bastion of male supremacy fell without the shedding of a single drop of blood.[17]

Her transition to Congress was frenetic. She had to close up Hale's congressional office, his majority leader's office, his Joint Economic Committee offices, and his Ways and Means subcommittee office. In addition, Hale had been a member of both the Warren Commission and the Eisenhower Commission.

As she assumed office, Lindy mused, "I went from being president of everything (referring to all the Washington organizations she had headed) to a mere member of Congress."[18] She had been close to Rep. Carl Albert, the Speaker, and to Rep. Thomas P. "Tip" O'Neill, who had been whip, when Hale was majority leader. The only specific decision that she had had to make before the House declared the seat vacant was when O'Neill called and said, "You know, there's going to be the election for the majority leader. Do you mind if I run?" Lindy, always political as well as sensitive, said, "No, I want you to run, and I want you to be elected, because when Hale comes back, you'll give his place back to him."

Lindy Boggs first sought election to the Banking Committee, on which her husband had also served and had helped to pass the Omnibus Housing Act of 1949. Louisiana had been the last state in the Union to allow this urban renewal program to come to the state, and New Orleans was the only city large enough to be eligible for it. When President Nixon impounded the program's funds, everything came to a halt. So when Speaker Albert asked Boggs on which committee she wanted to serve, she said: "I want to be on Banking and Currency, and I have to be on Financial Institutions and the HUD subcommittees. He didn't say a word, but Jerry Ford and Tip ... worked it out for me."

In addition to attempting to restore federal help for New Orleans, a community in which more than one-third of the population was low-income, Boggs used her position on the Banking and Currency Committee to open nondiscriminatory credit to women. In an amendment to the House mortgage bill, which prohibited discrimination according to age, race, and veteran status, she added the categories of sex and marital status. She attributes her awareness of this issue to the many women who had called or written to her about it.

When the Equal Credit Opportunity Act was passed, the Federal Reserve was given the responsibility for writing the regulations:

The head of the Federal Reserve, Arthur Burns, and his wife were friends of mine. When the preliminary regulations came out, incorporating most of the suggestions [from women's groups], all of the women's groups were so happy, but not one wrote and said thank you. When the final regulations came out, they were greatly altered and the women's groups thought they had been had, and were up in arms. So the congresswomen invited Mr. Burns up to talk and he arrived with five experts, three of whom were women. Some of the things were taken care of. But you know, we didn't get the women's business ownership situation straightened out until Rep. John LaFalce [D-N.Y.] took it over the year before I left Congress.

In 1976, the year Jimmy Carter was nominated for president and four years after Shirley Chisholm ran for president, Lindy Boggs became the first woman to preside over a national political convention. And, in that same year, her abiding interest in history and library science propelled her to the role she played as chairwoman of three bicentennial committees on the American Revolution.

Boggs eventually moved from the Banking Committee to the exclusive Appropriations Committee. When Otto E. Passman, D-La., was defeated for reelection in 1977, Rep. Joe D. Waggonner Jr., D-La., the head of the Louisiana delegation, asked Boggs to run for the opening created on the committee because he thought she could win. She became one of the handful of women who have ever sat on that committee, and to this day, she remains the longest-serving woman on it, having served there twelve years. She and Rep. Virginia Smith, R-Neb., were the only two women serving on the committee for many years. In that position, she worked for Louisiana oil and gas interests and, as a member of the Subcommittee on Energy and Water, for the New Orleans port.

Boggs continued her philanthropic work using the connections she had built over a lifetime, including such Republicans as Gil and Jane Gude. Her son, Thomas Boggs Jr., a Washington attorney and well-known lobbyist, had run unsuccessfully for Congress from Maryland in 1970 against Gil Gude. The Gudes asked Lindy Boggs to meet with Dr. Veronica Maz of Georgetown University, who was interested in helping the homeless elderly women of

Washington, D.C. Together, they helped start the House of Ruth to house deinstitutionalized mental patients. Boggs also served on the Subcommittee on Veterans Administration, Housing and Urban Development, and Independent Agencies, which had jurisdiction over veterans, housing, the environment, the National Aeronautics and Space Administration, and the National Science Foundation. In addition, she served on the Legislative Branch Subcommittee, which oversaw the Library of Congress, the National Archives, and the Botanical Gardens.

In the late 1970s she helped form the Congresswoman's Caucus:

We discovered the new Republican women members didn't even want to join the caucus. And then, along came 1982, and that was the first year of the gender gap, [when] two million more women than men voted. Suddenly, our male colleagues began to ask for information, research materials, for our newsletter, and to come and talk in their districts. Then we decided to open it up as a Congressional Caucus on Women's Issues and invite men as well.

Meanwhile, the population of Louisiana had grown and the demographics were shifting. After the 1980 census, Boggs's Second Congressional District kept losing territory outside New Orleans and finally was confined to the city itself. The black population in her district had grown to 58 percent. In discussing the first election after the redistricting, Boggs noted:

I had several black opponents. Among them was a really fine man, a state judge, highly respected, a legitimate candidate. It so infuriated the black women in my district that someone of his substance would oppose me, they formed a group called "100 Ladies for Lindy." In a couple of weeks, the 268 of them did what Hale and I had done back in our early youth, formed a ward-precinct organization. We won that election with 61 percent of the vote.

The rise of representation by minorities in Congress, particularly blacks in the South, presented a particular irony for Lindy. "When she left the House at the end of 1990, she was the only white Member of Congress representing a black majority U.S. House district."[19] She and Hale had been leaders in the civil rights struggle since their earliest years together, and it was perhaps fitting that progress was first witnessed in the Second Congressional District. As her older daughter, Barbara Sigmund, a former mayor of Princeton, New Jersey, would recall:

[L]ots of my childhood memories involve traveling the highways between Washington and New Orleans. We had our own direct experience with the foolishness of segregation on those trips back and forth. Oftentimes, the woman who helped raise us, Emma Cyprian, who was black, traveled with us. One night, when I was about 7 years old, we were driving around southern Virginia looking for a hotel. It was getting later and later, but Daddy kept coming out of every place we tried saying, "No soap." He meant no hotel would accept Emma. Finally around 1 o'clock in the morning, when he came out and announced there was no soap again, I asked him, "Daddy, why can't we bring in our own soap?"[20]

Boggs's other daughter, Cokie Roberts, Washington correspondent for National Public Radio and anchorwoman for ABC news, recalls:

I remember the night before the debate on the 1965 Voting Rights Bill. We were all giving Daddy a hard time, and he said, "I'm voting for it, leave me alone." We said we don't want you just to vote for it, we want you to talk as well. He said we were asking too much from somebody from the Deep South. But the next day he heard one of his colleagues saying there was no discrimination in Louisiana. He couldn't stand it, and he got up and gave the most phenomenal speech of his career.[21]

Boggs pursued her legislative interests with certainty and strength while always remaining very much the lady. Her daughter Barbara once said, "Whenever I want to do something directly, I think of what Daddy would have done. And whenever I want to accomplish something indirectly, I try to emulate what Mama would do."[22] Lindy Boggs became famous for this indirect style. Sen. J. Bennett Johnston, D-La., said, "dealing with Lindy was like a Chinese water torture ... drip. drip. drip."[23] Another Democratic representative from her state, James A. "Jimmy" Hayes, told this story:

We have a new kitten and her name is Mrs. Boggs. Do you want to know why? Well, you see, this morning I got up and I opened my dresser drawer to get out my underwear, and this kitten jumped in the drawer. And then I went into the bathroom to try to shave, and the kitten jumped up on the basin. And then I went into the kitchen for breakfast, and the kitten got up on the table. And then I was trying to get out of the kitchen into the garage, and the kitten got between me and the door. And I said, "We're going to name this cat Mrs. Boggs. She's everywhere."[24]

It was this persistence and skill at indirect pressure that marked Lindy's style as a progressive southern woman working to advance the cause of humanity. When asked to identify legislation of which she is most proud, she cites bills cosponsored on behalf of minorities, women, and children; her efforts to improve education from the elementary to the college level; her work on the children's task force on crisis intervention. She also counts as special areas of interest her efforts to open the National Museum of African Art in Washington, D.C., and to establish the Office of Historian in the House of Representatives. And she finally achieved Margaret Chase Smith's dream of making the rose the national flower.

To honor her commitment to the cause of women, the House of Representatives voted to rename a room off the central rotunda the Lindy Claiborne Boggs Congressional Women's Reading Room.[25] This private room is the only place in the Capitol that contains a full set of portraits of all the female members of Congress. "It always made me feel so proud," she said, "that that room was named for me, because I felt that Abigail Adams had finally succeeded. She had asked her husband, John, to 'remember the ladies' when the Constitution was drafted or they would foment a revolution. He had not done so, and so their son's final resting place is now occupied by women, and named for a woman." John Quincy Adams, the sixth president of the United States, had run for Congress after serving as president, and died in that very room in the Capitol.

During a congressional ceremony at Independence Hall in Philadelphia in July 1987, Boggs presided over the assembly commemorating the Great Compromise of the Federal Constitution.[26] In 1989, she chaired the bicentennial committees on the U.S. Constitution and the U.S. House of Representatives.[27] In this latter capacity, she achieved publication, through the Office of the House Historian, of two encyclopedic volumes: *Women in Congress, 1917–1990*, and *Black Members of Congress*, both published by the U.S. Government Printing Office.

Although Boggs was always circumspect about the treatment she received by the 1980s generation of feminist organizations—such as the National Organization for Women, the National Abortion Rights Action League, and the Women's Political Caucus—she was no doubt hurt by their lack of appreciation for the South she represented, the career she built, and her own manner of advancing people's concerns in the public realm. Many women's organizations largely ignored her potential during the 1984 presidential campaign, when the leadership of many Washington-based feminist groups championed Geraldine Ferraro, who had been in Congress six years, and promoted her nomination as vice president of the United States. Without question the issue that made the difference was abortion. Although Boggs's entire life stood for people's advancement, including women's, reporters and others constantly chided her. One reporter stated:

When asked for her evaluation of the battle over payments for abortions through Medicaid, Mrs. Boggs acknowledges only that she has a "personal inhibition" concerning abortion and that she believes a better result could be achieved through increased knowledge and facilities for family planning [for which she had sponsored legislation]. Women's rights advocates in Louisiana want to know just where Lindy stands. To date, however, no one has been able to secure a direct answer from her on this subject.[28]

In fact, Lindy Boggs had given a straight answer when she stated, "The right to life is the beginning of human rights."[29] She voted against federal funding of abortion but for family planning. As early as 1973, she and Rep. Leonor Sullivan, D-Mo., had sponsored a resolution that provided for states' rights on the matter.

For nearly twenty years the debate tore interest group from interest group. After the close of her congressional career, Boggs commented that she believed that such a hue and cry was made about abortion that "it became equated with ERA and helped to defeat it." She added,

We have failed to write the moral parameters around technological advances. So we get into trouble about euthanasia, for example. When the pill came out, everybody relaxed about all sorts of rules and regulations and moral behavior. Where are the moral parameters written around when life [should begin] or should be terminated? What are the circumstances that it should be induced? Life and death issues are very difficult when they're related to technological achievements.

Her daughter Barbara summed it up: "Mama is the only person I know who is truly pro-life rather than pro-punishment."[30] Lindy Boggs would say, "We women have been socialized to be more compassionate, to think about the future of children and the next generation, to be more gentle. We are the keepers of the culture. We have a nurturing quality that we bring to politics. We have a different political style from men's."[31]

In 1990, Boggs decided to leave Congress in the hope that she could spend more time with her daughter Barbara, who had been stricken with cancer. "I've always said `being a Congresswoman was an interruption in my regular life.' I can't hug Barbara from here."[32] Her daughter succumbed to cancer a few months later, in October 1990.

When she left Congress, half a century after she had first gone to Washington with her husband, Boggs set about assembling her and her husband's historical materials and archives at Tulane University. She completed a book about her life, entitled *Washington through a Purple Veil,* published in 1994. As she reflected on changes in Congress since her first election, she "sensed a tremendous frustration among the new members ... who do not seem as dedicated as previous freshmen classes.... The younger Members seem to be caught up in a feeling of obligation to do something now but then to move on to other things. The result is `stepping stone' members moving on to other positions."[33]

Boggs expressed concern for the loss of the experience that can come from making congressional work a lifelong endeavor. When she first came to Congress with Hale,

there was more stability among congressional families. On weekends, we did barbeques at each other's houses. A lot of problems were worked out over social settings. We didn't have as many organized think tanks. We would get groups of people together who were very proficient in different legislative areas, and it was dinner table conversation, after dinner table conversation.

Just like "in-plantation." She said, "Exactly."

NOTES

1. Judy Ball, "Lindy Boggs: Leaves Congress on a High Note," *St. Anthony's Messenger,* July 1991, 33.
2. Garry Clifford, "Family: Lindy Boggs Quits Congress to Close Ranks with Her Two Remarkable Daughters, One Gravely Ill with Cancer," *People,* August 18, 1990, 57.
3. Corinne Claiborne "Lindy" Boggs, interview by author, Washington, D.C., October 15, 1993. All quotations in this chapter that are not attributed to another source are from this interview.
4. Ibid.
5. Kathy Caruso, "The Lady Lindy," *New Orleans Courier,* October 27–November 2, 1977.
6. Michael Barone and Grant Ujifusa, *The Almanac of American Politics, 1996* (Washington, D.C.: National Journal, 1995), 574.
7. Rep. W. J. "Billy" Tauzin, D-La., interview by author, Washington, D.C., November 1994.
8. T. Harry Williams, *Huey Long* (New York: Knopf, 1969), 2.
9. Barone and Ujifusa, *Almanac of American Politics,* 564.
10. Ball, "Lindy Boggs," 31.
11. Lindy Boggs's remarks at Recognition Breakfast, Washington, D.C., September 14, 1990.
12. Member of Congress from adjacent state who wishes to remain anonymous, interview by author, Washington, D.C., June 1995.
13. Williams, *Huey Long,* 1–2.
14. Member of Congress from adjacent state, interview.
15. Mike Roccaforte, quoted by Caruso, "The Lady Lindy."
16. Tauzin, interview.
17. Roccaforte, quoted in Caruso, "The Lady Lindy."
18. Lindy Boggs, quoted in Clifford, "Family," 57.
19. Ball, "Lindy Boggs," 31.
20. Clifford, "Family," 64.
21. Ibid.
22. Ibid.
23. Ibid.
24. Rep. Jimmy Hayes, interview by author, Washington, D.C., November 1993.
25. Ball, "Lindy Boggs," 33.
26. U.S. Congress, House, Office of the Historian, *Women in Congress, 1917–1990* (Washington, D.C.: U.S. Government Printing Office, 1991), 18.
27. Ibid.
28. Caruso, "The Lady Lindy," 6.
29. Ball, "Lindy Boggs," 33.
30. Clifford, "Family," 58.
31. Ball, "Lindy Boggs," 33.
32. Clifford, "Family," 64.
33. Caruso, "The Lady Lindy."

Patricia S. Schroeder

Democrat–Colorado (1973–1997)

First Congresswoman Elected from Colorado

> *One reason changes in the workplace have been slow in coming is that our society is still,*
> *to an overwhelming degree, governed by older, upper-middle-class white men who know*
> *little of the family balancing act because their wives have insulated them from it.*
> Pat Schroeder, *Champion of the Great American Family*

At the opposite end of the twentieth century from Rep. Jeannette Rankin's pioneering journey to Congress, another woman of the West crashed against the wall of tradition circling the nation's Capitol. Still the only married woman who was not a "widow-successor" to rear two young children to adulthood while serving as a member of Congress, Patricia Nell Scott Schroeder embodies the contemporary, "working mother," middle-class feminist struggle first given voice by Betty Friedan in 1963 in *The Feminine Mystique.* "I have a brain and a uterus and I use both," Schroeder said.[1]

By century's end, women's educational advance along with economic necessity had given rise to a tension that whipsawed women between their traditional roles as homemakers and careers beyond the home. For Pat Schroeder, work represented more than an income-producing job–it also defined much about her persona. Making the personal political, she drove the issues of middle-class family life, parenting and child rearing, abortion and reproductive rights, and women's equity into national prominence. "Her plan was to get where the big spending action was and expose the strategic and economic follies of U.S. defense policies, and then to rally support to loosen chunks of tax money for healthier purposes."[2] She was untiring in her efforts to gain passage of the Family and Medical Leave Act that finally passed Congress in 1993. She regarded caring for children and aged parents as important because "the average family is having a child care crisis every six months

169

to a year."[3] As a member of the Armed Services Committee who eventually rose to chair the Subcommittee on Military Installations, Schroeder worked for and achieved the right of female military personnel to have abortions in military hospitals and to fly combat missions. But she also worked diligently to reduce the magnitude of the defense budget during Ronald Reagan's presidency and to exact increased sharing among U.S. allies of the costs of their defense.

Pat Schroeder perfectly reflected the hopes and career-family conflicts of the college-educated generation of the 1950s. Yet in her first election, she doubted she would win and thus kept her jobs through the election, "thinking I'd need something to go back to."[4] When she was sworn in, in January 1973, she was one of only fifteen women in the House of Representatives; there were none in the Senate. In 1988, after a truncated attempt to become the first female nominee of a major party for the presidency, she served eight additional years in Congress before announcing that she would retire at the end of the 104th Congress.

Born in Portland, Oregon, on July 30, 1940, this granddaughter of Irish immigrants hailed from the solid and rather comfortable white middle class. Both her parents were college-educated; her mother, Bernice Scott, was a public elementary school teacher, and her father, Lee Combs Scott, an army air force reservist and aviation insurance adjuster. Her father's career necessitated an "army brat" existence for her and her younger brother, Mike, from their earliest years. From the many moves the family made, Schroeder learned always to land on her feet:

Starting at three, whenever we moved I had to find kids to play with in the new neighborhood, so as soon as the moving truck pulled away, I would line up my toys on the sidewalk and sit down next to them. It worked. The toys were like flypaper! I made friends almost at once.[5]

Schroeder's determination shone through at an early age. She suffered from amblyopia, a condition that required her to wear glasses from the age of eighteen months and an eye patch during her early school years.[6] She became the butt of taunting and jokes by her contemporaries but reflects, "The experience with my eyes ... helped me to understand more clearly the sense of isolation felt by those whose problems—physical and emotional— were much more serious than mine."[7]

Schroeder attended grade school in Texas, junior high in Ohio, and high school in Iowa. Brought up by their parents to be resourceful and independent, she and her brother received their pilot's licenses at an early age. Later, she worked her way through the University of Minnesota with her own flying service, graduating magna cum laude and a member of Phi Beta Kappa after only three years.[8] Her college years awakened her natural political inclinations. She majored in history, philosophy, and political science.[9] Schroder describes her college days:

A quiet shift away from the conservatism of the post-war Midwest was beginning to take place. The civil rights movement was burgeoning and Senator Hubert Humphrey [later vice president] drew huge crowds when he spoke on campus. When, as Senate Majority Leader, he was able to shepherd through the Congress important civil rights legislation, I felt that anything was possible and that I could be a part of it.[10]

Yet her early goals were very traditional. She looked forward to working after college, then getting married and continuing to work until her first child was born. Maybe she would go back to work when the children were older.[11]

As Sen. Barbara Boxer later outlined in her book *Strangers in the Senate:*

What made the job of the feminists so hard in the '60s was that the voices of the '40s had been stilled in the '50s, as our society worried that women like Rosie the Riveter, who went toe to toe with any man on the assembly line, would refuse to step back and let the men regain their superior place in the American workplace.

In the '50s, it became almost unpatriotic to hold down a decent-paying job if you were a woman. First, you were made to feel that you were taking the job away from a man, unless you were a secretary or "helper"—and even a "helper" had to be sure she knew her place. When I was a teenager, I clearly remember my mother feeling extremely sorry for those women who "had" to work. But mixed in with her sympathy was a definite tone of disapproval.[12]

Schroeder's political roots went back to her great-grandparents and the independent, western prairie populism that swirled around reform Democrat William Jennings Bryan. In the 1860s her father's family had immigrated to Nebraska from Ireland, taking advantage of the Homestead Act, which opened public lands in the West to settlement by citizens or those who intended to become citizens.[13] Her great-grandfather was elected during the latter part of the 1800s to the Nebraska state legislature, serving with Bryan. Their election reflected the agrarian unrest and economic difficulties that swept the plains and the Midwest, pitting ordinary citizens against the big business interests of banking and commerce. Later, the Great Depression helped shape her parents' ideas on the role of government. During those years, growing numbers of unemployed Americans needed the government's help in finding jobs, food, and shelter.[14]

Schroeder had wanted to go to law school for as long as she could remember, and in 1961 she was accepted at Harvard Law School. The Great Depression had interfered with her father's dream of becoming a lawyer, and she helped fulfill that dream for him.[15] Her brother, Mike, became an attorney as well. At Harvard, Schroeder was one of only 19 women in a class of 554.[16] She later recolleceted her experience:

I found myself submerged in sexism. On my first day, one of my male classmates refused to take his assigned seat when he saw that he had been placed next to a woman—next to me, that is. He let me know that he had never gone to school with a girl before and he didn't think he should have to start now. Before he stomped off to have his seat changed, he also sniped that I should be ashamed of myself for taking up a spot in the class that should have gone to a man.[17]

Others in the class were more open. Many of them had been in the service and some had been pilots. One of the former servicemen was James Schroeder, who had graduated from Princeton but had then served in the navy before going to Harvard.

Within a year, Pat and Jim were married, and she confronted immediately the tension between family and career. Contraceptives were illegal in Massachusetts, and although she could get prescriptions for birth control pills at the student clinic, she could not fill them until she and Jim visited their families in Iowa or Illinois.[18] Technically, if she carried birth control pills into Massachusetts, she was in violation of the law. In 1965, state laws regarding access to birth control were overridden by the Supreme Court in its ruling in *Griswold v. Connecticut*, which gave married couples throughout the country the right to obtain contraceptives. Later, when the Schroeders moved to Denver, she did pro bono legal work for the Rocky Mountain Planned Parenthood organization until she was elected to Congress.[19] Thus Pat Schroeder's lifetime preoccupation with family planning and women's health grew from a set of deep, personal experiences. In 1964, just before completing her law degree, one of only fifteen women from the original class to do so, she began looking for postgraduate employment.[20] She describes the search:

The placement officer told me he thought it best that I not look for work with a law firm. He said, "No firm will hire a young married woman like you because they know you will be having children soon and they see it as a waste of time." He told me that firms would interview me if I insisted, but that I would never be hired. I did have several interviews—and was invariably asked if I could type! Since I wanted to practice law, I kept on looking, and soon accepted the offer of a job in the federal government.[21]

She became a field attorney for the National Labor Relations Board with responsibility for Colorado, Utah, and Wyoming. The couple relocated to Colorado after graduation. Two years later, in 1966, she became pregnant with their first child, Scott. During this pregnancy she and her husband were almost killed by a gas leak in the house, and it was months before they were sure the baby had not been harmed. After Scott's birth, she volunteered as a Democratic precinct committeewoman and taught law at the Community College of Denver in 1969 and 1970, at the University of Denver in 1969, and at Regis College from 1970 to 1972.[22] Two years later, she became pregnant again, but during the fourth month, something was clearly wrong:

My obstetrician explained that I was bleeding because I was "high-strung." On it went for months—I would complain about the bleeding, he would say ... that being a Harvard lawyer, I was just having trouble adjusting to life as a housewife!... Eight weeks before I was due, I went into labor and was rushed to the hospital.... [N]o one could find the doctor. For twelve hours I waited in a small room....

My doctor eventually arrived and the delivery proceeded.... He discovered I had twins—a boy and a girl. All he could say was "Oh, my God, we should have done a cesarean." The girl had died earlier in the pregnancy and this had been the cause of my hemorrhaging. She was born first and it was very difficult. The boy was alive, but barely, weighing only four and a half pounds. The delivery was very hard on him. We tried, with no luck, to get him into a hospital that had equipment to keep him alive. He died the next morning of a brain hemorrhage caused by the pressure of a difficult delivery.[23]

Schroeder's second pregnancy had been a nightmare. She changed doctors and found her next pregnancy, with her daughter, Jamie, in 1970, a pleasant experience. Soon after the delivery, however, Schroeder started hemorrhaging and remained at death's door for most of the next six weeks. She was warned not to have more children.[24] This set of experiences anchors Pat Schroeder's beliefs that

a woman has a right to decide what happens to her own body. That is a basic right, and it should not be curtailed by the government nor anyone else.... I have always been amazed that a fetus is assigned a personality immediately upon conception—girls have hair ribbons and are holding dolls in the womb, boys are playing with trucks—but the woman is rarely mentioned by conservatives in debates on reproduction. She is just an impersonal receptor.[25]

Within two years, Pat Schroeder would run for Congress at the urging of her husband, who offered her name at a political meeting of anti–Vietnam War activists after others had rejected the idea of running themselves.[26] She would quip, "I was the only person he could talk into it."[27]

Back in 1972, when most people thought of the Congressional race in Denver as a noble suicide mission for a Democrat, Jim convinced me to see it as an incredible challenge and an opportunity. Neither of us understood what the race would lead to....

In the old days, there were two ways for a woman to run for Congress: as the widow of an incumbent or as a challenger in a hopeless race. Scenario number two was how I was chosen to run.[28]

Throughout the primary and the general election, Schroeder continued her part-time jobs teaching law, working as a hearing officer of the Colorado state personnel systems, and volunteering her services as a counsel at Planned Parenthood. The reputation that dogged her throughout her political career—"an antic disposition"—had manifested itself early.[29] One year before her election, as a worker for Rocky Mountain Planned Parenthood, she had passed out love buttons on Valentine's Day that carried the message, "Vasectomy Means Never Having to Say You're Sorry."[30]

From the beginning, she had definite ideas about her campaign, and she traveled to Washington to gain the support of the Democratic National Committee:

I wanted to run a campaign on the issues—the Vietnam War, housing, the environment, children, the elderly. The DNC didn't think I would win that way—or any way—and they sent us home empty-handed....

So we raised money the same way we organized, at the grass roots. We had thousands of campaign posters printed on bright-colored paper because we "got a deal." It turned out that the bright colors were almost as controversial as the posters themselves. Few candidates defy the unspoken rule that campaign literature be printed in red, white, and blue, and that it show the candidate in front of the Capitol dome, with his family and the dog. (Republicans would always insert a horseback shot in their brochures, and the Democrats a bike-riding scene, to show their love of the outdoors.) Not only was the color of our paper unorthodox, my face didn't appear on any of my posters. Instead, one poster showed a field of tombstones in Arlington Cemetery with the headline "Yes, some American troops have already been withdrawn from Vietnam." Another had a picture of a young Hispanic child with the caption "This radical troublemaker wants something from you. Hope."[31]

Because Schroeder had never run for office before (her husband had lost a race for the state legislature in 1970), the Democratic establishment of Denver would not back her. "Organized labor wouldn't put its money on a candidate who looked like a loser. Another big problem. People kept saying a mother belongs with her children."[32] Sometimes she would take her children with her to campaign events and at other times she would chide voters, "I'm that nut you've heard about, the one who keeps her kids in a freezer."[33]

On election day, in November 1972, Pat Schroeder, then thirty-one years of age, defeated the Republican incumbent, James D. "Mike" McKevitt, and won with nearly 52 percent of the vote, having defeated the Democratic primary opponent in September by a thin margin of 4,000 votes.[34] Schroeder became the first woman from Colorado to be elected to Congress in a state that had granted voting rights to women in 1893. It had taken seventy-nine years for a woman to become a serious candidate for Congress. This initial victory was all the more impressive in that it occurred in the presidential year in which the Republican Richard Nixon defeated the anti–Vietnam War candidate George McGovern.

Schroeder carried diapers in her purse when she went to the floor of the House to be sworn in.[35] When Rep. Bella Abzug called to congratulate her on becoming the fourteenth woman in the House of Representatives, Abzug questioned her about managing her congressional duties as the mother of two young children. Schroeder replied that she really was not sure and had hoped that Abzug would give the answer, not ask the question.[36] Her greatest fear as a freshman in Congress was "losing my housekeeper," a young Japanese woman who served as both baby-sitter and maid.[37]

Schroeder came to realize that women officeholders were considered aberrations. Although a growing number of women with children under three years old were working outside the home—27 percent during the 1970s—few were in Congress. And there were no women in the Senate: Margaret Chase Smith had left just as Schroeder was sworn in. Schroeder plowed new ground, not just in Congress, but as a symbol of trends transforming society at large. "In the United States," she stated, "we have defined the family as your problem, not our future."[38] Her sensitivity to the changing nature of the American family helped coin now-familiar expressions such as "two-parent family," "single-parent family," "blended family," "extended family," and "empty-nest family." "[E]ach of these," she said, "comes with particular stresses and needs."[39]

Somewhat surprisingly, her first political move as a member of Congress was to seek election to the all-male Armed Services Committee. Lack of money for the kinds of programs she cared about and her interest in ending the Vietnam War decided her to do so:

> Being a liberal freshman woman made me a long shot for the slot. It also didn't help that the chairman of the committee, F. Edward Hebert, a conservative Southern Democrat who boasted about his male chauvinism, did not consider me worthy of the seat. Women, he claimed, knew nothing of combat, since historically they had never been a part of it. His reasoning seemed to me to be completely bogus, since many of the male committee members, in spite of their rhetoric, had never served in the armed forces either. I studied the war records of all the committee members, and when those who had never served in the armed forces tried to embarrass me by asking, "How can you serve on this committee? You have never been in combat," I would calmly reply, "Then you and I have a lot in common."[40]

She achieved appointment to the committee in her first term, a committee that the future Speaker Thomas P. "Tip" O'Neill would define as one on which no liberal wished to sit. Hebert, from Louisiana, revealed the scorn with which he viewed her appointment when "he scrawled an inscription in a copy of his book, *Creed of a Congressman:* `For the House Armed Services Committee's first lovely den mother—with hope you could better understand your chairman after reading between these covers.' "[41] *Current Biography* recounts Hebert's contempt for her: "He even refused to okay her appointment to the United States delegation to a SALT disarmament conference on chemical warfare in Geneva, Switzerland, telling her, `I wouldn't send you to represent this committee at a dogfight.' "[42] Eventually, she would help mastermind a move to replace him as chair of the committee in 1975. A decade later, she and two allies on the committee—Ron Dellums, D-Calif., and Les

Aspin, D-Wis., again deposed a sitting chairman, Mel Price, D-Ill., replacing him with Les Aspin. That move ushered in an era of Democratic defense budgets that met her standard of "reasonable strength," not "unreasonable redundancy."[43]

As a new member of Congress, she simultaneously spoke out against the war in Vietnam and in support of an expanded role of the federal government to support education and to assist families and children, including funding for day care. She explains, "In 1971, amid the clamor of the Vietnam War, Congress passed the first comprehensive child care bill. President Nixon vetoed it. This veto set the stage for a fifteen-year fight over the federal government's relationship to the American family."[44]

And for fifteen years, Pat Schroeder stood at the center of that "butter vs. guns" maelstrom. She would run head up against the vested interests of the defense establishment and the Pentagon: "However useless a defense concept," she stated, "however extravagant its cost, an argument to proceed is deemed conclusive on one of two grounds. Either the Russians are doing it, and so we must do it to avoid falling behind, or the Russians are not doing it and therefore we must in order to stay ahead."[45] She opposed the MX missile system, which would have benefited contractors near Denver, on the grounds that not only was it wasteful but that the fixed silos were sitting targets for enemy attack. She hoped to shift spending priorities by moving some of the 40 percent of the national budget devoted to defense to improving society.

After years of fighting in the trenches for attention to day care in public policy, she commented in 1989: "Family issues don't confer power on their advocates. Family issues aren't as prestigious as defense and foreign policy. Charting America's international destiny sounds like a more powerful cause than ensuring that fathers pay child support."[46]

Her dogged determination to force public debate about family issues placed her at the raw edge of the values debate about the roles of men and women in society and the opportunities available to each beyond their home and child-rearing responsibilities. As always, she reflected on her own family's experience:

My mother was a schoolteacher and returned to the classroom as soon as I started kindergarten. I don't think my family was unusual: women have always worked, in circumstances that varied with class and geography. Poor and immigrant women either worked outside the home or took in work. Almost all women did housework....

The view of men as breadwinners and women as wives and mothers continues to have a strong hold on some policymakers, educators, and corporate executives. It is mirrored in legislative policy that puts women at a disadvantage, discriminates against them in the workplace, and undermines their economic security.... I think we need to take back the traditional definition of the family as an economic unit and basic building block of our society and get on with reinforcing it....

The economy did more to put women in the workplace than feminism did or, certainly, than progressive legislation did.[47]

In an ironic twist of fate, on January 22, 1973, three weeks after Schroeder was sworn in, the Supreme Court handed down its historic decision *(Roe v. Wade)* on a woman's right to choose whether or not to have a baby and preventing states from restricting that right before viability. Schroeder was immediately thrust into the center of a debate for which she seemed to have been sent to Congress, and one she personally cared deeply about. It was a debate that was to shadow her throughout her public life, and one on which she cast her shadow as well:

> *Roe v. Wade* dramatically changed the scale of the controversy over birth control. It made a woman's right to an abortion the law of the land and virtually eliminated illegal abortions, with their alarmingly high mortality rates. Even though, prior to the ruling, seventeen states had adopted laws making certain abortions legal, and nearly 600,000 women had obtained legal abortions in 1972, the Center for Disease Control estimates that another 130,000 women had to resort to illegal or self-induced procedures.
>
> *Roe v. Wade* sparked a fervent nationwide debate that has not faded to this day. Despite what the critics say, I am pro-life *as well as* pro-choice.... Abortion became a moral battlefield on which conservatives and liberals fought out the definition of women's role in society.... With the legal authority to make decisions about childbearing, women gained power over their own lives.... [T]here are two lives involved in an abortion. I don't think it is within my power as a lawmaker to decide which life has the greater right to exist.... I wish [the pro-life groups] would join me in supporting research to find a safe and totally effective contraceptive so the question of abortion would be moot.[48]

She attempted, unsuccessfully, to codify the *Roe v. Wade* decision through introduction of the Freedom of Choice Bill. The prospects for passage are dim in that the Congress, and the public at large, are averse to supporting legislation that appears to condone abortion or ease access to it beyond those situations where the mother's life is imperiled or in instances of rape or incest.

During her first decade of service, Schroeder introduced several bills aimed at gaining economic parity for women. In 1977, she, along with eighty-one colleagues, introduced the Pregnancy Discrimination Bill to remove the workplace stigma that denied women health benefits related to pregnancy. When Congress passed the Civil Rights Act in 1964, prohibiting discrimination on several bases, a southern conservative had added the word "sex" to the list in a last-minute effort to kill the bill altogether. But the Equal Employment Opportunity Commission, the implementor of the bill, could not make a final decision as to whether pregnancy fell within the law. Meanwhile, women were being fired and denied disability and maternity benefits:

> By 1976, things came to a head. The Supreme Court agreed to hear the case of *General Electric Co. v. Gilbert* (429 U.S. 125) to decide whether GE had discriminated against

its female employees by excluding pregnancy from coverage under its disability plan.... To my utter surprise, the Supreme Court, reversing the decisions of seven federal courts of appeal and numerous lower federal courts throughout the country, found that discriminating against pregnancy does not constitute sex discrimination. They held that pregnancy is not a sex-related condition! Had any members of the then entirely male Court been pregnant? ... [P]art of the Court's thinking rested on the premise that pregnancy was a "voluntary" condition and therefore did not have to be included in a disability benefit package. But GE's disability plan covered voluntary conditions like sports injuries, attempted suicides, venereal disease, disabilities incurred in the commission of a crime or during a fight, and vasectomies. The only voluntary activity not covered was procreation.[49]

The Pregnancy Discrimination Act became law in 1978, and henceforth, employers had to treat pregnancy like any other temporary disability. Although defining *pregnancy* as a "disability" seems convoluted to a non-lawyer, the result was that women were finally accorded better insurance coverage.

Schroeder's quest to gain passage of this landmark legislation paled in comparison to her decade-long endeavor, beginning in 1984, to pass the Family and Medical Leave Bill. Originally, this measure was aimed at creating a national mandated benefit requiring employers to grant employees "up to eighteen weeks of unpaid, job-protected leave to care for a newborn, newly adopted, or seriously ill child. Disability leave of up to twenty-six weeks was to be granted to workers if they were unable to work because of a temporary serious medical condition, including pregnancy."[50] Normally, one would consider such benefits to be covered through health insurance in the private sector and to be available to all Americans who desire them. However, such family coverage was not offered broadly. In order to gain passage, Schroeder kept whittling the bill down to dampen opposition from the business community. By 1985, she was successful in gaining hearings on the issues, altering the bill to exempt businesses with fewer than fifty employees; three years later, that number was lowered to thirty-five. An employee would have to work one year before becoming eligible, and the leave itself was reduced from eighteen weeks to ten over a two-year period. Added to the bill was a section allowing employees to take time off to care for an extremely ill parent, a provision that picked up votes for passage.

Schroeder was motivated not just by humanitarian and family concerns. She recognized the economic reliance the modern family placed on women's wages. "Wives who work full-year, full-time jobs contributed 40 percent [of a family's annual income].... Furthermore, women alone support about 10.2 million families—16 percent of all families in the United States."[51] In February 1993 the Family and Medical Leave Act was signed into law.

Schroeder's dedication to advancing the cause of women and families found expression along other avenues in Congress. She helped establish, and eventually chaired, the Select Committee on Children, Youth, and Families. Although a nonlegislative committee, it held hearings and helped focus attention on family issues throughout the 1980s. It was disbanded in 1995 after the Republicans took charge of Congress, ending forty years of Democratic control. She also served on the Judiciary Committee, co-chaired the Congressional Women's Caucus for several years, and served on the Post Office and Civil Service Committee, where she chaired the Subcommittee on Civil Service from the 96th to the 100th Congress.[52] In these capacities she led the fight for a range of issues: passage of the proposed Equal Rights Amendment; pay equity; retirement equity for women, including the wives of foreign service officers and women in the military, the civil service, and the Central Intelligence Agency; child support enforcement; health research for women, particularly on breast and ovarian cancer and osteoporosis; and a block grant to fund day care centers for school-age children.

Her work on the Armed Services Committee was equally rich. Early on, she led the effort to impose a ban on nuclear testing. In her later career she was most often acknowledged for her work in successfully advancing the sharing by U.S. allies of the cost of the defense of the free world. Schroeder also painstakingly worked to improve family housing and facilities for military service members. She fought for several years before achieving for military personnel the right to have abortions in military hospitals. And in 1991 she was able to persuade the Armed Services Committee that women in the military should be allowed to fly combat missions, since they were already flying back-up missions into hostile territory.[53] Women, she believes, do not lack courage. She cites the fact that "during World War I, more women died during childbirth in the United States, than American soldiers were killed in battle."[54]

Schroeder's abiding interest, however, has been family issues, an interest that most politicians do not share. She writes:

I've noticed that the only ones who "get it" are men who have become grandparents and have witnessed the dizzying pace of their children's lives; young men whose generation clearly expects both men and women to shoulder child-rearing responsibilities in marriage; and women who have had to balance career and family obligations.[55]

In 1987, after co-chairing Gary Hart's presidential campaign, which faltered because of personal allegations against him, she was drawn briefly and belatedly into that presidential race, running for the office herself. Drawing support initially from the National Organization for Women and other Washington-based feminist organizations, she confronted the serious challenge of whether she could be more than "the women's candidate."[56] Schroeder's entry into the race seemed a logical extension of Geraldine Ferraro's selection as the vice-presidential candidate on the Democratic ticket in 1984. *Business*

Week reported that female officeholders were increasing their numbers: there were 94 mayors of cities with populations of more than 30,000 and there were 1,164 women in state legislatures. Those figures were up from 1971 when only 7 mayors and 362 legislators were women.

Yet, her entry into the race was marked by a curious naiveté. "I never even thought about doing this. Gary Hart had been the front-runner, and then the whole bizarre thing blew up, and people started calling and saying, `Well, you get in.' And I said `huh? wha? huh?' "[57] And then apparently while she was doing something like doodling on a napkin in a restaurant, she just decided to give it a try. "I wanted to see if a woman could really be President of the United States."[58] The press called her "Snow White" and the other Democratic contenders the "Seven Dwarfs."[59] She recalls the rigors of the campaign trail, traveling 75,000 miles in twenty-nine states, fueled by junk food ("I'm turning my body into a hazardous waste dump"), and catching only a few hours of sleep a night, an "unbelievable nightmare."[60] She called the entire process "dehumanizing," and after three months of campaigning, she withdrew from the race in an emotional press conference. Choking back tears, she finished her speech and threw herself into her husband's arms. As she retells it: "I could not figure out how to run and not be separated from those I serve."[61] Her lack of a national campaign organization, fund-raising shortfalls, and lack of delegates resulted in an early withdrawal from the race. Some speculated she may actually have run to launch her name as a potential vice-presidential candidate.[62] With humor, she recalls, "What began on June 5, 1987, as an exciting quest for the presidency of the United States ended three months later, on September 28, as a search for Kleenex."[63] She would comment dejectedly:

It had been a tough weekend. I'd had the whole family together, telling all of them and then all the staff that it was no go, and everybody was all upset. But it was really having two thousand friends out there, who have given up their vacations, their summers, their weekends, everything. They want you to say "By golly, we are going to go on." You really feel like you are just throwing cold water on their dream. But you have to deal with your limits if you are talking about a rendezvous with reality. Finally, when I announced I wasn't going to run, there was this incredible groan; it was like a knife going through the old heart. I suddenly thought I really did let everybody down, and they didn't let me down. I felt so crappy.[64]

Eight years later, at fifty-six years of age, still young by congressional standards, and with twenty-three years seniority, Schroeder announced that she would not run for Congress in 1996. A quick-witted feminist and attorney with impressive legislative achievements, Pat Schroeder has made her mark on the nation's consciousness. Although her critics may not agree with her views, there is no question that she holds her ground and their respect. She appears gratified by her achievements and has overcome many of her initial reservations about

the common mythology that a woman couldn't be a member of Congress and especially that a mother couldn't and shouldn't combine career and family. Despite my education and the changing times, I had to disprove these myths for myself. I learned to overcome them, but I thank goodness my daughter will not have the same doubts. I hope she will also have fewer of the problems.[65]

Shortly after her announcement, she mused with characteristic feistiness: "Women have had the right to vote for 76 years. My contention is they haven't used it very well.... If you think the angry white male was something, wait for the angry woman."[66] That attitude perfectly reflected the answer she had given to a *Ms.* magazine interviewer more than a decade earlier. When asked, "If you had one piece of advice, one last word to share with the readers of *Ms.,* what would that be?" She replied, "Don't be intimidated."[67]

NOTES

1. Susan Ferraro, "The Prime of Pat Schroeder," *New York Times Magazine,* July 1990.
2. Ilene Barth, "Congresswoman Pat Schroeder," *Ms.,* June 1976, 62.
3. John Michael Kelly, "Women, Government Need Each Other Pat Schroeder Says," *Toledo Blade,* April 30, 1996, 3.
4. Patricia Matson, "Pat Schroeder: Congresswoman from Colorado," *Saturday Evening Post,* November 1974, 9.
5. Pat Schroeder, *Champion of the Great American Family,* large print ed. (Thorndike, Me.: Thorndike Press, 1989), 28.
6. Ibid., 147.
7. Ibid., 148.
8. Michael Barone and Grant Ujifusa, *Almanac of American Politics, 1994* (Washington, D.C.: National Journal, 1993), 223.
9. Ferraro, "The Prime of Pat Schroeder."
10. Schroeder, *Champion of the Great American Family,* 148.
11. Ibid., 149.
12. Barbara Boxer, *Strangers in the Senate* (Bethesda, Md.: National Press Books, 1994), 75.
13. Schroeder, *Champion of the Great American Family,* 198.
14. Ibid., 197.
15. Ibid., 149.
16. Ferraro, "The Prime of Pat Schroeder."
17. Schroeder, *Champion of the Great American Family,* 43.
18. Ibid., 59.
19. Ibid.
20. "Pat Schroeder's Ambition to Be First Lady in the Oval Office Nears the Moment of Truth," *People,* September 7, 1987, 49.
21. Schroeder, *Champion of the Great American Family,* 216.
22. *Current Biography 1978,* s.v. "Schroeder, Patricia S(cott)."
23. Schroeder, *Champion of the Great American Family,* 55–56.
24. Ibid., 57.
25. Ibid., 57–58.
26. Barone and Ujifusa, *Almanac of American Politics,* 223.

27. Winzola McLendon, "This Woman's Place Is in the House," *McCall's*, January 1980, 28.
28. Schroeder, *Champion of the Great American Family*, 14, 26.
29. Alessandra Stanley, "Run, Pat, Run," *Time*, August 3, 1987, 20.
30. "People on the Cover," *Redbook*, November 1973, 4.
31. Schroeder, *Champion of the Great American Family*, 27–28.
32. "Who's That Pretty Young Thing on the Armed Services Committee?" *Family Circle*, July 1975, 28.
33. Ibid.
34. Schroeder, *Champion of the Great American Family*, 29.
35. "A Vote for Two Careers," *Newsweek*, November 24, 1975, 77.
36. Schroeder, *Champion of the Great American Family*, 29.
37. Ferraro, "The Prime of Pat Schroeder."
38. Kelly, "Women, Government Need Each Other," 3.
39. Schroeder, *Champion of the Great American Family*, 289.
40. Ibid., 46.
41. "Who's That Pretty Young Thing," 26.
42. *Current Biography 1978.*
43. Ibid.
44. Schroeder, *Champion of the Great American Family*, 37.
45. Barth, "Congresswoman Pat Schroeder," 62.
46. Schroeder, *Champion of the Great American Family*, 276.
47. Ibid., 41.
48. Ibid., 59–60.
49. Ibid., 79–82.
50. Ibid., 85.
51. Ibid., 84.
52. U.S. Congress, House, Office of the Historian, *Women in Congress, 1917–1990* (Washington, D.C.: U.S. Government Printing Office, 1991), 232.
53. Barone and Ujifusa, *Almanac of American Politics*, 224.
54. Patricia S. Schroeder, interview by author, Washington, D.C., October 1995.
55. Schroeder, *Champion of the Great American Family*, 275–276.
56. Douglas Harbrecht and Richard Fly, "Can Pat Schroeder Be More than 'The Women's Candidate'?" *Business Week*, October 5, 1987, 35.
57. Jane O'Reilly and Gloria Jacobs, "Watch Pat Run," *Ms.*, February 1988, 47.
58. Ibid.
59. Ferraro, "The Prime of Pat Schroeder."
60. Ibid.; Maureen Dowd, "Patricia Schroeder, Uncompromising Free Spirit," *Newsweek*, August 17, 1987, 76.
61. Ferraro, "The Prime of Pat Schroeder."
62. O'Reilly and Jacobs, "Watch Pat Run," 51.
63. Schroeder, *Champion of the Great American Family*, 11.
64. O'Reilly and Jacobs, "Watch Pat Run," 44–46.
65. Ibid., 49.
66. Kelly, "Women, Government Need Each Other," 3.
67. Shelah Leader and Sheila Tobias, "Pat Schroeder: The Congresswoman Who Asks Tough Questions," *Ms.*, March 1983, 87.

CARDISS COLLINS
Democrat–Illinois (1973–1997)

Longest-Serving African American Congresswoman

> *No other ethnically or nationally identifiable group has more right to be involved in foreign decision-making than [blacks] do. We as Blacks are a foreign affair!*
> Cardiss Collins, "Do Our Votes Count?" *Essence,* November 1980

C ardiss Collins is a big-city woman, savvy, steady, determined, quick to smile, somewhat enigmatic— but all these qualities fail to capture fully her poker-playing genius. The longest-serving African American congresswoman in U.S. history, she has been an unwavering defender of working-class people, minorities, and the dispossessed. At once street smart but reserved, her demeanor has helped her endure in Congress for more than two decades. Her legislative achievements and struggles cover wide and often controversial ground, embraced by the jurisdiction of her major committees: Energy and Commerce (renamed the Commerce Committee in 1994) and Government Operations. Collins has worked to eliminate discrimination in mortgage insurance (legislation still awaiting reconsideration), to achieve equal opportunity for women in education and gender equity in college sports, and to improve airline safety. She has also introduced and gained passage of important legislation concerning the health and general welfare of minorities, women, and children.

Born on September 24, 1931, in St. Louis, Missouri, Cardiss Robertson Collins began her journey to Congress in the lower working class. That alone would set her apart from the majority of members with whom she would serve in Congress. Her parents, a manual laborer named Finley Robertson and a domestic worker, separated when she, their only child, was a baby. Her mother, Rosie, could afford only a two-room apartment with no refrigerator or gas stove.[1] The families whose homes her mother cleaned gave her their hand-me-down clothes for her daughter. "They sent their boys' clothes," Collins recalls. "I've worn many a shirt that was a boy's shirt. But nobody laughed because everybody was doing it."[2] When Collins was ten, she and her mother moved to Detroit, and she completed high school there.

After graduation, with no work, Collins moved to Chicago to live with her grandmother. Her first job was as a seamstress at a mattress factory. She was fired for talking too much, but she had high ambitions. She took night courses in accounting at Northwestern University while working during the day as a stenographer at the Illinois Department of Labor. It took twelve painstaking years, but Collins eventually learned enough about accounting and business so that she could rise through the ranks of the Illinois civil service in the audit department of the Illinois Department of Revenue, first as an accountant and then as a revenue auditor.

When she was twenty-six she married George M. Collins, a budding Chicago politician well liked by the local Democratic party organization. She became involved in his campaigns for alderman, committeeman, and congressman and even held a minor post in the Democratic machine herself as committeewoman of the Twenty-fourth Ward Regular Democratic Organization.[3] This level of "helpmate" grass-roots political activity was characteristic of many other congresswomen before they were elected, such as Lindy Boggs and Margaret Chase Smith.

In 1972 George Collins, who had been serving his second term in Congress, was killed in a plane crash. The legendary Chicago Democratic machine, in the person of Mayor Richard Daley Sr., asked Cardiss Collins, then forty-two years of age, to run to fill her husband's unexpired term to maintain the continuity of the seat. Collins agreed, partly out of the loyalty she felt to the party for supporting her husband in his campaigns. She expected only to finish his term.

Daley's organization gave Collins her opportunity because her husband had been a faithful lieutenant and rising star in the wards where the machine needed roots. With the support of this machine, her victory in the special election was virtually assured. It has been said that the district from which she was running "was so politically controlled, it once elected a dead man to Congress."[4] The old Daley machine based its initial strength in the Irish and Eastern European working- and middle-class neighborhoods of Chicago's South Side. But the African American population of Chicago was expanding, and Chicago ward politics built from the block upward to city hall. The machine prided itself on delivering practical results, rewarding loyalty; this was the politics of who got potholes filled and garbage collected.

George Collins had helped the Democratic organization sink its roots in Chicago's South and near West Sides, but Cardiss Collins's involvement had been at the margins. During the years when her husband had been advancing to the City Council and then into Congress, Collins continued to work as an auditor for the Illinois Revenue Department.[5] Still, she knew that, as the machine candidate, outspoken opinions or controversial causes were frowned upon.[6] She won the special election in 1973 with 85 percent of the vote, and her broad acceptance within party circles helped avoid a divisive succession battle by other aspiring politicians.

Chicago's Seventh Congressional District contains perhaps the greatest extremes in lifestyle America could offer. It stretches from the downtown Loop to the "Magnificent Mile" of upscale stores along Michigan Avenue to the troubled Cabrini-Green public housing projects, from the splendor and wealth along the Gold Coast to the despair and poverty of the Robert Taylor Homes and the struggling black neighborhoods on the West and South Sides. Along the way, it picks up the downtown skyscrapers, Soldier Field, and the prosperous suburbs of Oak Park and River Forest.[7]

When Collins arrived in Washington as the new congresswoman from Chicago, she was caught by surprise. "I guess I must have been in Congress all of 24 hours when I realized that, as the wife of a politician, I had just been a political spectator—not really playing the game. The difference started rolling in, like a sledgehammer." Her political inexperience was exacerbated because she entered Congress midsession and missed the orientation session other freshmen members received. Her hardest lesson, she revealed, was "realizing that I was not in the city of Chicago, which was controlled by a master politician."[8] In Washington, she was on her own.

Collins instinctively knew, however, where her focus should lie in representing her district, beginning with her knowledge of accounting and the struggle of working-class families to move up the ladder of economic opportunity. Two days after her election, she began to work on a bill to eliminate credit discrimination against women. As the daughter of a single black mother, and a single mother herself, Collins stood at once with the concerns of women and their need for equal credit rights.

But making the transition to congressional life was not automatic or easy. Overcoming the grief at her husband's sudden death was a major hurdle for Collins. Like other widows in Congress before her—Margaret Chase Smith, Mary Norton, and Lindy Boggs—she was forced to rise above family tragedy. One day, standing in the halls of Capitol Hill, Collins realized that she was wearing the same dress she had worn when her husband was sworn in as a representative, and she was overcome by emotion.[9]

A further difficulty was that her thirteen-year-old son, Kevin, chose to stay in Chicago after his mother's election to Congress. This dilemma was solved by Collins's mother, who left retirement to take care of her grandson. "I knew he was being well taken care of, and he got a chance to be spoiled by his grandmother."[10] Even so, Collins felt pain and guilt about not spending more time with her son, and she had to cope with the sense that she was missing important moments in his life. "The worst thing was suddenly looking around and discovering my son, Kevin, was a man. He had grown up without me. When I returned to my district on weekends, I only saw him asleep. Then he started dating. I saw him at the doorway—he was going out when I was coming in."[11]

With her mind and heart pulled in different directions, it is no wonder that Collins had the reputation of being a reserved, hesitant member. In 1973, when she was sworn in, African American members of Congress were few, and black women members even fewer. Shirley Chisholm of New York had been sworn in in 1969, and Yvonne Brathwaite Burke of California and Barbara Jordan of Texas in 1973, six months before Collins. The media tended to favor these members over the more reticent Collins. As Collins herself would humbly comment,

I came to Congress at the same time as Yvonne Brathwaite Burke and Barbara Jordan. Shortly after Yvonne was in, she became the first expectant mother ever to sit on the floor of the House. [Burke left after the birth of her child.] Then, shortly after that, you had Watergate, which just drew Barbara to national and international attention. So competition was pretty stiff. Besides, I had to learn the ropes, and I'm not as vocal as a lot of members of Congress.[12]

By the early 1980s, however, these members had retired (Chisholm after fourteen years and Jordan and Burke after six years each), and for nearly ten years Collins was the only black woman in Congress. She is now the longest-serving African American woman in Congress, having served twenty-four years. In 1995 she announced she would retire at the end of the 104th Congress (in January 1997).

To the uncritical observer, Collins's temperate demeanor belied her persevering grit. Early in her career she gained election to the prestigious Energy and Commerce Committee and remained the only woman on that powerful committee for nearly two decades. *Ebony* magazine, widely circulated in the African American community, reported in 1979: "Congresswoman Cardiss Collins wins the biggest poker pots by carefully 'reading' all the other hands and making extremely conservative but correct decisions."[13] Those skills would mark her legislative style as well.

As she gained experience, Collins made a natural transition to becoming a kind of at-large representative for blacks nationally. At the urging of Rep. Ronald V. Dellums, D-Calif., former chair of the Congressional Black Caucus, who served as her mentor, she was elected chair of the Congressional

Black Caucus in the Ninety-sixth Congress, in 1979. The caucus then numbered seventeen members. Her colleague William L. Clay, D-Mo., would muse:

You've got a women's caucus, a steelworker's caucus, an Italian Caucus. Each state has a caucus. You got three cotton caucuses, two potato caucuses. Every interest group has a caucus. But none of them are as meaningful or powerful as the Black Caucus. Its power is multiplied by the substantial presence of Black voters in the districts of 90 Congressmen. Those are the first 90 votes we look for in addition to our 17.[14]

When she took the office, Collins declared, "we move now to the arena of power politics." She personally made the same kind of move, as the position thrust her into the national media spotlight.[15] Because of her nonthreatening style, Collins was successful in gaining the confidence of the largely male membership of the Black Caucus. Unlike Shirley Chisholm, who had offended the caucus's leadership and not sought to work with it, Collins was viewed by the caucus as trustworthy. Her Chicago political roots served her well.

During her term as chair of the Congressional Black Caucus, Collins became embroiled in highly charged legislative and political struggles. The first arose in 1979, shortly after she became chair, and centered on the incendiary issue of public school busing. A controversial constitutional amendment to prevent school busing used to promote racial integration had been introduced by the conservative Democratic representative Ronald M. Mottl of eastern Ohio. Essentially, the amendment would have prohibited students from being required to attend public schools other than those closest to their homes. Since similar measures had been stalled in congressional committees for years, Mottl had used an obscure procedure to force the bill to the floor for a vote. Collins, in her new role, launched an all-out blitz to defeat this measure. She enlisted her colleague Louis Stokes, D-Ohio, to lead the House fight, set up strategy meetings with the Speaker of the House, Thomas P. "Tip" O'Neill, and involved the vice president of the United States, Walter Mondale. She organized outside support with representatives of more than a hundred groups throughout the United States, debated Mottl on national television, and spoke to organizations throughout the nation. It was a credit to her leadership that the amendment lost, in a bitter fight, 216–209, far shy of the two-thirds vote required for passage.[16]

As caucus chair, Collins packed the agenda. She fought to restore proposed cuts made by Jimmy Carter's administration in education, housing, and health programs; made sure that the 1980 Census did not undercount minority groups; worked to maintain current levels of Social Security; struggled to give full House and Senate representation to the District of Columbia; and pushed for economic sanctions to promote majority rule in South Africa and Rhodesia.[17] Collins also embarked on a risky strategy of protest for the black electorate in the upcoming election for president. She urged blacks to vote but, in protest against the lack of a presidential candidate who addressed their concerns, to vote only for congressional, state, and local offices, abstaining from the presidential race.[18] Not only would this protest highlight black dissatisfaction with the presidential candidates of the major parties, but it would also demonstrate that blacks had a voice in the future selection of candidates.

It is important to recall that Collins's tenure with the Congressional Black Caucus began during the late 1970s, not long after the civil rights movement's most historic victories, when blacks first began to wield authority in the political realm. This was a time when few African Americans were as nationally prominent as the Reverend Jesse Jackson. Many black Democrats were unhappy with the record of Democratic president Carter, under whom, Collins said, blacks could expect more unemployment, inflation, and cuts to vital social programs.[19] The Republican Party offered no alternative. Collins openly supported Sen. Edward Kennedy, D-Mass., for the presidential nomination, and when he failed in that effort, she weakly endorsed President Carter for reelection. Disillusionment with Carter, however, led to the landslide election of the Republican nominee, Ronald Reagan, in 1980. The Congressional Black Caucus, under Collins, continued to function as the only representation many blacks felt they had in national politics.

As a member of the House, Collins has risen steadily in stature and responsibility. Her seniority on the Energy and Commerce Committee lifted her, finally, to chair its Subcommittee on Commerce, Consumer Protection and Competitiveness from 1991 to 1994. She became the first woman, and the first African American, to chair a subcommittee of this prestigious committee. Her agenda was jam-packed.

With the subcommittee often at the cutting edge of new technology, one of her first efforts was made in gaining passage of legislation to permit blank digital audio recording tapes to be made readily available in the commercial market. In 1994 she conducted widely publicized hearings on the influence of "gansta rap" on the violent and degrading behavior of youth in the United States. And she called recording industry executives to task for not doing more than simply placing a parental advisory label on the records and discs. During the protracted congressional debate in 1992 on the North American Free Trade Agreement (NAFTA), Chairwoman Collins traveled as a member of a congresswomen's delegation to Mexico to investigate firsthand the working conditions in Mexico.

Her wide range of legislative achievements with the subcommittee has often encompassed other pathbreaking or controversial issues. For example, she wrote and the House passed the Anti-Redlining Insurance Disclosure Bill. This bill would have required insurance companies to disclose where they sell mortgage insurance policies to ensure they do not "redline," or charge inflated rates, in certain neighborhoods. Generally, such firms underserve inner city and rural areas. After her hard work in gaining passage of the bill in the full House, its journey to passage in the Senate was blocked by Reps. Joseph Kennedy, D-Mass., and Henry Gonzalez, D-Texas. Kennedy and Gonzalez claimed that Collins's bill was not strong enough to change industry behavior, since it only required disclosure. Kennedy chaired the rival Subcommittee on Insurance and Consumer Affairs of the Banking Committee, which Gonzalez chaired. However, the Banking Committee was not able to gain passage of a bill of its own, and Collins's legislation languished in the limbo between the House and Senate.

Collins was responsible for investigations that led to gender equity in college sports, for which, in 1994, the Black Coaches Association named her "Sportsperson of the Year."[20] On projects large and small, she has been a tireless advocate of business interests in Chicago. She was successful in persuading the U.S. Department of Agriculture to release its crop reports in the early morning hours, conveniently benefiting the Chicago futures markets and locking out the Tokyo exchanges, which were put at a disadvantage because of the international time difference.

Long an advocate of universal health insurance, as a member of the Health Subcommittee of the Energy and Commerce Committee, she wrote special legislation to create the Office on Minority Health in the National Institutes of Health. She achieved passage of annual resolutions designating October as National Breast Cancer Awareness Month, and in 1990 she wrote the law that expanded Medicare coverage for screening mammography for millions of elderly and disabled women. She sponsored legislation to expand Medicaid coverage for Pap smears for early detection of cervical and uterine cancer. She gained passage of the Child Safety Protection Act of 1993, which required warning labels to be placed on dangerous toys and established federal safety standards for bicycle helmets.[21] And she has been successful in advocating for health clinics in high schools, especially in underserved areas.

Collins also chaired the Government Operations Subcommittee on Government Activities and Transportation, where she gained national prominence in her efforts to regulate the interstate transport of toxic materials. In 1987, she spearheaded investigations on the safety of U.S. air travel. Her widely publicized investigations of Eastern Airlines equipment failures led to an unprecedented review of the company and eventual indictment of Eastern Airlines and nine of its managers. Passage of the Aviation Security Act of 1990 upgraded the nation's aviation security system.

As chair of this subcommittee, Collins also worked steadfastly to help minority concerns—for minority broadcasters to gain access to the telecommunications and broadcasting field; to improve the quality of minority health care; and to reserve 10 percent of all airport concessions for disadvantaged business enterprises (minorities) and women. Collins consistently has championed issues that women, particularly black and working women, care about. She sponsored a bill in 1980 to give federal subsidies for day care to poor and middle-class families.[22] As a mother who had to balance career and child rearing, Collins identified with the need for day care and for mothers to know that their children are well cared for while they are working. Not every working mother can be as fortunate as Collins was to have her own mother care for her child. As a member of the Government Operations Committee and its Subcommittee on Government Oversight and Investigations, Collins examined the quality and availability of child care facilities for federal workers. The legislation she wrote became law in 1990 and has resulted in more than sixty-five new day care centers for the children of federal workers, a tripling of the prior number.

Collins also fought hard for the proposed Equal Rights Amendment (ERA) to the Constitution during the push for ratification. She considered it not only a women's issue but "a basic bread-and-butter issue that relates directly to poverty and the working poor.... It's long past time for this nation to establish constitutional protection against sex discrimination, just as was done earlier in the century with regard to race discrimination."[23]

Although efforts to ratify the ERA were unsuccessful, Collins took other steps to combat gender discrimination. In 1993–1994 (the 103d Congress), she conducted investigations of college sports and proposed legislation to force college athletic departments to divulge how their financial assets were divided between men's and women's programming. She argued that Title IX of the Civil Rights Act of 1972, which mandated nondiscrimination in all education programs, included sports at institutions of higher learning receiving federal aid. Her battle was aimed at affording women gender equity in education. When she was within striking distance of a legislative victory, she introduced her bill as House Resolution 921 to signify that it was twenty-one years after passage of the original act. As part of her investigation of college and university compliance with Title IX, she called for equal athletic opportunities for men and women athletes. Among the tangible results of her work was a certification program for Division I schools (that is, the top schools, like Yale, Princeton, and Harvard), including a section on gender equity. Collins also introduced a bill that would require all universities to disclose the number of students and amount of money in men's and women's athletic programs. For her work in achieving gender equity in sports education, she was inducted into the Women's Sports Hall of Fame in Oberlin, Ohio, in October 1994.

Collins views the controversy over abortion rights from the pro-choice perspective and has voted for women to retain the legal right to abortion through constitutional protection. She virulently opposed the 1980 Supreme

Court decision that denied federal government funding to poor women who wanted abortions. "The implication of this action is enormous.... We have gone from color segregation to financial segregation."[24]

The same prohibition on federal funding of abortions, the main effects of which are felt by poor women, has been upheld more recently by amendments offered by Rep. Henry J. Hyde, R-Ill., to the appropriations bill funding the Department of Health and Human Services. In 1993, the debate on this amendment demonstrated the degree to which this controversial issue inflames racial and class-based tensions:

[Rep.] Cynthia A. McKinney of Georgia, who is black, charged that the Hyde restriction "is nothing but a discriminatory policy against poor women who happen to be disproportionately black...."

Hyde responded: "We tell poor people, `You can't have a job, you can't have a good education, you can't have a decent place to live.... I'll tell you what we'll do, we'll give you a free abortion because there are too many of you people, and we want to kind of refine, refine the breed.'"

Collins then leapt to her feet and rushed to the microphone. "I am offended by that kind of debate," she shouted. Hyde said to her, "I'm going to direct my friend to a few ministers who will tell her just what goes on in her community."

Other black women Democrats ran up and joined Collins, crowding around the microphone, as she demanded that Hyde's words be expunged from the record....

Collins and Hyde eventually apologized to each other, and his words were removed from the record.

[Her point made, Collins, typically understated, remarked,] "I don't think there is any acrimony. Henry Hyde is a decent person. In the heat of the debate, he got carried away."[25]

Collins has long since overcome her inexperience of the early 1970s, when she first arrived in Congress—by her own admission a naive replacement for her husband. In 1994, at the height of her power, the House changed from a Democratic to a Republican majority for the first time in forty years. Forced to relinquish her subcommittee chairmanships on Commerce, Consumer Protection and Competitiveness and on Government Activities and Transportation to assume the role of ranking minority member of the full committee on Government Reform and Oversight, she used the opportunity to fight against the undermining of federal support for the causes to which she has dedicated her life. She continues to use her seniority as a powerful member, albeit minority, and found herself as the leading Democratic voice on several issues moved to the floor in 1995, including product liability reform and regulatory reform legislation. Overcoming her own shyness to speak out where she sees injustice or discrimination, Collins has become not only an able representative of her various constituents in Chicago, along with blacks and working women across the country, but also, as a ranking member in a Republican-controlled Congress, a vociferous advocate for positions assumed by the House Democratic Caucus.

Among the committees Collins has served on is the Foreign Affairs Committee. When she became a member of its Subcommittee on Africa, she began to develop an international perspective on human rights and the advance of democracy abroad. "No other ethnically or nationally identifiable group has more right to be involved in foreign decision making than we do. Our history, if nothing else, sets the precedent."[26] Collins was a leader in the call for sanctions against South Africa to protest apartheid.

Even after nearly a quarter-century of service, it is still striking that her legislative interests and successes are likely to be reported only in the minority press—*Ebony, Essence, Jet* magazine. Rarely has the mainstream press chosen to highlight this seasoned woman, who has shunned stridency and inflammatory rhetoric. She has been a steady workhorse, not a show horse. In fact, it could be argued that the mainstream press shows its prejudice by gravitating to the more controversial and voluble African Americans who claim to speak for the causes of minorities, in the process ignoring the solid, moderate views of the majority of minorities best exemplified by a representative like Collins.

Her dedication remains steadfast. As she has observed:

There are very few Blacks who can do something about the plight of the 25 or 30 million Blacks in this country. There are only 17 of us in Congress [40 by 1996]; relatively few Black judges, few Blacks in high places. So whenever the highest elected tribunal in the nation can help write the last word on issues affecting minorities—well, that's tremendous satisfaction. It's worth whatever sacrificing, whatever suffering; whatever self-denial. Victory like that is sweet.[27]

Her political godfathers, Mayor Richard Daley Sr. and Rep. Ron Dellums of California, would be proud of her advance. So is her only granddaughter, Candice, whom Collins jubilantly carried onto the floor of Congress as a newborn, as the 1990s ushered in the last decade of the twentieth century.

NOTES

1. Alex Poinsett, "The New Cardiss Collins," *Ebony,* December 1979, 66.
2. Ibid.
3. U.S. Congress, House, Office of the Historian, *Women in Congress, 1917–1990* (Washington, D.C.: U.S. Government Printing Office, 1991), 50.
4. Poinsett, "The New Cardiss Collins," 64.
5. Michael Barone and Grant Ujifusa, *Almanac of American Politics 1994* (Washington, D.C.: National Journal, 1993), 413.
6. Poinsett, "The New Cardiss Collins," 64.
7. Barone and Ujifusa, *Almanac of American Politics 1994,* 412.
8. Rep. Cardiss Collins, "Do Our Votes Count?" *Essence,* November 1980, 102.
9. Jacqueline Trescott, "The Coming Out of Cardiss Collins," *Washington Post,* September 21, 1979, 27.
10. Collins, "Do Our Votes Count?" 85.
11. Ibid.
12. Poinsett, "The New Cardiss Collins," 64.

13. Ibid., 68.
14. Ibid., 64.
15. Ibid., 63.
16. Ibid., 66.
17. Ibid.
18. Collins, "Do Our Votes Count?" 102.
19. Ibid.
20. "BCA Names Rep. Collins Sportsperson of the Year," *Jet,* May 23, 1994.
21. "Cardiss Collins," Office of Rep. Cardiss Collins, Washington, D.C., July 1994.
22. Collins, "Do Our Votes Count?" 105.
23. Ibid., 105.
24. Ibid.
25. Barone and Ujifusa, *Almanac of American Politics 1994,* 411.
26. Ibid.
27. Poinsett, "The New Cardiss Collins," 68.

NANCY LANDON KASSEBAUM

Republican–Kansas (1979–1997)

First Woman to Chair a Major Senate Committee

There's never any certainty.... [W]e're voting here until 11 p.m. We had the filibuster on the Interior Appropriations [bill] because of the grazing fee issue. So I stayed here and worked a bit and watched the World Series and then took some work home with me. It's midnight before we get caught up with everything. No, it's not an easy life. I don't think people have any idea.

Nancy Kassebaum, interview by author, October 24, 1993

N ancy Landon Kassebaum of Kansas—down-to-earth prairie patrician—has moved along a political path that has brought her close to the highest office in the nation, one that eluded her father, Alf Landon, a half-century earlier. The backgrounds of the suffragist Jeannette Rankin and Kassebaum are not that dissimilar; like Kassebaum, Rankin held an advanced degree, had a reputation for independence, was unmarried at the time of her election (Kassebaum was separated and near a divorce), and was a Republican.

Yet from Rankin to Kassebaum a vast divide exists. Rankin, the first congresswoman, served only four years in the House; her only memorable legislative accomplishments were her votes for women's suffrage and against both world wars. Kassebaum has now served almost eighteen years in the Senate and in 1995 rose to chair the powerful Labor and Human Resources Committee. She is the first and only woman ever to chair a major Senate committee.[1] The most popular elected official in Kansas, she was, for most of her tenure, one of just two women in the Senate. She has remained the most senior.

And her election marked the first time a woman was elected to the Senate who was not the widow of a congressman.[2] In subsequent elections, she won handily—with 76 percent of the vote in 1984 and 74 percent in 1990.

Nancy Landon Kassebaum was born to Alfred Mossman Landon and Theo Cobb Landon in Topeka, Kansas, on July 29, 1932, during the Great Depression. As the daughter of an oil magnate, who was elected governor of Kansas in 1932 and who ran for the presidency against Franklin D. Roosevelt in 1936, she experienced none of the want that faced most of the nation. Her family stood at the apex of the banking and political world of rural Kansas.

Kassebaum grew up in Topeka, the capital of the Sunflower State, attending public schools there. This unassuming city is the hub of America's breadbasket. Midway between the Atlantic and Pacific Oceans, it has long been a rail center, home of the Atchison, Topeka, and Santa Fe Rail System. As the gateway to the wheat fields and cattle ranges that stretch westward, the city abounds in America's western folklore—Wyatt Earp, Wild Bill Hickok, Bat Masterson, rugged men with rawhide integrity who knew how to shoot and kept the peace in the sprawling boom towns at the edges of the range.

Kassebaum's father, who had been born in Pennsylvania, completed high school in Marietta, Ohio, then graduated from the University of Kansas and went to law school there. He built his life in the oil business and never practiced law. Her mother, the daughter of a banker, graduated from Washburn University in Topeka and was a fine musician, both a pianist and harpist. Theo Landon demonstrated an interest in business "because she always worked in the bank, as did her mother."[3] Kassebaum recalled that her mother was also active in community projects:

I remember during World War II, she headed up the Home Nursing Program, in which retired nurses would go out and help in the homes when people needed nurses due to shortages in medical personnel. I remember she was always on the phone, trying to round up hospital beds, or health care providers for people that needed care in the house.

Still, her mother had no great taste for politics, although she welcomed her husband's friends readily into her home. Nancy's father had promised her mother, before they married, that he would not enter politics. Shortly thereafter, in the year of Kassebaum's birth, he ran successfully for governor of Kansas.

When Kassebaum was four years old she was swept into the political tides and decked in campaign ribbons on her father's presidential campaign trail.[4] Throughout her childhood, she was surrounded by such major political figures as William Howard Taft and the Taft family, who were personal friends of her father's.[5] Like Rep. Frances Bolton of Ohio and Rep. Lindy Boggs of Louisiana, Kassebaum experienced the give and take of political debate through the constantly changing array of political figures who came into the Landon home and stayed for political discussions.[6] She recalls, as a child, after going to bed at night, listening to the political debates of her father's contemporaries through a ceiling vent that allowed their voices to be heard upstairs.[7]

Of course, Kassebaum never consciously planned to go into politics herself. "I lived in the country and grew up on the river. I'd just spend my days on the sandbars. It was really a Huck Finn existence." Neither her brother, who was born during Governor Landon's first term, nor her older half-sister ever took much interest in politics either.[8] But Nancy's natural intellect, love of reading, openness, and curiosity never dulled. Her greening at her family's dinner table sparked her consciousness of public opinion that was to last a lifetime.

Like many young women in the 1940s and 1950s, Kassebaum never gave much thought to a future career outside the home. Perhaps her upbringing led her to choose political science as her college major, but even her politician father asked her what she would do with such a degree. In fact, Kassebaum already knew what she would do before she graduated from the University of Kansas in 1954. She would marry a former classmate, Philip Kassebaum, who had graduated from the University of Kansas and had gone on to study law at the University of Michigan in Ann Arbor.[9] She worked only briefly, as a struggling typist and receptionist at Hallmark Cards in Kansas City—as she describes it, "a filler job"—before she married him during his final year in law school.

Oddly, however, at the same time that she was becoming a newly married homemaker, Kassebaum was also pursuing a master's degree in diplomatic history at the University of Michigan. She received her degree in 1956, with a master's thesis on the division of Poland at the Yalta Conference. While she may not have had an inkling that she would one day serve on the prestigious Senate Foreign Relations Committee, Kassebaum did dream of being a foreign service officer.[10] In the 1950s, however, married women couldn't join the officer corps, so perhaps she was simply asserting the independent strain for which she is well known. Kassebaum thought she might teach, in a college or private school setting, but marriage and motherhood quickly engulfed her energies and the family moved to a farm near Maize, Kansas.[11]

Nevertheless, education was never far from her mind when she was a young mother. Her first child, John, was born in 1958, and three more children followed within five years—Linda, Richard, and William. Nancy's husband, an attorney with a large city firm, had little time for child rearing, so Kassebaum took on nearly all the responsibility. As in her own family, dinnertime was time for intelligent discussion. Remembering her childhood, when the dinner topics had ranged from Topeka politics to the progress of

World War II, Kassebaum briefly attempted to organize her children's evening conversation by assigning each child a particular topic.[12] As they grew up, however, the children had little patience with that approach, so Kassebaum abandoned that tradition. During this time she also worked as vice president of the family-owned Kassebaum Communications, which operated radio stations KFH and KBRA.

She began her public service career, as many women do, on the local school board, serving a single term, as president, from 1973 to 1975. It was her only elective office before she won her seat in the Senate.[13] As an involved parent, Kassebaum had initiated a tutoring program for the Maize schools and had secured funding to provide an elementary school library.[14] She also served on the Kansas Governmental Ethics Commission and the Kansas Committee on the Humanities. She stayed in touch with her Republican Party heritage by volunteering on some campaigns. But her husband was much more involved. He served as local precinct chair, which required the Kassebaums to drive around the Kansas countryside, visiting farm after farm.[15] This political travel probably helped Nancy Kassebaum, as it had Margaret Chase Smith, build a base and gain recognition for her own future campaigns. In addition, Philip Kassebaum became Kansas chairman for the Republican presidential candidate Nelson Rockefeller in 1968. Both Kassebaums attended the 1968 Republican convention.

In 1975 Nancy and Philip Kassebaum were divorced. As she explains it, around "1973 and 1974 [we] just [had] family difficulties, and in 1975 Phil and I mutually thought it might be a good idea for us to sort of separate and see how things would work out." Hardly one to play the victim, Kassebaum dealt with the prospect of single motherhood by calling a familiar politician, Sen. James B. Pearson of Kansas.[16] She used her estranged husband's service as Pearson's campaign chair as her point of contact, having no real political credentials of her own. Drawing on her adventurous spirit, and with substantial courage and midwestern practicality, she accepted Senator Pearson's offer of a position as caseworker on his staff.

With pets in tow, the family drove cross-country to Washington, D.C., so that Kassebaum could take the job for one year, 1975–1976. Three of Kassebaum's four children were still living at home, the youngest in the ninth grade, and the transition to Washington was not painless. At the end of that year, they returned to Kansas, and, as Kassebaum put it, "I was really ready to go home." Upon her return, she again helped manage the radio stations in Wichita.

In 1978, Senator Pearson announced that he would not run for reelection. When Kassebaum considered entering the race, it was her mother and mother-in-law who encouraged her to do so. Her father "didn't want me to [do it] at all. I think he thought I would lose." Kassebaum's demeanor at first seems almost too gentle for the rough-and-tumble theatrics of the U.S. Senate, and she was initially deterred from running when another female Republican, Rep. Jan Meyers, from the eastern part of the state near Kansas City, threw her hat into the primary ring. But by March of that year, Kassebaum had reconsidered, later saying, "I didn't know why I should necessarily not run just because Jan was running. . . . The men don't look at it that way." Still, Nancy's sense of fairness and courtesy prevailed on her to call Jan Meyers before entering the race. The primary field included not only Jan Meyers but eight other candidates as well, all men, largely from the eastern part of the state. Their numbers meant that these candidates would have to split the vote, and that gave Kassebaum, from Topeka (farther west and south) an advantage. Still, this roster of opponents forced her to jump higher hurdles in her campaign than she had contemplated. "We had a lot of debates. I was really scared to death before the first one, because I just had never done anything like that, never been on TV, and never debated."

Kassebaum's fears proved to be unwarranted when she swept right through both the primary and the general elections on the slogan "A Fresh Face: A Trusted Kansas Name," landing a seat in the otherwise all-male U.S. Senate. She won election without the support of the national women's organizations like the Women's Political Caucus or National Organization for Women. Even though Kassebaum supported the proposed Equal Rights Amendment, she did not gain the support of these groups because she did not favor "an extension of time for its passage if it couldn't have made it through in the time span allowed initially." But her personal wealth enabled her to benefit her own campaign by contributing a major sum of $115,000 to the effort, out of $841,287 raised.[17]

Kassebaum experienced an amazing, meteoric rise to the Senate, compared with nearly every woman who had served there before her. Her only political experiences had been her two years on the local school board and her stint with Senator Pearson. Furthermore, she did not follow or complete a term for her husband, nor had she ever served in the House of Representatives. But the Landon name was a legend in Kansas and in Republican politics. She herself would admit, "It has been said I am riding on the coattails of my dad, but I can't think of any better coattails to ride on."[18]

After taking her seat in January 1979, Kassebaum jumped right into serious responsibilities in the Senate. Because of the year she had already spent on Capitol Hill as a staff member, she knew what to expect. She "knew that it was not a lot of glory, [that] there was a lot of nitty-gritty and hard work, and that you didn't come to just set all the wrongs aright. You couldn't even if you would like to, and you just had to sort of take one day at a time." Yet, as the only woman, it took her a long time to feel at home in the Senate. "There is a senators' dining room . . . and then across the hall from that there's one that has one long table that's Democrat and one long table where the Republicans sit.... I bet a year [passed] before I went in there. I didn't go because I was intimidated." And she would joke of her position as the lone woman in the Senate, "There's so much work to do, the coffee to make and the chamber to vacuum. There are Pat Moynihan's hats to brush and the buttons to sew on Bob Byrd's red vests, so I keep quite busy."[19]

In her early years in the Senate, Kassebaum received assignment to several major committees and was exposed to the array of legislation emanating from diverse committees—Banking, Housing, and Urban Affairs; Budget; Commerce, Science, and Transportation; and the Special Committee on Aging. The Republicans' success in the 1980 election allowed her to exchange her seat on Banking for one on Foreign Relations. She immediately became chair of the Subcommittee on African Affairs and retained this position until the Republicans lost control of the Senate in 1986. She also served as chair of the Aviation Subcommittee of the Commerce, Science, and Transportation Committee. During those years, Kassebaum was captivated by her work on the Foreign Relations Committee. Her involvement in international relations no doubt stemmed from her early dream of being a foreign service officer and her education toward that goal. During her career, she has supported arms control initiatives and democracy building in foreign lands. Although she knew nothing about Africa at the start, she would develop a fascination with that continent. Against the dictates of her party, she firmly pressed for limited sanctions against the South African government to protest apartheid, and she helped draft the legislation to outline how to remove the sanctions systematically. She continued to serve on that subcommittee after 1986 and was especially vocal in 1992 in calling for arming the United Nations relief workers in Somalia. "I was there in July of '92, and really believe that nothing was going to make a difference there unless we could make sure that relief got through.... I would still argue that we did a very honorable mission."

Kassebaum's instincts in foreign relations have often seemed, to many observers, extremely forward-looking. She and Rep. Dan Glickman, a fellow Kansan and Democrat, proposed a cutoff of credit guarantees to Saddam Hussein in June 1990, a move that might have prevented the invasion of Kuwait and the Persian Gulf War, or at least hindered Saddam Hussein from stockpiling weapons as quickly as he did. Unfortunately, the administration of George Bush opposed this policy, a position it would later come to regret. Political commentators often viewed Kassebaum's leadership on foreign affairs as visionary. Had others paid heed earlier to her call for armed peacekeepers in Somalia, the loss of life and collateral damage and the need for American troops might also not have been as great as it was.[20]

When, in November 1994, the Republican Party recaptured the Senate after being out of command for almost a decade, Kassebaum achieved a milestone unmatched by any other woman. With her seniority of sixteen years, she rose to chair the Committee on Labor and Human Resources. Historically, this committee has been the one to which women were assigned. Although its jurisdiction was viewed as "more feminine," involving as it does the major federal social services programs, income safety net benefits, and labor relations, no other female senator has ever chaired such a major committee. In fact, no woman had chaired any Senate committee since 1955, when Margaret Chase Smith chaired a Special Committee on Rates and Compensation that had very narrow responsibilities. As chair of the Labor and Human Resources Committee, Kassebaum has had her hand in most of the major, controversial social proposals currently in Congress—education, labor relations, minimum wage, substitution of employer-sanctioned worker committees for collective bargaining, devolving job training to the states, health insurance reform, and welfare reform. Her committee's jurisdiction carried her to wider audiences, bringing her much media attention on such topics in the 104th Congress as proposals to raise the minimum wage, which Kassebaum opposes (along with the majority of her party). "I don't think that's the answer.... Especially if you're thinking of moving people off of welfare into entry-level jobs."[21] At the same time, Congress is debating the bipartisan health insurance reform legislation, entitled the Kassebaum-Kennedy Health Insurance Reform Act of 1996, which she and Sen. Edward Kennedy, D-Mass., wrote. The bill would allow for greater portability of benefits by workers from job to job as well as coverage of individuals with preexisting conditions. It is a pared back version of her "BasiCare" benefit bill (which included coverage for basic long-term care) that had been introduced in 1992 and 1993 and attempted to expand health insurance to the uninsured through the creation of a uniform benefits package.[22]

Kassebaum has developed a reputation as a moderate Republican, whose centrism has often perplexed and angered her more conservative colleagues. She stands out even more in the 104th Congress's sharply ideological and partisan climate. *Time* magazine reports:

She is famous for the independent streak that led her to oppose Ronald Reagan on school prayer, Star Wars, and a balanced budget amendment while supporting abortion rights, and sanctions against South Africa. Despite powerful pressure from her own party, she was the only Republican to vote against George Bush's choice of John Tower to be his Secretary of Defense.[23]

The wisdom of this last decision was later borne out when Tower was forced to resign under the mantle of personal indiscretions. She would later call on the Republican senator Bob Packwood of Oregon to resign after he came under investigation by the Senate Ethics Committee for sexual harassment.[24]

Kassebaum often serves as a mediator when the battle lines are drawn, and she has been able to gain her colleagues' respect even on highly divisive issues. Disagreeing with the Republican Party position on abortion, she is pro-choice. However, she entered into a high-profile debate in 1995 over the nomination by President Bill Clinton of Dr. Henry Foster as surgeon general, which her committee considered. When questions arose about Dr. Foster's inability to say how many abortions he had performed, Kassebaum expressed concern over the misleading information.[25] Dr. Foster failed to achieve confirmation.

Kassebaum has also differed with her party on international family planning, which she supports. In December 1992, she cofounded the Republican Majority Coalition, whose goal is to combat the rise of the religious right as a force in the Republican Party.[26] Her credentials as a moderate Republican were solidified during President Reagan's presidency when many of her opinions were in sharp contrast to prevailing opinion.[27] Although Kassebaum's positions have changed somewhat on certain issues, particularly her support of the balanced budget amendment, she has remained independent of her party on many subjects.

Kassebaum claims little legislative frustration with a diverse and active legislative agenda. She mentions, however, that while serving for six years as chair of the Aviation Subcommittee of the Commerce Committee she could not succeed in passing aviation product liability laws. She was able to pass the bill out of committee but could not get a vote on the floor.[28]

Kassebaum's stature and respect within the Republican Party are unmistakable, especially when she is mentioned as a possible vice-presidential candidate, as she was in the 1992 election cycle. She did not make the final cut as George Bush's choice, but the fact that she was considered puts her at the top tier of Republican women. Whether she would be willing to run might be another story, for, as she says,

I've always thought that a woman considering this type of race in the United States today has to be prepared for a three- or four-year endeavor, constantly going around the country, enormous amounts of money.... Are we not requiring so much today that it really is more style than substance? As women, are we geared to doing all this that shouldn't be important, but is?[29]

Here again, Kassebaum's voice is a voice of reason, crying out to those who would not be as thoughtful as she, or who perhaps are governed largely by ambition. At sixty-four, she is still frequently mentioned as the only Republican woman qualified for the presidency and vice presidency in long lists dominated by males with whom she has worked.[30] In 1996, as another Kansan, Robert Dole, became the Republican nominee for president, Kassebaum announced she would not seek another term in the U.S. Senate.

Kassebaum has often been called soft-spoken, demure, reserved. She once said, "Someday I'm going to hit someone over the head for calling me diminutive and soft-spoken," and then added, laughing, "But then, I am!"[31]

She dislikes being compared to Dorothy in the *Wizard of Oz,* but she is light-hearted enough to permit her staff to make reference to the movie on an intricate patchwork quilt they gave her that is now displayed in her Senate office reception area.[32] Her manner remains easy as a Kansas breeze, and her style studious. While she may not make her point with a raised voice and a fist, she leaves little doubt where she stands. She has come to command that elusive quality called "respect."

Some of her friends feel that Kassebaum never really leaves Kansas. One said, "If she had a chance to go to Rome, Paris, Bangkok, or Topeka, she would choose Topeka."[33] That certainly helps account for her landslide election victories in which she continues to rack up margins that tip the scales at 75 percent majorities. She wistfully reflected in 1989, perhaps foreshadowing her personal decision to retire at the end of her third term: "The land. Someday one must go back to the land. You understand what I mean, don't you?"[34] Her experience and wisdom often rush forward:

Before I leave, there are two things I'd really like to do. One, I've written my own comprehensive health care reform bill. Of course, the longer I've worked with it, the less sure one gets of what that should be. And the other is our need to reform Congress. What I've been pressing for is combining committee structures, by function rather than by appropriation and authorizing committees. I don't think checks and balances [in Congress] work any more; it gets more and more confusing, and accountability gets more and more convoluted, particularly when you do the budget and then you do authorization and then appropriation. [It's too] disconnected now.... I don't think it'll come to pass; it's probably too big a change.

As the chair of the Senate Committee on Labor and Human Resources, and a member of the Republican leadership of the Senate, Kassebaum has spent the closing months of her career attempting to gain passage of the health measure she wrote with Senator Kennedy, which has been blocked, ironically, by Dole, the majority leader and 1996 presidential candidate. At issue was Dole's insistence that amendments be included that were not present in her original bill, thus ensuring that she would not be able to muster the necessary votes to clear a final measure. Moving any health reform bill through Congress requires the most careful balancing of interests. "By attaching an MST [Medical Saving Account] and a mental health amendment ... Dole put her in the difficult position of either violating her pledge or appearing disloyal to him."[35] Her eleventh-hour efforts—this former 4-H leader, mother, and wife—were devoted to clearing an acceptable measure that would gain passage in her final term. The rare opportunity she had been afforded to exercise her power as chair in advancing a cause so vital to millions of the nation's families offered no easy path to one who, as a result of seniority, seemed so well-poised to achieve a final, sweet victory.

Kassebaum's plain Kansas wisdom concerning women's ascendant role in the nation's politics will leave a vacuum in the Senate. When she was selected deputy chair of the 1988 Republican convention with some speculation that President Bush might choose her as his vice-presidential running mate, she chose to spend the time in Abilene, Kansas, commenting to a Wichita newspaper: "I'm happy to speak on substantial issues. But to be treated as a bauble on the tree is not particularly constructive, is it?"[36]

NOTES

1. Michael Barone and Grant Ujifusa, *Almanac of American Politics, 1994* (Washington, D.C.: National Journal, 1993), 509.
2. *Current Biography 1982*, s.v. "Kassebaum, Nancy Landon," 190–191.
3. Nancy Landon Kassebaum, interview by author, Washington, D.C., October 24, 1993. All quotations in this chapter that are not attributed to another source are from this interview.
4. Maya Angelou, "From Kansas to the Senate to the Land," *Working Woman*, September 1989, 122.
5. Kassebaum, interview.
6. Ibid.
7. *Current Biography 1982*, 191.
8. Kassebaum, interview.
9. Ibid.
10. Angelou, "From Kansas to the Senate," 122.
11. Kassebaum, interview.
12. Ibid.
13. Barone and Ujifusa, *Almanac of American Politics, 1994*, 508.
14. Kassebaum, interview.
15. Ibid.
16. Ibid.
17. *Current Biography,1982*, 192.
18. Quoted in ibid.
19. "There's so much work to do . . ." quoted in ibid.
20. Barone and Ujifusa, *Almanac of American Politics, 1995*, 491.
21. Barone and Ujifusa, *Almanac of American Politics, 1994*, 509.
22. "Kassebaum Reintroduces Health Care Coverage," *Best's Review*, March 1993.
23. "Five Who Fit the Bill: From Kansas with Plenty of Moxie," *Time*, May 20, 1991.
24. William Eaton, "Kassebaum Calls on Packwood to Resign," *Los Angeles Times*, December 18, 1993, A19.
25. Phillip D. Duncan and Christine C. Lawrence, eds., *Politics in America, 1996* (Washington, D.C.: CQ Press, 1995), 510.
26. Barone and Ujifusa, *Almanac of American Politics, 1995*, 492.
27. "Five Who Fit the Bill."
28. Kassebaum, interview.
29. "Nancy Kassebaum and Barbara Mikulski," *Ms.*, September 1988, 59.
30. "Five Who Fit the Bill."
31. Barone and Ujifusa, *Almanac of American Politics, 1994*, 508.
32. Kassebaum, interview.
33. Angelou, "From Kansas to the Senate," 122.
34. Ibid.
35. Jamie Stiehm, "Kansas Allies Dole, Kassebaum Clash over Competing Interests on Health Insurance," *The Hill*, May 8, 1996, 8.
36. "Five Who Fit the Bill."

Reference Materials

TABLE A-1 WOMEN IN CONGRESS, BY CONGRESS

Congress	House	Senate
THE PIONEERS: 1917–1939		
65th (1917–1919)	Jeannette Rankin[a]	—
66th (1919–1921)	—	—
67th (1921–1923)	Winnifred Sprague Mason Huck, Mae Ella Nolan, Alice Mary Robertson	Rebecca Latimer Felton
68th (1923–1925)	Mae Ella Nolan	—
69th (1925–1927)	Florence Prag Kahn, Mary Teresa Norton, Edith Nourse Rogers	—
70th (1927–1929)	Florence Prag Kahn, Katherine Gudger Langley, Mary Teresa Norton, Edith Nourse Rogers, Pearl Peden Oldfield	—
71st (1929–1931)	Florence Prag Kahn, Katherine Gudger Langley, Ruth Hanna McCormick, Mary Teresa Norton, Pearl Peden Oldfield, Ruth Bryan Owen, Ruth Sears Baker Pratt, Edith Nourse Rogers, Effiegene Locke Wingo	—
72d (1931–1933)	Willa McCord Blake Eslick, Florence Prag Kahn, Mary Teresa Norton, Ruth Bryan Owen, Ruth Sears Baker Pratt, Edith Nourse Rogers, Effiegene Locke Wingo	Hattie Wyatt Caraway
73d (1933–1935)	Marian Williams Clarke, Isabella Selmes Greenway, Virginia Ellis Jenckes, Florence Prag Kahn, Kathryn McCarthy, Mary Teresa Norton, Edith Nourse Rogers	Hattie Wyatt Caraway
74th (1935–1937)	Isabella Selmes Greenway, Virginia Ellis Jenckes, Florence Prag Kahn, Mary Teresa Norton, Caroline Love O'Day, Edith Nourse Rogers	Hattie Wyatt Caraway, Rose McConnell Long
75th (1937–1939)	Elizabeth Hawley Gasque, Nan Wood Honeyman, Virginia Ellis Jenckes, Mary Teresa Norton, Caroline Love Goodwin O'Day, Edith Nourse Rogers	Hattie Wyatt Caraway, Dixie Bibb Graves, Gladys Pyle

THE GREENING YEARS: 1939–1971

76th (1939–1941)	Frances Payne Bolton, Florence Reville Gibbs, Clara Gooding McMillan, Mary Teresa Norton, Caroline Love O'Day, Edith Nourse Rogers, Margaret Chase Smith, Jessie Sumner	Hattie Wyatt Caraway
77th (1941–1943)	Veronica Grace Boland, Frances Payne Bolton, Katharine Edgar Byron, Mary Teresa Norton, Caroline Love O'Day, Jeannette Rankin, Edith Nourse Rogers, Margaret Chase Smith, Jessie Sumner	Hattie Wyatt Caraway
78th (1943–1945)	Frances Payne Bolton, Willa Lybrand Fulmer, Clare Boothe Luce, Mary Teresa Norton, Edith Nourse Rogers, Margaret Chase Smith, Winifred Claire Stanley, Jessie Sumner	Hattie Wyatt Caraway
79th (1945–1947)	Frances Payne Bolton, Emily Taft Douglas, Clare Boothe Luce, Helen Douglas Mankin, Mary Teresa Norton, Eliza Jane Pratt, Edith Nourse Rogers, Margaret Chase Smith, Jessie Sumner, Chase Going Woodhouse	Helen Gahagan Douglas
80th (1947–1949)	Frances Payne Bolton, Vera Bushfield, Georgia Lee Lusk, Mary Teresa Norton, Edith Nourse Rogers, Katharine Price St. George, Margaret Chase Smith	Helen Gahagan Douglas
81st (1949–1951)	Frances Payne Bolton, Reva Zilpha Beck Bosone, Cecil Murray Harden, Edna Flannery Kelly, Mary Teresa Norton, Edith Nourse Rogers, Katharine Price St. George, Chase Going Woodhouse	Margaret Chase Smith, Helen Gahagan Douglas
82d (1951–1953)	Frances Payne Bolton, Reva Zilpha Beck Bosone, Vera Daerr Buchanan, Marguerite Stitt Church, Cecil Murray Harden, Maude Elizabeth Kee, Edna Flannery Kelly, Edith Nourse Rogers, Katharine Price St. George, Ruth Thompson	Margaret Chase Smith
83d (1953–1955)	Frances Payne Bolton, Vera Daerr Buchanan, Marguerite Stitt Church, Mary Elizabeth Farrington, Cecil Murray Harden, Maude Elizabeth Kee, Edna Flannery Kelly, Gracie Bowers Pfost, Edith Nourse Rogers, Katharine Price St. George, Leonor Kretzer Sullivan, Ruth Thompson	Eva Kelly Bowring, Margaret Chase Smith
84th (1955–1957)	Iris Faircloth Blitch, Frances Payne Bolton, Vera Daerr Buchanan, Marguerite Stitt Church, Mary Elizabeth Farrington, Katherine Elizabeth Granahan, Edith Starrett Green, Martha Wright Griffiths, Cecil Murray Harden, Maude Elizabeth	Margaret Chase Smith

TABLE A-1 *(Continued)*

Congress	House	Senate
85th (1957–1959)	Kee, Edna Flannery Kelly, Coya Gjesdal Knutson, Gracie Bowers Pfost, Edith Nourse Rogers, Katharine Price St. George, Leonor Kretzer Sullivan, Ruth Thompson	Margaret Chase Smith
86th (1959–1961)	Iris Faircloth Blitch, Frances Payne Bolton, Marguerite Stitt Church, Florence Price Dwyer, Katherine Elizabeth Granahan, Edith Starrett Green, Martha Wright Griffiths, Cecil Murray Harden, Maude Elizabeth Kee, Edna Flannery Kelly, Coya Gjesdal Knutson, Gracie Bowers Pfost, Edith Nourse Rogers, Katharine Price St. George, Leonor Kretzer Sullivan	Maurine Neuberger, Margaret Chase Smith
87th (1961–1963)	Iris Faircloth Blitch, Frances Payne Bolton, Marguerite Stitt Church, Florence Price Dwyer, Katherine Elizabeth Granahan, Edith Starrett Green, Martha Wright Griffiths, Julia Butler Hansen, Maude Elizabeth Kee, Edna Flannery Kelly, Catherine Dean May, Gracie Bowers Pfost, Edith Nourse Rogers, Katharine Price St. George, Edna Oakes Simpson, Leonor Kretzer Sullivan, Jessica McCullough Weis	Maurine Neuberger, Margaret Chase Smith
88th (1963–1965)	Iris Faircloth Blitch, Frances Payne Bolton, Marguerite Stitt Church, Florence Price Dwyer, Katherine Elizabeth Granahan, Edith Starrett Green, Martha Wright Griffiths, Julia Butler Hansen, Maude Elizabeth Kee, Edna Flannery Kelly, Catherine Dean May, Catherine Dorris Norrell, Gracie Bowers Pfost, Louise Goff Reece, Corrine Boyd Riley, Katharine Price St. George, Leonor Kretzer Sullivan, Jessica McCullough Weis	Maurine Neuberger, Margaret Chase Smith
88th (1963–1965)	Irene Bailey Baker, Frances Payne Bolton, Florence Price Dwyer, Edith Starrett Green, Martha Wright Griffiths, Julia Butler Hansen, Maude Elizabeth Kee, Edna Flannery Kelly, Catherine Dean May, Charlotte Thompson Reid, Katharine Price St. George, Leonor Kretzer Sullivan	Maurine Neuberger, Margaret Chase Smith
89th (1965–1967)	Frances Payne Bolton, Florence Price Dwyer, Edith Starrett Green, Martha Wright Griffiths, Julia Butler Hansen, Edna Flannery Kelly, Catherine Dean May, Patsy Takemoto Mink, Charlotte Thompson Reid, Leonor Kretzer Sullivan, Lera Millard Thomas	Maurine Neuberger, Margaret Chase Smith

Congress (Years)	Representatives	Senators
90th (1967–1969)	Frances Payne Bolton, Florence Price Dwyer, Edith Starrett Green, Martha Wright Griffiths, Julia Butler Hansen, Margaret M. Heckler, Edna Flannery Kelly, Catherine Dean May, Patsy Takemoto Mink, Charlotte Thompson Reid, Leonor Kretzer Sullivan	Margaret Chase Smith
91st (1969–1971)	Shirley Anita Chisholm, Florence Price Dwyer, Edith Starrett Green, Martha Wright Griffiths, Julia Butler Hansen, Margaret M. Heckler, Catherine Dean May, Patsy Takemoto Mink, Charlotte Thompson Reid, Leonor Kretzer Sullivan	Margaret Chase Smith

THE MODERN ERA: 1971 TO THE PRESENT

Congress (Years)	Representatives	Senators
92d (1971–1973)	Bella Abzug, Elizabeth B. Andrews, Shirley Anita Chisholm, Florence Price Dwyer, Ella Tambussi Grasso, Edith Starrett Green, Martha Wright Griffiths, Julia Butler Hansen, Margaret M. Heckler, Louise Day Hicks, Patsy Takemoto Mink, Charlotte Thompson Reid, Leonor Kretzer Sullivan	Elaine Edwards, Margaret Chase Smith
93d (1973–1975)	Bella Abzug, Corinne C. "Lindy" Boggs, Yvonne Brathwaite Burke, Cardiss Collins, Ella Tambussi Grasso, Edith Green, Martha Wright Griffiths, Julia Butler Hansen, Margaret M. Heckler, Marjorie S. Holt, Elizabeth Holtzman, Barbara C. Jordan, Patsy Takemoto Mink, Patricia S. Schroeder, Leonor Kretzer Sullivan	—
94th (1975–1977)	Bella Abzug, Corinne C. "Lindy" Boggs, Yvonne Brathwaite Burke, Shirley Anita Chisholm, Cardiss Collins, Millicent Fenwick, Margaret M. Heckler, Marjorie S. Holt, Elizabeth Holtzman, Barbara C. Jordan, Martha Elizabeth Keys, Marilyn Lloyd, Helen Stevenson Meyner, Patsy Takemoto Mink, Shirley N. Pettis, Patricia S. Schroeder, Virginia Smith, Gladys Noon Spellman, Leonor Kretzer Sullivan	—
95th (1977–1979)	Corinne C. "Lindy" Boggs, Yvonne Brathwaite Burke, Shirley Anita Chisholm, Cardiss Collins, Millicent Fenwick, Margaret Heckler, Marjorie Holt, Elizabeth Holtzman, Barbara C. Jordan, Martha Elizabeth Keys, Marilyn Lloyd, Helen Stevenson Meyner, Barbara Ann Mikulski, Mary Rose Oakar, Shirley N. Pettis, Patricia S. Schroeder, Virginia Smith, Gladys Noon Spellman	Maryon P. Allen, Muriel Humphrey
96th (1979–1981)	Corinne C. "Lindy" Boggs, Beverly Byron, Shirley Anita Chisholm, Cardiss Collins, Millicent Fenwick, Geraldine Ferraro, Margaret M. Heckler, Marjorie S.	Nancy Landon Kassebaum

TABLE A-1 *(Continued)*

Congress	House	Senate
97th (1981–1983)	Holt, Elizabeth Holtzman, Marilyn Lloyd, Barbara Ann Mikulski, Mary Rose Oakar, Patricia S. Schroeder, Virginia Smith, Olympia J. Snowe, Gladys Noon Spellman	
	Jean Ashbrook, Corinne C. "Lindy" Boggs, Beverly Byron, Shirley Anita Chisholm, Cardiss Collins, Millicent Fenwick, Geraldine Ann Ferraro, Bobbi Fiedler, Katie Hall, Margaret M. Heckler, Marjorie S. Holt, Barbara Bailey Kennelly, Marilyn Lloyd, Lynn M. Martin, Barbara Ann Mikulski, Mary Rose Oakar, Margaret Scafati Roukema, Claudine Schneider, Patricia S. Schroeder, Virginia Smith, Olympia J. Snowe	Paula Hawkins, Nancy Landon Kassebaum
98th (1983–1985)	Corinne C. "Lindy" Boggs, Barbara Boxer, Sala Burton, Beverly Byron, Cardiss Collins, Geraldine Ann Ferraro, Bobbi Fiedler, Katie Hall, Marjorie S. Holt, Nancy L. Johnson, Marcy (Marcia Carolyn) Kaptur, Barbara Bailey Kennelly, Marilyn Lloyd, Lynn M. Martin, Barbara Ann Mikulski, Mary Rose Oakar, Margaret Scafati Roukema, Claudine Schneider, Patricia S. Schroeder, Virginia Smith, Olympia J. Snowe, Barbara Vucanovich	Paula Hawkins, Nancy Landon Kassebaum
99th (1985–1987)	Helen Delich Bentley, Corinne C. "Lindy" Boggs, Barbara Boxer, Sala Burton, Beverly Byron, Cardiss Collins, Bobbi Fiedler, Marjorie S. Holt, Nancy L. Johnson, Marcy (Marcia Carolyn) Kaptur, Barbara Bailey Kennelly, Marilyn Lloyd, Cathy Long, Lynn M. Martin, Jan Meyers, Barbara Ann Mikulski, Mary Rose Oakar, Margaret Scafati Roukema, Claudine Schneider, Patricia S. Schroeder, Virginia Smith, Olympia J. Snowe, Barbara Vucanovich	Paula Hawkins, Nancy Landon Kassebaum
100th (1987–1989)	Helen Delich Bentley, Corinne C. "Lindy" Boggs, Barbara Boxer, Sala Burton, Beverly Byron, Cardiss Collins, Nancy L. Johnson, Marcy (Marcia Carolyn) Kaptur, Barbara Bailey Kennelly, Marilyn Lloyd, Lynn M. Martin, Jan Meyers, Constance A. Morella, Mary Rose Oakar, Elizabeth J. Patterson, Nancy Pelosi, Margaret Scafati Roukema, Patricia F. Saiki, Claudine Schneider,	Paula Hawkins, Nancy Landon Kassebaum

	Patricia S. Schroeder, Louise M. Slaughter, Virginia Smith, Olympia J. Snowe, Barbara Vucanovich	Nancy Landon Kassebaum, Barbara Ann Mikulski
101st (1989–1991)	Helen Delich Bentley, Corinne C. "Lindy" Boggs, Barbara Boxer, Beverly Byron, Cardiss Collins, Nancy L. Johnson, Marcy (Marcia Carolyn) Kaptur, Barbara Bailey Kennelly, Marilyn Lloyd, Jill Long, Nita M. Lowey, Lynn M. Martin, Jan Meyers, Patsy Takemoto Mink, Susan Molinari, Constance A. Morella, Mary Rose Oakar, Elizabeth J. Patterson, Nancy Pelosi, Ileana Ros-Lehtinen, Margaret Scafati Roukema, Patricia F. Saiki, Claudine Schneider, Patricia S. Schroeder, Louise M. Slaughter, Virginia Smith, Olympia J. Snowe, Jolene Unsoeld, Barbara Vucanovich	Nancy Landon Kassebaum, Barbara Ann Mikulski
102d (1991–1993)	Helen Delich Bentley, Barbara Boxer, Beverly Byron, Barbara-Rose Collins, Cardiss Collins, Rosa DeLauro, Joan Kelly Horn, Nancy L. Johnson, Marcy (Marcia Carolyn) Kaptur, Barbara Bailey Kennelly, Marilyn Lloyd, Jill Long, Nita M. Lowey, Jan Meyers, Patsy Takemoto Mink, Susan Molinari, Constance A. Morella, Eleanor Holmes Norton,[b] Mary Rose Oakar, Elizabeth J. Patterson, Nancy Pelosi, Ileana Ros-Lehtinen, Margaret Scafati Roukema, Patricia S. Schroeder, Louise M. Slaughter, Olympia J. Snowe, Jolene Unsoeld, Barbara Vucanovich, Maxine Waters	Jocelyn Burdick, Nancy Landon Kassebaum, Barbara Ann Mikulski
103d (1993–1995)	Helen Delich Bentley, Corrine Brown, Leslie L. Byrne, Maria Cantwell, Eva Clayton, Barbara-Rose Collins, Cardiss Collins, Pat Danner, Rosa DeLauro, Jennifer Dunn, Karan English, Anna G. Eshoo, Tillie Fowler, Elizabeth Furse, Jane Harman, Eddie Bernice Johnson, Nancy L. Johnson, Marcy (Marcia Carolyn) Kaptur, Barbara B. Kennelly, Blanche Lambert Lincoln, Marilyn Lloyd, Jill Long, Nita Lowey, Cynthia McKinney, Carolyn Maloney, Marjorie Margolies-Mezvinsky, Carrie Meek, Jan Meyers, Patsy Takemoto Mink, Susan Molinari, Constance A. Morella, Eleanor Holmes Norton,[b] Nancy Pelosi, Deborah Pryce, Ileana Ros-Lehtinen, Lucille Roybal-Allard, Margaret Scafati Roukema, Lynn Schenk, Patricia S. Schroeder, Karen Shepherd, Louise M. Slaughter, Olympia J. Snowe, Karen L. Thurman, Jolene Unsoeld, Nydia M. Velazquez, Barbara F. Vucanovich, Maxine Waters, Lynn Woolsey	Barbara Boxer, Dianne Feinstein, Kay Bailey Hutchison, Nancy Landon Kassebaum, Barbara Ann Mikulski, Carol Moseley-Braun, Patty Murray

TABLE A-1 *(Continued)*

Congress	House	Senate
104th (1995–1997)	Corrine Brown, Helen Chenoweth, Eva Clayton, Barbara-Rose Collins, Cardiss Collins, Barbara Cubin, Pat Danner, Rosa DeLauro, Jennifer Dunn, Anna G. Eshoo, Tillie Fowler, Elizabeth Furse, Enid Greene, Jane Harman, Sheila Jackson-Lee, Eddie Bernice Johnson, Nancy L. Johnson, Marcy (Marcia Carolyn) Kaptur, Sue W. Kelly, Barbara B. Kennelly, Blanche Lambert Lincoln, Zoe Lofgren, Nita M. Lowey, Carolyn B. Maloney, Karen McCarthy, Juanita M. McDonald,[d] Cynthia A. McKinney, Carrie P. Meek, Jan Meyers, Patsy Takemoto Mink, Susan Molinari, Constance A. Morella, Sue Myrick, Eleanor Holmes Norton,[b] Nancy Pelosi, Deborah Pryce, Lynn Rivers, Ileana Ros-Lehtinen, Marge Roukema, Lucille Roybal-Allard, Patricia Schroeder, Andrea Seastrand, Louise M. Slaughter, Linda Smith, Karen L. Thurman, Nydia M. Velazquez, Barbara F. Vucanovich, Maxine Waters, Lynn Woolsey	Barbara Boxer, Dianne Feinstein, Sheila Frahm,[c] Kay Bailey Hutchison, Nancy Landon Kassebaum, Barbara Ann Mikulski, Carol Moseley-Braun, Patty Murray, Olympia J. Snowe

Source: Compiled by the author.

[a] Rankin served before the Nineteenth Amendment to the Constitution was passed in 1920. This amendment gave women the right to vote.

[b] Nonvoting delegate from the District of Columbia.

[c] Frahm was appointed to take Sen. Bob Dole's place when he resigned in June 1996 to run for president.

[d] McDonald won a special election in March 1996.

TABLE A-2   THE WOMEN OF CONGRESS, ALPHABETICALLY BY CONGRESSWOMAN

Name	Dates of Service	Length of Service	Age When Sworn In	Brief Profile
THE PIONEERS: 1917–1939				
HOUSE				
Marian Williams Clarke (R-N.Y.)	12-28-33 to 1-3-35	1 year	53	Succeeded her 6-term husband and announced her intention to run for reelection; withdrew before the primary.
Willa McCord Blake Eslick (D-Tenn.)	8-4-32 to 3-3-33	6 months	54	Filled her husband's seat after he died on the Chamber floor in 1932.
Elizabeth Hawley Gasque (D-S.C.)	9-13-38 to 1-3-39	4 months	42	Never sworn in because Congress adjourned.
Isabella Selmes Greenway (D-Ariz.)	10-3-33 to 1-3-37	3-1/4 years	47	A friend of the Roosevelt family; married three times; ran in a special election.
Nan Wood Honeyman (D-Ore.)	1-3-37 to 1-3-39	2 years	56	Lost a bid for reelection.
Winnifred Mason Huck (R-Ill.)	11-7-22 to 3-3-23	1 year	40	A journalist who succeeded her father; defeated in reelection bid.
Virginia Ellis Jenckes (D-Ind.)	3-4-33 to 1-3-39	6 years	56	Defeated by a Republican.
Florence Prag Kahn (R-Calif.)	3-4-25 to 1-3-37	12 years	59	Succeeded her husband, then lost in the Democratic landslide
Katherine Gudger Langley (R-Ky.)	3-4-27 to 3-3-31	4 years	39	Succeeded her husband after his conviction for selling liquor; lost her seat in 1930.
Kathryn O'Laughlin McCarthy (D-Kan.)	3-4-33 to 1-3-35	2 years	39	Defeated a Republican, then lost her seat two years later.
Ruth Hanna McCormick (R-Ill.)	3-4-29 to 3-3-31	2 years	49	A progressive Republican who lost a bid for the Senate in 1930.

TABLE A-2   *(Continued)*

Name	Dates of Service	Length of Service	Age When Sworn In	Brief Profile
Mae Ella Hunt Nolan (R-Calif.)	1-23-23 to 3-3-25	2 years	37	First woman to chair a House committee (Post Office); declined renomination.
Mary Teresa Norton (D-N.J.)	3-4-25 to 1-3-51	26 years	50	First woman elected from the east; chaired Labor Committee and District of Columbia Committee.
Caroline Love Goodwin O'Day (D-N.Y.)	1-3-35 to 1-3-43	8 years	60	A friend of Eleanor Roosevelt; a peace and settlement house activist.
Pearl Peden Oldfield (D-Ark.)	1-11-29 to 3-3-31	2 years	53	Succeeded husband.
Ruth Bryan Owen (D-Fla.)	3-4-29 to 3-3-33	4 years	44	Daughter of William Jennings Bryan; lost her seat because she favored Prohibition.
Ruth Sears Baker Pratt (R-N.Y.)	3-4-29 to 3-3-33	4 years	52	A "silk stocking" district representative; served in the New York Assembly; supported Hoover and private funding for unemployment.
Jeannette Rankin (R-Mont.)	3-4-17 to 3-3-19; 1-3-41 to 1-3-43	4 years	37	A suffragist and a peace activist; the first woman to serve in Congress.
Alice Mary Robertson (R-Okla.)	3-4-21 to 3-3-23	2 years	67	Daughter of missionaries; the second woman elected to the House, after defeating a three-term incumbent Democrat.
Edith Nourse Rogers (R-Mass.)	6-30-25 to 9-10-60	35 years	44	Longest-serving woman in Congress; succeeded her husband; chaired the Veterans Committee; died in office at age 79.

TABLE A-2 *(Continued)*

Name	Dates of Service	Length of Service	Age When Sworn In	Brief Profile
Effiegene Locke Wingo (D-Ark.)	11-4-30 to 3-3-33	2 years	47	Interested in the environment; helped set up a student internship.

SENATE

Name	Dates of Service	Length of Service	Age When Sworn In	Brief Profile
Hattie Wyatt Caraway (D-Ark.)	11-13-31 to 1-2-45	13-1/2 years	53	First woman elected to Senate; succeeded her husband; championed by Huey Long.
Rebecca Latimer Felton (D-Ga.)	11-21-22 to 11-22-22	1 day	87	First woman senator; appointed to fill the term of a senator who had died; served one day and resigned.
Dixie Bibb Graves (D-Ala.)	8-20-37 to 1-10-38	4 months	55	Appointed by her husband to fill the seat vacated when Hugo Black was appointed to the Supreme Court.
Rose McConnell Long (D-La.)	1-31-36 to 1-3-37	11 months	44	Appointed to fill a vacancy caused by the assassination of her husband, Huey Long.
Gladys Pyle (R-S.D.)	11-9-38 to 1-3-39	2 months	48	First Republican woman elected to Senate; filled a vacancy caused by death of incumbent; never sworn in, because Senate adjourned early.

THE GREENING YEARS: 1939–1971

HOUSE

Name	Dates of Service	Length of Service	Age When Sworn In	Brief Profile
Irene Bailey Baker (R-Tenn.)	3-10-64 to 1-3-65	10 months	63	Succeeded husband.
Iris Faircloth Blitch (D-Ga.)	1-3-55 to 1-3-63	8 years	43	A state officeholder who won election to Congress; switched parties after leaving Congress.

TABLE A-2 *(Continued)*

Name	Dates of Service	Length of Service	Age When Sworn In	Brief Profile
Veronica Grace Boland (D-Pa.)	11-3-42 to 1-3-43	2 months	43	Succeeded husband.
Frances Payne Bolton (R-Ohio)	2-27-40 to 1-3-69	29 years	55	A debutante philanthropist who succeeded her husband; defeated after redistricting.
Reva Zilpha Beck Bosone (D-Utah)	1-3-49 to 1-3-53	4 years	54	An accomplished attorney and judge; a self-made leader.
Vera Daerr Buchanan (D-Pa.)	7-24-51 to 11-26-55	4-1/2 years	49	Succeeded her husband and died in office.
Katharine Edgar Byron (D-Md.)	5-27-41 to 1-3-43	1-1/2 years	38	Succeeded her husband. (Years later her son was elected to the same seat, died, and was succeeded by his wife.)
Shirley Anita Chisholm (D-N.Y.)	1-3-69 to 1-3-83	14 years	45	First African American congresswoman; ran for president in 1972.
Marguerite Stitt Church (R-Ill.)	1-3-51 to 1-3-63	12 years	59	Succeeded her husband and imposed retirement on herself.
Emily Taft Douglas (D-Ill.)	1-3-45 to 1-3-47	2 years	46	Elected on her own, served one term, and was defeated. (Her husband, Paul Douglas, was elected senator in 1948.)
Florence Price Dwyer (R-N.J.)	1-3-57 to 1-3-73	16 years	55	Self-made; by background, a lobbyist for business and professional women.
Mary Elizabeth Pruett Farrington (R-Hawaii)	7-31-54 to 1-3-57	2-1/2 years	56	A publisher who succeeded her husband, then won on her own.
Willa Lybrand Fulmer (D-S.C.)	11-7-44 to 1-3-45	2 months	60	Succeeded husband.
Florence Reville Gibbs (D-Ga.)	10-1-40 to 1-3-41	3 months	50	Succeeded husband.

TABLE A-2   *(Continued)*

Name	Dates of Service	Length of Service	Age When Sworn In	Brief Profile
Kathryn Elizabeth Granahan (D-Pa.)	11-6-56 to 1-3-63	6 years	62	Succeeded husband; forced to resign because of illness.
Edith Starrett Green (D-Ore.)	1-3-55 to 12-31-74	19 years	45	Dedicated to education; later became a Republican because of her belief that social programs do not work.
Martha Wright Griffiths (D-Mich.)	1-3-55 to 12-31-74	19 years	43	An accomplished lawyer who ran for Congress and lost, then ran again; first woman to serve on Ways and Means Committee; held an abiding interest in women's rights
Julia Butler Hansen (D-Wash.)	11-8-60 to 12-31-74	14 years	53	Elected to the House after 22 years of public service in local and state office.
Cecil Murray Harden (R-Ind.)	1-3-49 to 1-3-59	10 years	55	A Republican Party organizer whose husband was active politically; lost her sixth bid for reelection.
Margaret M. Heckler (R-Mass.)	1-3-67 to 1-3-83	16 years	36	Defeated an 81-year-old; concentrated on veterans affairs; defeated after redistricting.
Maude Elizabeth Kee (D-W.Va.)	7-17-51 to 1-3-65	14 years	56	A columnist who succeeded her husband and was succeeded by her son.
Edna Flannery Kelly (D-N.Y.)	11-8-49 to 1-3-69	20 years	43	Rose through ranks of Democratic Party after death of husband; lost seat in redistricting.
Coya Gjesdal Knutson (D-Minn.)	1-3-55 to 1-3-59	4 years	43	Lost election after her husband publicly said her career was damaging their marriage and asked her to come home; divorced him after election.

TABLE A-2   *(Continued)*

Name	Dates of Service	Length of Service	Age When Sworn In	Brief Profile
Clare Boothe Luce (R-Conn.)	1-3-43 to 1-3-47	4 years	40	Wife of publisher Henry Luce; keynote speaker at 1944 Republican convention.
Georgia Lee Lusk (D-N.M.)	1-3-47 to 1-3-49	2 years	54	A widow, educator, and rancher who won election over six opponents.
Helen Douglas Mankin (D-Ga.)	2-12-46 to 1-3-47	11 months	52	As representative, fought for the vote for black Americans; denied reelection under Georgia law by "county unit" vote.
Catherine Dean May (R-Wash.)	1-3-59 to 1-3-71	12 years	45	Defeated a Democrat; focused on agriculture in the House.
Clara Gooding McMillan (D-S.C.)	11-7-39 to 1-3-41	1-1/4 years	45	Succeeded husband.
Patsy Takemoto Mink (D-Hawaii)	1-3-65 to 1-3-77; 9-22-90 to present	16 years	38	After losing Senate race in 1976 returned to the House thirteen years later; focused on education, civil rights, and women's rights.
Catherine Dorris Norrell (D-Ark.)	4-18-61 to 1-3-63	2 years	60	A music teacher who succeeded her husband.
Mary Teresa Norton (D-N.J.)	3-4-25 to 1-3-51	26 years	50	See previous section.
Caroline Love Goodwin O'Day (D-N.Y.)	1-3-35 to 1-3-43	8 years	60	See previous section.
Gracie Bowers Pfost (D-Idaho)	1-3-53 to 1-3-63	10 years	47	A chemist and county officeholder who fought for federal development of Hell's Canyon on Snake River; lost 1962 Senate bid.

TABLE A-2   *(Continued)*

Name	Dates of Service	Length of Service	Age When Sworn In	Brief Profile
Eliza Jane Pratt (D-N.C.)	5-25-46 to 1-3-47	6 months	44	A former newspaper editor who worked for a House member, then succeeded him; did not seek reelection.
Jeannette Rankin (R-Mont.)	3-4-17 to 3-3-19; 1-3-41 to 1-3-43	4 years	37	See previous section.
Louise Goff Reece (R-Tenn.)	5-16-61 to 1-3-63	2 years	63	Daughter of a U.S. senator; succeeded husband.
Charlotte Thompson Reid (R-Ill.)	1-3-63 to 10-7-71	8 years	50	Succeeded husband who died while campaigning.
Corrine Boyd Riley (D-S.C.)	4-10-62 to 1-3-63	9 months	69	Succeeded husband.
Edith Nourse Rogers (R-Mass.)	6-30-25 to 9-10-60	35 years	44	See previous section.
Edna Oakes Simpson (R-Ill.)	1-3-59 to 1-3-61	2 years	68	Succeeded husband.
Margaret Chase Smith (R-Maine)[a]	6-3-40 to 1-3-49	32-1/2 years	43	Former telephone operator and teacher who succeeded her husband.
Winnifred Claire Stanley (R-N.Y.)	1-3-43 to 1-3-45	2 years	34	Interrupted her legal career to run for Congress.
Katharine Price Collier St. George (R-N.Y.)	1-3-47 to 1-3-65	18 years	53	A wealthy cousin of Roosevelts; worked in husband's coal brokerage firm before House career; defeated for a tenth term at age 70.
Leonor Kretzer Sullivan (D-Mo.)	1-3-53 to 1-3-77	24 years	51	Worked for her husband while he was in Congress; after his death worked for another member; elected in her own right in 1952; author of food stamp program.

TABLE A-2   *(Continued)*

Name	Dates of Service	Length of Service	Age When Sworn In	Brief Profile
Jessie Sumner (R-Ill.)	1-3-39 to 1-3-47	8 years	41	An isolationist who criticized FDR's New Deal.
Lera Millard Thomas (D-Texas)	3-26-66 to 1-3-67	9 months	66	Succeeded husband.
Ruth Thompson (R-Mich.)	1-3-51 to 1-3-57	6 years	64	A lawyer; first woman to serve on Judiciary Committee.
Jessica McCullough Weis (R-N.Y.)	1-3-59 to 1-3-63	4 years	58	A wealthy Republican whose avocation was party politics.
Chase Going Woodhouse (D-Conn.)	1-3-45 to 1-3-47; 1-3-49 to 1-3-51	4 years	55	An economist and academic who defeated an incumbent; lost her seat in 1946 but won in 1948.
SENATE				
Hazel Hempel Abel (R-Neb.)	11-8-54 to 12-31-54	1 month	66	Elected to fill a two-month vacancy; voted to censure Sen. Joseph McCarthy.
Eva Kelly Bowring (R-Neb.)	4-16-54 to 11-7-54	6 months	62	Appointed to fill a vacancy.
Vera Cahalan Bushfield (R-S.D.)	10-6-48 to 12-26-48	3 months	59	Filled out term of her husband, who had succeeded his father.
Hattie Wyatt Caraway (D-Ark.)	11-13-31 to 1-2-45	13-1/2 years	53	See previous section.
Maurine Brown Neuberger (D-Ore.)	11-8-60 to 1-3-67	7 years	53	She and her husband both served in the Oregon State Senate; she helped him get elected to U.S. Senate then succeeded him.
Margaret Chase Smith (R-Maine)[a]	1-3-49 to 1-3-73	32-1/2 years	52	Elected to Senate after serving in House; longest serving woman senator; defeated for a fourth term at age 75. See under House.

TABLE A-2   *(Continued)*

Name	Dates of Service	Length of Service	Age When Sworn In	Brief Profile
THE MODERN ERA: 1971–Present				
HOUSE				
Bella Savitsky Abzug (D-N.Y.)	1-21-71 to 1-3-77	6 years	50	Ran for the Senate in 1976 but lost in primary to Daniel Patrick Moynihan.
Elizabeth Bullock Andrews (D-Ala.)	4-10-72 to 1-3-73	9 months	61	Succeeded husband; declined to run for reelection.
Jean Spencer Asbrook (R-Ohio)	7-12-82 to 1-3-83	5 months	60	Succeeded husband.
Helen Delich Bentley (R-Md.)	1-3-85 to 1-3-95	10 years	61	Defeated Democratic incumbent; ran for governor of Maryland in 1994 but was defeated in Republican primary.
Corinne C. "Lindy" Boggs (D-La.)	3-27-73 to 1-3-91	18 years	57	Succeeded her husband, Hale Boggs, a rising star in the House leadership; proceeded to rise in stature in her own right.
Barbara Boxer (D-Calif.)[b]	1-3-83 to 1-5-93	13 years	42	Defeated five candidates for the Democratic nomination to the House.
Corrine Brown (D-Fla.)	1-5-93 to present	3 years	46	Won hotly contested primary; elected in a minority district.
Yvonne Brathwaite Burke (D-Calif.)	1-3-73 to 1-3-79	5-3/4 years	40	Declined to run for reelection; returned to California to pursue a legal career and motherhood.
Sala Burton (D-Calif.)	6-21-83 to 2-1-87	3-1/2 years	58	Succeeded husband and won reelection; died in office.
Leslie Larkin Byrne (D-Va.)	1-5-93 to 1-3-95	2 years	46	Defeated in her bid for a second term. (Both of her races were highly contested.)

TABLE A-2   *(Continued)*

Name	Dates of Service	Length of Service	Age When Sworn In	Brief Profile
Beverly Butcher Byron (D-Md.)	1-15-79 to 1-3-93	14 years	46	Succeeded husband; first woman to chair Armed Services Subcommittee.
Maria Cantwell (D-Wash.)	1-5-93 to 1-3-95	2 years	34	Defeated in her bid for a second term.
Shirley Anita Chisholm (D-N.Y.)	1-3-69 to 1-3-83	14 years	44	See previous section.
Eva Clayton (D-N.C.)	11-5-92 to present	3-1/2 years	58	First African American representative in N.C. since the late 1890s.
Barbara-Rose Collins (D-Mich.)	1-3-91 to present	5 years	51	Ran against the 78-year-old Democratic incumbent in 1988; he won but bowed out in next election.
Cardiss Collins (D-Ill.)	6-7-73 to present	23 years	41	Succeeded husband; remains the longest-serving African American woman in U.S. history.
Barbara Cubin (R-Wyo.)	1-3-95 to present	1 year	49	First congresswoman from Wyoming.
Patsy Ann "Pat" Danner (D-Mo.)	1-5-93 to present	3 years	58	Formerly a state senator and served in Jimmy Carter's administration.
Rosa DeLauro (D-Conn.)	1-3-91 to present	5 years	47	Before Congress, served as director of the pro-choice group Emily's List and was a congressional aide.
Jennifer Dunn (R-Wash.)	1-5-93 to present	3 years	51	Served as the chair of the Washington State Republican Party.
Florence Pryce Dwyer (R-N.J.)	1-3-57 to 1-3-73	16 years	55	See previous section.
Karan English (D-Ariz.)	1-5-93 to 1-3-95	2 years	43	Served as a county supervisor and state representative; defeated in reelection bid.

TABLE A-2   *(Continued)*

Name	Dates of Service	Length of Service	Age When Sworn In	Brief Profile
Anna G. Eshoo (D-Calif.)	1-5-93 to present	3 years	50	Former county supervisor who ran unsuccessfully for the House in 1988.
Millicent Hammond Fenwick (R-N.J.)	1-3-75 to 1-3-83	8 years	34	Editor of *Vogue* magazine before her election to Congress; defeated in Senate race in 1982.
Geraldine Ferraro (D-N.Y.)	1-15-79 to 1-3-85	6 years	43	First woman nominated by a major political party for vice president.
Bobbi Fiedler (R-Calif.)	1-5-81 to 1-3-87	6 years	43	Defeated incumbent Democrat to win House seat; lost Senate bid in primary.
Tillie Fowler (R-Fla.)	1-5-93 to present	3 years	50	An attorney and former city council president.
Elizabeth Furse (D-Ore.)	1-5-93 to present	3 years	56	Peace activist.
Ella T. Grasso (D-Conn.)	1-21-71 to 1-3-75	4 years	51	Elected governor of Connecticut in 1974 and 1978; the first woman elected governor in her own right.
Edith Starrett Green (D-Ore.)	1-3-55 to 12-31-74	19 years	45	See previous section.
Enid Greene (R-Utah)	1-3-95 present	1 year	36	Decided not to run for reelection after a scandal involving her husband and campaign finances.
Martha Wright Griffiths (D-Mich.)	1-3-55 to 12-31-74	19 years	43	See previous section.
Katie Beatrice Hall (D-Ind.)	11-2-82 to 1-3-85	2 years	44	Introduced bill to make Martin Luther King Jr.'s birthday a federal holiday; defeated in the primary.

TABLE A-2 *(Continued)*

Name	Dates of Service	Length of Service	Age When Sworn In	Brief Profile
Julia Butler Hansen (D-Wash.)	11-8-60 to 12-31-74	14 years	53	See previous section.
Jane Harman (D-Calif.)	1-5-93 to present	3 years	47	A lawyer and business-woman; defeated in reelection bid by another woman.
Margaret M. Heckler (R-Mass.)	1-13-67 to 1-3-83	16 years	36	See previous section.
Louise Day Hicks (D-Mass.)	1-21-71 to 1-3-73	2 years	47	An anti-busing standard bearer who lost the race for mayor of Boston then lost her seat after re-districting.
Marjorie Holt (R-Md.)	1-3-73 to 1-3-87	14 years	52	Focused on national defense; decided to retire from in 1987.
Elizabeth Holtzman (D-N.Y.)	1-3-73 to 1-5-81	8 years	31	Defeated fifty-year veteran Democrat; filed a lawsuit to stop the war in Cambodia; lost a Senate bid to Alfonse D'Amato.
Joan Kelly Horn (D-Mo.)	1-3-91 to 1-3-93	2 years	55	A political consultant who won her first congressional race.
Sheila Jackson-Lee (D-Texas)	1-3-95 to present	1 year	44	A municipal court judge and city council member who won her first House race.
Eddie Bernice Johnson (D-Texas)	1-5-93 to present	3 years	57	A nurse and business-woman who served as a state senator and repre-sentative before running for Congress.
Nancy Johnson (R-Conn.)	1-3-83 to present	13 years	47	A former state senator and community activist; serves on Ways and Means and chairs Ethics Committee.

TABLE A-2 *(Continued)*

Name	Dates of Service	Length of Service	Age When Sworn In	Brief Profile
Barbara Jordan (D-Texas)	1-3-73 to 1-3-79	6 years	35	An attorney and university professor; the first African American woman to address the Democratic National Convention (in 1976); retired in 1978.
Marcy (Marcia Carolyn) Kaptur (D-Ohio)	1-3-83 to present	13 years	36	A member of the Appropriations Committee and a Carter White House advisor; a city/regional planner by profession; "daughter of blue-collar America."
Barbara Kennelly (D-Conn.)	1-25-82 to present	14 years	45	A member of the Ways and Means Committee; daughter of a Democratic National Committee chairman.
Martha Elizabeth Keys (D-Kan.)	1-14-75 to 1-3-79	4 years	44	A member of the Ways and Means Committee; defeated in a reelection bid.
Blanche Lambert Lincoln (D-Ark.)	1-5-93 to present	3 years	32	One of youngest women ever elected; former legislative aide to a member of Congress.
Marilyn Lloyd (D-Tenn.)	1-14-75 to 1-3-95	20 years	55	A businesswoman and broadcaster; member of the House Select Committee on Aging.
Zoe Lofgren (D-Calif.)	1-3-95 to present	1 year	48	A lawyer who was a legislative aide for her predecessor.
Catherine Small Long (D-La.)	3-30-85 to 1-3-87	2 years	60	Succeeded husband.

TABLE A-2   *(Continued)*

Name	Dates of Service	Length of Service	Age When Sworn In	Brief Profile
Jill Lynnette Long (D-Ind.)	4-5-89 to 1-3-95	7 years	36	A business professor and farmer who was defeated in a reelection bid.
Nita M. Lowey (D-N.Y.)	1-3-89 to present	7 years	51	A member of the Appropriations Committee; worked for the secretary of state in New York.
Carolyn Maloney (D-N.Y.)	1-5-93 to present	3 years	44	Former New York City Council member; mother of two young children when elected.
Marjorie Margolies-Mezvinsky (D-Pa.)	1-5-93 to 1-3-95	2 years	50	A television broadcaster and journalist; defeated in reelection bid.
Lynn Martin (R-Ill.)	1-5-81 to 1-3-91	10 years	41	Left House to seek a Senate seat, but lost; appointed secretary of labor.
Karen McCarthy	1-3-95 to present	1 year	47	Former state legislator; won first congressional race.
Juanita M. McDonald (D-Calif.)	4-6-96 to present	—	56	Elected in special election.
Cynthia McKinney (D-Ga.)	1-5-93 to present	2 years	37	A former state representative; elected in a minority district.
Carrie Meek (D-Fla.)	1-5-93 to present	2 years	66	A former state senate president pro tempore; elected in a minority district.
Jan Meyers (R-Kan.)	1-3-85 to present	11 years	56	Served as a state senator and city council member; chairs the House Small Business Committee.
Helen Stevenson Meyner (D-N.J.)	1-14-75 to 1-3-79	4 years	45	Wife of governor of New Jersey; elected in her own right; defeated in 1978.

TABLE A-2   *(Continued)*

Name	Dates of Service	Length of Service	Age When Sworn In	Brief Profile
Barbara Ann Mikulski (D-Md.)[c]	1-4-77 to 1-6-87	20 years	40	A social worker before she was elected to the House.
Patsy Takemoto Mink (D-Hawaii)	1-3-65 to 1-3-77; 9-22-90 to present	16 years	38	See previous section.
Susan Molinari (R-N.Y.)	3-20-90 to present	6 years	32	Succeeded father; keynote speaker at 1996 Republican convention.
Constance A. Morella (R-Md.)	1-3-87 to present	9 years	56	An educator and mother; served in the Maryland General Assembly.
Eleanor Holmes Norton (D-D.C.)[d]	1-3-91 to present	5 years	53	First woman to chair the Equal Employment Opportunity Commission.
Mary Rose Oakar (D-Ohio)	1-3-77 to 1-3-93	12 years	36	Former city council member; defeated in bid for reelection.
Elizabeth J. Patterson (D-S.C.)	1-3-87 to 1-3-93	7 years	47	Daughter of a former senator and governor; defeated in reelection bid.
Nancy Pelosi (D-Calif.)	6-2-87 to present	9 years	47	Democratic Party activist and finance chair for California Democratic Party; member of Appropriations Committee.
Shirley Neil Pettis (R-Calif.)	4-29-75 to 1-3-79	3-1/2 years	50	A journalist who succeeded her husband;
Deborah Pryce (R-Ohio)	1-5-93 to present	3 years	41	Served as municipal court judge and prosecutor.
Charlotte Thompson Reid (R-Ill.)	1-3-63 to 10-7-71	8 years	50	See previous section.

TABLE A-2   *(Continued)*

Name	Dates of Service	Length of Service	Age When Sworn In	Brief Profile
Lynn Rivers (D-Mich.)	1-3-95 to present	1 year	38	Education activist who won House seat.
Ileana Ros-Lehtinen (R-Fla.)	8-29-89 to present	7 years	36	Teacher and mother of two children; first Cuban American in Congress.
Margaret Scafati Roukema (R-N.J.)	1-3-81 to present	15 years	51	An educator and school board member; chairs the Banking Subcommittee.
Lucille Roybal-Allard (D-Calif.)	1-5-93 to present	3 years	51	A former state assembly-woman; first Mexican American woman in Congress.
Patricia Saiki (R-Hawaii)	1-3-87 to 1-3-91	4 years	56	State party chair in Hawaii State House and Senate; left the House to run for Senate, but lost.
Lynn Schenk (D-Calif.)	1-5-93 to 1-3-95	2 years	48	An attorney; lost bid for reelection.
Claudine Schneider (R-R.I.)	1-5-81 to 1-3-91	10 years	33	Left the House to run for Senate, but lost.
Patricia Schroeder (D-Colo.)	1-3-73 to present	23 years	32	One of youngest woman elected to the House; cochaired Women's Caucus; announced plans to retire after the 104th Congress.
Andrea Seastrand (R-Calif.)	1-3-95 to present	1 year	53	A teacher and mother; appointed assistant majority whip.
Karen Shepherd (D-Utah)	1-5-93 to 1-3-95	2 years	52	A former state senator, teacher, and social services director; defeated in bid for reelection.
Louise M. Slaughter (D-N.Y.)	1-3-87 to present	9 years	57	A former county and state assembly woman; elected to the Rules Committee.

TABLE A-2   *(Continued)*

Name	Dates of Service	Length of Service	Age When Sworn In	Brief Profile
Linda Smith (R-Wash.)	1-3-95 to present	1 year	57	A former state senator; first person in Washington State to qualify for general election ballot as a write-in candidate.
Virginia Dodd Smith (R-Neb.)	1-3-75 to 1-3-91	16 years	63	A farm wife; served on the Appropriations Committee before her retirement.
Olympia J. Snowe (R-Maine)[e]	1-3-79 to 1-3-95	18	31	Won open House seat and served eight terms before running for Senate.
Gladys Spellman (D-Md.)	1-14-75 to 2-24-81	6 years	56	A teacher and county official, had a heart attack at age 62 when campaigning for reelection. (Her husband ran in her stead, but failed.)
Leonor Kretzer Sullivan (D-Mo.)	1-3-53 to 1-3-77	24 years	51	See previous section.
Karen Thurman (D-Fla.)	1-5-93 to present	3 years	41	Served as state senator and mayor before election to Congress.
Jolene Unsoeld (D-Wash.)	1-3-89 to 1-3-95	6 years	57	A former state representative and lobbyist; defeated in bid for a fourth term.
Nydia Velazquez (D-N.Y.)	1-5-93 to present	3 years	39	A former member of the New York City Council; first Puerto Rican woman to win election to Congress.
Barbara Vucanovich (R-Nev.)	1-3-83 to present	13 years	61	A businesswoman and congressional aide to a former senator; member of the Appropriations Committee.
Maxine Waters (D-Calif.)	1-3-91 to present	5 years	52	A former state assemblywoman; represents a minority district.

TABLE A-2   *(Continued)*

Name	Dates of Service	Length of Service	Age When Sworn In	Brief Profile
Lynn Woolsey (D-Calif.)	1-5-93 to present	3 years	56	A small business owner who previously served on the city council.
SENATE				
Maryon P. Allen (D-Ala.)	6-8-78 to 1-3-79	6 months	52	Appointed to fill the vacancy caused by the death of her husband.
Barbara Boxer (D-Calif.)[b]	1-5-93 to present	13 years	52	Second Democratic woman elected to the Senate in her own right. See under House.
Jocelyn Burdick (D-N.D.)	9-16-92 to 12-4-92	3 months	70	Appointed to fill the vacancy caused by the death of her husband.
Elaine Edwards (D-La.)	8-1-72 to 11-13-73	5 months	43	Appointed by her husband, Gov. Edwin Edwards, to fill vacancy caused by death of incumbent.
Dianne Feinstein (D-Calif.)	11-10-92 to present	3 years	59	Elected to fill the vacancy caused by resignation of Pete Wilson, who ran for governor.
Sheila Frahm (R-Kan.)	6-11-96 to present	—	51	Appointed to fill Bob Dole's Senate seat when he resigned to run for president.
Paula Hawkins (R-Fla.)	1-5-81 to 1-3-87	6 years	53	First woman senator whose male relative did not precede her.
Muriel Humphrey (D-Minn.)	2-6-78 to 3-3-79	1 year	66	Appointed to fill vacancy caused by death of her husband, Hubert H. Humphrey.
Kay Bailey Hutchison (R-Texas)	6-14-93 to present	3 years	49	Elected to fill vacancy caused by resignation of Lloyd Bentsen to become secretary of Treasury.

TABLE A-2   *(Continued)*

Name	Dates of Service	Length of Service	Age When Sworn In	Brief Profile
Nancy Landon Kassebaum	12-23-78 to present	18 years	46	One of two women in history to serve more than two Senate terms; daughter of Alf Landon.
Barbara Ann Mikulski (D-Md.)[c]	1-6-87 to present	20 years	51	First Democratic woman to be elected to the Senate in her own right. See under House.
Carol Moseley-Braun (D-Ill.)	1-5-93 to present	3 years	45	First African American woman elected to the Senate.
Patty Murray (D-Wash.)	1-5-93 to present	3 years	42	Elected as "a mom in tennis shoes."
Olympia J. Snowe (R-Maine)	1-3-95 to present	18 years	48	A cochair of the Women's Caucus. See under House.

Source: Compiled by the author.

[a] Smith was elected to the Senate in 1948. The length of service includes both House and Senate. See under Senate.

[b] Boxer was elected to the Senate in 1992. The length of service includes both House and Senate. See under Senate.

[c] Mikulski was elected to the Senate in 1986. The length of service includes both House and Senate. See under Senate.

[d] Nonvoting delegate.

[e] Snowe was elected to the Senate in 1994. The length of service includes both House and Senate. See under Senate.

Table A-3   CONGRESSWOMEN WHO SERVED TEN YEARS OR MORE,
BY YEARS OF SERVICE

Representative/Senator	Years of Service	Dates of Service
Edith Nourse Rogers (R-Mass.)	35	1925–1960
Margaret Chase Smith (R-Maine)	33	1940–1973
Frances Payne Bolton (R-Ohio)	29	1940–1969
Mary Teresa Norton (D-N.J.)	26	1925–1951
Cardiss Collins (D-Ill.)	24	1973–present[a]
Patricia S. Schroeder (D-Colo.)	24	1973–present[a]
Leonor Kretzer Sullivan (D-Mo.)	24	1953–1977
Marilyn Lloyd (D-Tenn.)	22	1975–1995
Edith Starrett Green (D-Ore.)	20	1955–1974[b]
Martha Wright Griffiths (D-Mich.)	20	1955–1974[b]
Edna Flannery Kelly (D-N.Y.)	20	1949–1969
Barbara A. Mikulski (D-Md.)	20	1977–present
Corinne Claiborne "Lindy" Boggs (D-La.)	18	1973–1991
Nancy Landon Kassebaum (R-Kan.)	18	1979–present[a]
Patsy T. Mink (D-Hawaii)	18	1965–1977; 1990–present[c]
Katharine Price St. George (R-N.Y.)	18	1947–1965
Olympia J. Snowe (R-Maine)	18	1979–present
Beverly Butcher Byron (D-Md.)	16	1979–1993
Florence Price Dwyer (R-N.J.)	16	1957–1973
Margaret M. Heckler (R-Mass.)	16	1967–1983
Mary Rose Oakar (D-Ohio)	16	1977–1993
Margaret S. Roukema (R-N.J.)	16	1981–present
Virginia Dodd Smith (R-Neb.)	16	1975–1991
Barbara B. Kennelly (D-Conn.)	15	1982–present
Shirley A. Chisholm (D-N.Y.)	14	1969–1983
Julia Butler Hansen (D-Wash.)	14	1960–1974
Marjorie Sewell Holt (D-Md.)	14	1973–1987
Nancy L. Johnson (R-Conn.)	14	1983–present
Marcy (Marcia C.) Kaptur (D-Ohio)	14	1983–present
Maude Elizabeth Kee (D-W.Va.)	14	1951–1965
Barbara F. Vucanovich (R-Nev.)	14	1983–present[a]
Hattie Wyatt Caraway (D-Ark.)	13	1931–1945[d]
Marguerite Stitt Church (R-Ill.)	12	1951–1963
Florence Prag Kahn (R-Calif.)	12	1925–1937
Catherine Dean May (R-Wash.)	12	1959–1971
Jan Meyers (R-Kan.)	12	1985–present[a]
Helen Delich Bentley (R-Md.)	10	1985–1995

Table A-3   *(Continued)*

Representative/Senator	Years of Service	Dates of Service
Barbara Boxer (D-Calif.)	10	1983–present
Cecil Murray Harden (R-Ind.)	10	1949–1959
Lynn Martin (R-Ill.)	10	1981–1991
Gracie Bowers Pfost (D-Idaho)	10	1953–1963
Claudine Schneider (R-R.I.)	10	1981–1991

Source: Compiled by the author.

Note: Most terms of Congress begin and end on January 3. Although some women were sworn in after January or ended their service somewhat before January, those years of service are counted as full years, except where otherwise noted.

[a] Retiring at end of the 104th Congress.
[b] Term ended December 31, 1974.
[c] Term began September 22, 1990; the year is not counted in calculation of years of service.
[d] First term began November 13, 1931; the year is not counted in calculation of years of service.

Table A-4   NUMBER OF WOMEN IN CONGRESS, BY STATE

State	104th Congress (1995–1997)	Historical Number	Percentage of All Women in Congress
Alabama	0	3	2%
Alaska	0	0	0
Arizona	0	2	1
Arkansas	1	5	3
California	11	19	10
Colorado	1	1	a
Connecticut	3	6	3
Delaware	0	0	0
D.C.[b]	1	1	a
Florida	5	7	4
Georgia	1	5	3
Hawaii	1	3	2
Idaho	1	2	1
Illinois	2	10	6
Indiana	0	4	2
Iowa	0	0	0
Kansas	3	5	2
Kentucky	0	1	a
Louisiana	0	4	2
Maine	1	2	1
Maryland	2	7	4
Massachusetts	0	3	2
Michigan	2	4	2
Minnesota	0	2	1
Mississippi	0	0	0
Missouri	2	4	2
Montana	0	1	a
Nebraska	0	3	2
Nevada	1	1	a
New Hampshire	0	0	0
New Jersey	1	5	3
New Mexico	0	1	6
New York	6	17	10
North Carolina	2	3	2
North Dakota	0	1	a
Ohio	2	5	3
Oklahoma	0	1	a
Oregon	2	5	3

Table A-4   *(Continued)*

State	104th Congress (1995–1997)	Historical Number	Percentage of All Women in Congress
Pennsylvania	0	4	2
Rhode Island	0	1	a
South Carolina	0	5	3
South Dakota	0	2	1
Tennessee	0	4	2
Texas	3	5	3
Utah	1	3	2
Vermont	0	0	0
Virginia	0	1	a
Washington	2	6	3
West Virginia	0	1	a
Wisconsin	0	0	0
Wyoming	1	1	a
Total	58	176	
Democrats	37	111	
Republicans	21	65	

Source: Compiled by the author.

[a] Less than 1 percent.
[b] The delegate from the District of Columbia is nonvoting.

TABLE A-5 WOMEN OF THE 104TH CONGRESS (1995–1997)

Member	Birthdate	Year and Age Sworn In	Religion	Family Status When First Elected
HOUSE				
Corrine Brown (D-Fla.)	1946	1993 46	Baptist	Divorced, 1 adult child
Helen Chenoweth (R-Idaho)	1938	1995 57	Christian	Divorced, 2 adult children
Eva Clayton (D-N.C.)	1934	1993 58	Presbyterian	Married, 4 adult children, 3 grandchildren
Barbara-Rose Collins (D-Mich.)	1939	1991 51	Pan African Orthodox Christian	Widowed, 2 adult children
Cardiss Collins (D-Ill.)	1931	1973 41	Baptist	Widowed, 1 son
Barbara Cubin (R-Wyo.)	1949	1995 45	Episcopalian	Married, 2 adult children
Pat Danner (D-Mo.)	1934	1993 58	Roman Catholic	Married, 4 adult children
Rosa DeLauro (D-Conn.)	1943	1991 47	Roman Catholic	Married, 3 stepchildren
Jennifer Dunn (R-Wash.)	1941	1993 51	Episcopalian	Divorced, 2 adult children
Anna G. Eshoo (D-Calif.)	1942	1993 50	Roman Catholic	Divorced, 2 adult children

Professional Background	Key Committees	Political Interest[a]
State representative, community college counselor	Transportation and Infrastructure, Veterans'Affairs	"Making Congress work for my district," and "bringing projects home."
Director of state Republican Party	Agriculture, Resources	"Concerned about federal agriculture and natural resources policies affecting the west and economic policies affecting the nation."
Business owner, N.C. Community Development Dept.	Agriculture, Small Business	"Rural economic development and housing; support for families such as Family and Medical Leave Act; immigration; Women's, Infants, and Children [WIC] funding."
Detroit City Council, state representative	Government Reform and Oversight, Transportation and Infrastructure	"I'm a black activist. Elected to school boards in [the] '70s, elected to state legislature for seven years, and now to Congress. I found you could do a whole lot more at the negotiating table than demonstrating."
Accountant/auditor in Illinois Dept. of Revenue	Commerce, Government Reform and Oversight	"Consumer protection—air safety, minority business, women's health, maintaining competitive financial market place."
Physician-husband's office manager	Resources, Science	"My family and I felt we needed to be a part of a peaceful revolution."
State senator	Transportation and Infrastructure	"Fiscal responsibility."
Director, Emily's List; Senate office chief of staff	National Security	"I come from a family devoted to public service. My mother served on city council for thirty years. My dad was an alderperson. I see myself as an advocate for people on behalf of jobs and health care."
State Republican Party chair	House Oversight, Ways and Means	"This is the most fascinating, challenging career I could imagine where I can make the most difference."
City supervisor	Commerce	"Improve the nation for the next generation. We're caretakers of the environment."

TABLE A-5   *(Continued)*

Member	Birthdate	Year and Age Sworn In	Religion	Family Status When First Elected
Tillie Fowler (R-Fla.)	1942	1993 50	Episcopalian	Married, 2 children
Elizabeth Furse (D-Ore.)	1936	1993 56	Protestant	Married, 2 adult children
Enid Greene (R-Utah)	1958	1995 36	Mormon	Married[b]
Jane Harman (D-Calif.)	1945	1993 47	Jewish	Married, 4 children
Sheila Jackson-Lee (D-Texas)	1950	1995 45	Seventh-day Adventist	Married, 2 children
Eddie Bernice Johnson (D-Texas)	1935	1993 57	Baptist	Divorced, 1 adult child
Nancy L. Johnson (R-Conn.)	1935	1983 47	Unitarian	Married, 3 children
Marcy (Marcia Carolyn) Kaptur (D-Ohio)	1946	1983 36	Roman Catholic	Single
Sue W. Kelly (R-N.Y.)	1936	1995 58	Presbyterian	Married, 4 adult children
Barbara B. Kennelly (D-Conn.)	1936	1982 45	Roman Catholic	Married, 4 children
Blanche Lambert Lincoln (D-Ark.)	1960	1993 32	Episcopalian	Single

Professional Background	Key Committees	Political Interest[a]
City council, legislative assistant	National Security, Transportation and Infrastructure	"Congressional reform to improve esteem of Congress."
Director, Oregon Peace Institute, Oregon Legal Services	Commerce	"I believe people can make a difference."
Attorney, corporate counsel, gubernatorial office chief of staff	Rules	"We needed significant changes on issues at the federal level that were having a detrimental impact on my state."
Corporate lawyer, Senior Senate staff member	National Security, Science	"Public service is the highest calling. I care intensely about certain issues—saving the industrial base, helping working families, educating all kids."
Houston city council, municipal judge, attorney	Judiciary, Science	"To be a change maker."
Businesswoman, state senator	Science, Transportation and Infrastructure	"Infrastructure and a free trader."
State senator, community activist	Standards of Official Conduct, Ways and Means	"I want to make democracy and government work better for people, and it's not as easy as I thought."
White House policy adviser, city and regional planner, party activist	Appropriations	"To assure America's political and social stability, raise the standard of living for all families, and advance democracy abroad by strengthening the U.S. economy and enacting fair trade laws."
Small business, patient advocate, woman-building rehabilitation	Banking and Financial Services, Small Business, Transportation and Infrastructure	"I care ardently that we have sound fiscal policies as well as a strong concern for the well-being of our nation's children."
Secretary of state, city council	Ways and Means	"I became the first woman to serve on [the] Intelligence Committee."
Congressional staff assistant	Commerce	"Environment, agriculture, budget, safe drinking water, aquaculture, Superfund, recycling, rural development."

TABLE A-5   *(Continued)*

Member	Birthdate	Year and Age Sworn In	Religion	Family Status When First Elected
Zoe Lofgren (D-Calif.)	1947	1995 48	Protestant	Married, 2 children
Nita M. Lowey (D-N.Y.)	1937	1989 51	Jewish	Married, 3 adult children
Carolyn B. Maloney (D-N.Y.)	1948	1993 44	Presbyterian	Married, 2 children
Karen McCarthy (D-Mo.)	1947	1995 47	Roman Catholic	Divorced
Juanita M. McDonald[c] (D-Calif.)	1938	1996 56	Baptist	Married, 5 adult children
Cynthia A. McKinney (D-Ga.)	1955	1993 37	Roman Catholic	Divorced, 1 son
Carrie P. Meek (D-Fla.)	1926	1993 66	Baptist	Divorced, 3 adult children
Jan Meyers (R-Kan.)	1928	1985 56	Methodist	Married, 2 adult children
Patsy T. Mink (D-Hawaii)	1927	1965[d] 37	——	Married, 1 child
Susan Molinari (R-N.Y.)	1958	1990 32	Roman Catholic	Divorced

Professional Background	Key Committees	Political Interest[a]
County supervisor	Judiciary, Science	"Our community found a dead body outside my son's elementary school. I thought I could make a difference here on education, prevention."
Assistant to New York secretary of state	Appropriations	"Life has been good to me. This gives me a chance to make a difference in other people's lives. It's a privilege to serve."
New York City Council, teacher, education administrator	Banking and Financial Services, Government Reform and Oversight	"What greater way to help people by impacting on social and economic policy."
Missouri House of Representatives, teacher	Science, Transportation and Infrastructure	"I thought I could make a difference, especially on fiscal policy."
California House of Representatives, Carson City mayor, teacher, education administrator	Small Business, Transportation and Infrastructure	"The former congressman resigned. This congressional district constituted 75% of my former [state] house district. I felt my community needed experienced representation."
State representative	Agriculture, International Relations	"Civil rights; economic development; code of conduct: don't sell arms to dictators."
State senator, college professor	Budget, Government Reform and Oversight	To "improve the lot of women and minorities."
Advertising, public relations	Economic and Educational Opportunities, International Relations, Small Business	"I view this as public service. My specific interests are small business, foreign affairs, welfare reform."
Attorney; state legislature	Budget, Economic and Educational Opportunities	"Our children are our future."
New York City Council	Budget, Economic and Educational Opportunities	It's "an honor to serve. Make sure community service improves the lot of women."

TABLE A-5   *(Continued)*

Member	Birthdate	Year and Age Sworn In	Religion	Family Status When First Elected
Constance A. Morella (R-Md.)	1931	1987 55	Roman Catholic	Married, 9 children (6 adopted)
Sue Myrick (R-N.C.)	1941	1995 53	Methodist	Married, 5 adult children
Eleanor Holmes Norton[e] (D-D.C.)	1937	1991 53	Episcopalian	Married, 2 adult children
Nancy J. Pelosi (D-Calif.)	1940	1987 47	Roman Catholic	Married, 5 children
Deborah Pryce (R-Ohio)	1951	1993 41	Presbyterian	Married, 2 adult children
Lynn Rivers (D-Mich.)	1956	1995 38	Protestant	Married, 2 children
Ileana Ros-Lehtinen (R-Fla.)	1952	1989 36	Roman Catholic	Married, 2 children, 2 stepchildren
Marge Roukema (R-N.J.)	1929	1981 51	Protestant	Married, 2 adult children[f]
Lucille Roybal-Allard (D-Calif.)	1941	1993 51	Roman Catholic	Married, 2 stepchildren

Professional Background	Key Committees	Political Interest[a]
State representative, college professor	Government Reform and Oversight, Science	"It was a relief to get out of the house for another challenge. I gain satisfaction in helping others. . . . Equity for women—credit, housing, employment, education, ERA. I'll leave when I lose enthusiasm."
Mayor of Charlotte, city council, advertising firm president	Budget, Science, Small Business	"To try to make the world better for my grandchildren."
Law professor, chair of Equal Employment Opportunity Commission	Government Reform and Oversight, Transportation and Infrastructure	"I guess I'm crazy . . . to try to put action where my mouth is . . . to empower District of Columbia."
State Democratic Party chair, business	Appropriations, Select Intelligence, Standards of Official Conduct	"Human rights, AIDS awareness/treatment, environment, housing, health."
Municipal court judge	Rules	To "raise level of awareness in my community on women; set a role model for my daughter and her friends. And, I was bored being a judge."
School board, state house of representatives	Budget, Science	"I thought I could do more at the federal level."
Teacher	Government Reform and Oversight, International Relations	To "change opinions in Washington, D.C., to liberate my native land, Cuba. Foreign policy [is] a divisive force."
Teacher, activist	Banking and Financial Services, Economic and Educational Opportunities	"This is my third career, having been a teacher, a mother, and now public policy and government; notice, I didn't say 'politics,' but public policy and government."
State assembly, alcohol/drug abuse counselor	Banking and Financial Services	"So much of what I wanted to do in my work was stopped by policies in Washington. Narrow guidelines limited our ability to serve the public, particularly in alcohol and drug abuse."

TABLE A-5   *(Continued)*

Member	Birthdate	Year and Age Sworn In	Religion	Family Status When First Elected
Patricia Schroeder (D-Colo.)	1940	1973 32	United Church of Christ	Married, 2 children
Andrea Seastrand (R-Calif.)	1941	1995 53	Roman Catholic	Widowed, 2 adult children
Louise M. Slaughter (D-N.Y.)	1929	1987 57	Episcopalian	Married, 3 adult children, 3 grandchildren
Linda Smith (R-Wash.)	1950	1995 44	Assembly of God	Married, 2 adult children
Karen L. Thurman (D-Fla.)	1951	1993 41	Episcopalian	Married, 2 children
Nydia M. Velazquez (D-N.Y.)	1953	1993 39	Roman Catholic	Divorced
Barbara F. Vucanovich (R-Nev.)	1921	1983 61	Roman Catholic	Married, 5 adult children
Maxine Waters (D-Calif.)	1938	1991 52	Christian	Married, 2 adult children
Lynn Woolsey (D-Calif.)	1937	1993 56	Presbyterian	Separated, 4 adult children

Professional Background	Key Committees	Political Interest[a]
Attorney	Judiciary, National Security	"In law, change comes a case at a time; here change is faster. My major concerns—women, family, defense."
State house of representatives, elementary teacher	Science, Transportation and Infrastructure	"I had been involved in grass-roots politics for 30 years and concerned about my kids participating in the American dream, even owning a home. Congress is not just a place for the privileged. My grandparents came from Poland; only in America could [my coming to Congress] happen."
State and county legislator	Budget, Government Reform and Oversight	"When you work in a place where laws are made, it's the most important job in the world."
Tax consulting firm manager, state house of representatives and senate	Resources, Small Business	"I didn't run for Congress; I was drafted to serve following a historic write-in campaign. I was picked by the people to fight for a cleaner government closer to the people. It's what I did at the state level and why I believe the voters wanted me in Congress."
Middle school math teacher	Agriculture, Government Reform and Oversight	To "try to bridge the gap between local, state, and federal governments to make it more efficient. Make the government more friendly and work for people."
New York City Council; director, N.Y. Puerto Rico Community Affairs Office	Banking and Financial Services	"Empowerment of my community, economic development, combating redlining by financial institutions."
Small business, managed Senate district office	Appropriations	"[I] believe I'm making a difference for my state, my fifteen grandchildren and 3 great-grandchildren."
State legislature, community activist loan guarantee	Banking and Financial Services, Veterans' Affairs	"Urban revitalization, youth. I worked hard to gain passage of authority for cities' economic development as part of disaster relief bill—$2 billion per year over five years."
Business, human resource management; city council, vice mayor	Budget, Economic and Educational Opportunities	To "make government work for people. Make education our No. 1 priority."

TABLE A-5   *(Continued)*

Member	Birthdate	Year and Age Sworn In	Religion	Family Status When First Elected
SENATE				
Barbara Boxer (D-Calif.)	1940	1993[g] 52	Jewish	Married, 2 children
Dianne Feinstein (D-Calif.)	1933	1993 59	Jewish	Married, 1 adult child, 3 stepchildren, 1 grandchild
Sheila Frahm[h] (R-Kan.)	1945	1996	United Methodist	Married, 3 children
Kay Bailey Hutchison (R-Texas)	1943	1993 49	Episcopalian	Married, 2 stepchildren, 4 grandchildren
Nancy Landon Kassebaum (R-Kan.)	1932	1978 46	Episcopalian	Separated, 4 children (2 adult)
Barbara A. Mikulski (D-Md.)	1936	1987[i] 51	Roman Catholic	Single
Carol Moseley-Braun (D-Ill.)	1947	1993 45	Roman Catholic	Divorced 1 son
Patty Murray (D-Wash.)	1950	1993 42	Roman Catholic	Married, 2 children

Professional Background	Key Committees	Political Interest[a]
City supervisor, congressional assistant, journalist, U.S. House	Banking, Housing, and Urban Affairs; Budget; Environment and Public Works; Special Whitewater	"I was against the war in Vietnam and therefore became involved in politics. My key issues are environment and women's concerns."
Mayor of San Francisco, city board of supervisors, state women's parole board	Foreign Relations, Judiciary, Rules and Administration	"California, if it were a nation, would rank No. 6 in the world . . . The economy [is] at the top of my list."
Kansas lieutenant governor, state senate, state board of education	Armed Services; Banking, Housing, and Urban Affairs	—
Business owner, attorney, state treasurer and legislator, TV correspondent	Armed Services; Commerce, Science, and Transportation; Small Business	"I wanted to send a message to Washington . . . to cut taxes and stand up to Bill Clinton."
Senate staffer, school board member	Foreign Relations, Indian Affairs, Labor and Human Resources	"[I] feel strongly about need to reform Congress . . . health care reform . . . an abiding interest in foreign relations."
Social work administrator, community organizer, Baltimore City Council, U.S. House	Appropriations, Labor and Human Resources	"Spousal impoverishment and women's agenda . . . along with committee responsibilities like space exploration."
Cook County recorder, state representative, assistant majority leader	Special Aging; Banking, Housing, and Urban Affairs; Finance; Special Whitewater	Assumed office on a tide of women's sentiment opposing nomination of Clarence Thomas to the Supreme Court.
School board president, teacher, state legislature	Appropriations, Banking and Urban Affairs, Budget, Select Ethics, Veterans' Affairs, Special Whitewater	Elected during the "Year of the Woman" as a "mom in tennis shoes." Focus on pocketbook issues and family concerns.

TABLE A-5   *(Continued)*

Member	Birthdate	Year and Age Sworn In	Religion	Family Status When First Elected
Olympia J. Snowe (D-Maine)	1947	1995[j] 48	Greek Orthodox	Married

Professional Background	Key Committees	Political Interest[a]
State house and senate, U.S. House	Budget; Commerce, Science, and Transportation; Foreign Relations; Small Business	"I've always been motivated by serving others, not necessarily in public service. Always wanted to help."

Sourc: Compiled by the author.

[a] Quotes are from interviews with the author, Washington, D.C., May-June 1996.

[b] Enid Greene Waldholtz divorced her husband in her first term and announced that she would not run for reelection.

[c] After winning a special election, McDonald was sworn into the House in April 1996.

[d] Mink served from 1965 to 1977 and from 1990 to the present.

[e] Norton is a nonvoting delegate.

[f] Another son had died in his early twenties before Roukema was elected.

[g] Boxer served in the House of Representatives from 1983 until her election to the Senate.

[h] Frahm was appointed to take Sen. Bob Dole's place when he resigned in June 1996 to run for president.

[i] Mikulski served in the House of Representatives from 1977 until her election to the Senate.

[j] Snowe served in the House of Representatives from 1979 until her election to the Senate.

Selected Readings

Abzug, Bella. *Bella! Mrs. Abzug Goes to Washington.* New York: Saturday Review Press, 1972.

Block, Judy Rachel. *The First Woman in Congress: Jeannette Rankin.* New York: Contemporary Perspectives, 1978.

Boggs, Lindy, with Katherine Hatch. *Washington through a Purple Veil: Memoirs of a Southern Woman.* New York: Harcourt, Brace, 1994.

Brownmiller, Susan. *Shirley Chisholm: A Biography.* Garden City, N.Y.: Doubleday, 1971.

Bryant, Ira B. *Barbara Charline Jordan: From the Ghetto to the Capitol.* Houston, Texas: D. Armstrong, 1977.

Caraway, Hattie Wyatt. *Silent Hattie Speaks: The Personal Journal of Hattie Caraway,* edited by Diane D. Kincaid. Westport, Conn.: Greenwood Press, 1979.

Chamberlin, Hope. *A Minority of Members: Women in the United States Congress.* New York: Praeger, 1973.

Chisholm, Shirley. *Unbought and Unbossed.* Boston: Houghton Mifflin, 1970.

Clopton, Beverly. *Her Honor, the Judge: The Story of Reva Beck Bosone.* Ames: Iowa State University Press, 1980.

Douglas, Helen Gahagan. *A Full Life.* Garden City, N.Y.: Doubleday, 1982.

Evans, Sara M. *Born for Liberty: A History of Women in America.* New York: Free Press, 1989.

Fenwick, Millicent. *Speaking Up.* New York: Harper and Row, 1982.

Ferraro, Geraldine. *My Story.* New York: Bantam Books, 1985.

Fleming, Alice. *The Senator from Maine: Margaret Chase Smith.* New York: Thomas Y. Crowell, 1969.

Foote, Frieda Lillian. "Role Stress and Cultural Resources: A Study of the Role of the Woman Member of Congress." Ph.D. diss., Michigan State University, 1967.

Gehlen, Frieda. "Women Members of Congress: A Distinctive Role." In *A Portrait of Marginality: The Political Behavior of the American Woman,* edited by Marianne Githins and Jewel Prestage. New York: David McKay, 1977.

George, Emily. *Martha W. Griffiths.* Lanham, Md.: University Press of America, 1982.

Giles, Kevin S. *Flight of the Dove: The Story of Jeannette Rankin.* Beaverton, Ore.: Touchstone Press, 1980.

Githins, Marianne, and Jewel Prestage, eds. *A Portrait of Marginality: The Political Behavior of the American Woman.* New York: David McKay, 1977.

Gould, Alberta. *First Lady of the Senate: A Life of Margaret Chase Smith.* Mount Desert, Maine: Windswept House, 1990.

Harris, Ted Carlton. "Jeannette Rankin: Suffragist, First Woman Elected to Congress, and Pacifist." Ph.D. diss., University of Georgia, 1972.

Hatch, Alden. *Ambassador Extraordinary: Clare Boothe Luce.* New York: Henry Holt, 1955.

Jordan, Barbara, and Shelby Hearon. *Barbara Jordan: A Self-Portrait.* Garden City, N.Y.: Doubleday, 1979.

Josephson, Hannah. *Jeannette Rankin: First Lady in Congress.* New York: Bobbs-Merrill, 1974.

Kidd, Benjamin. *The Science of Power.* London: Methuen, 1918.

Kinyon, Jeannette, and Jean Walz. *The Incredible Gladys Pyle.* Vermillion, S.D.: Dakota Press, 1985.

Kirkpatrick, Jeane. *Political Woman.* New York: Basic Books, 1974.

Lamson, Peggy. *Few Are Chosen: American Women in Political Life Today.* Boston: Houghton Mifflin, 1968.

Loth, David. *A Long Way Forward: The Biography of Congresswoman Frances Payne Bolton.* New York: Longmans, Green, 1957.

Lyons, Joseph. *Clare Boothe Luce.* New York: Chelsea House, 1989.

Malone, David. *Hattie and Huey: An Arkansas Tour.* Fayetteville: University of Arkansas Press, 1989.

Martin, Ralph. *Henry and Clare: An Intimate Portrait of the Luces.* New York: Putnam's, 1991.

Never Underestimate . . . The Life and Career of Margaret Chase Smith: Through the Eyes of the Political Cartoonist. Waterville, Me.: Northwood University, Margaret Chase Smith Library, 1993.

Norton, Mary T. "Autobiography." Jersey City Public Library, Jersey City, N.J.

Paxton, Annabel. *Women in Congress.* Richmond, Va.: Dietz Press, 1945.

Poole, Keith T., and L. Harmon Zeigler. *Women, Public Opinion, and Politics: The Changing Political Attitudes of American Women.* New York: Longman, 1985.

Roosevelt, Eleanor, and Lorena A. Hickok. *Ladies of Courage.* New York: Putnam's, 1954.

Rosenberg, Marie C. Barovic. "Women in Politics: A Comparative Study of Congresswomen Edith Green and Julia Butler Hansen." Ph.D. diss., University of Washington, 1973.

Ross, Ishbel. *Sons of Adam, Daughters of Eve.* New York: Harper and Row, 1969.

Schaffer, Ronald. "Jeannette Rankin: Progressive-Isolationist." Ph.D. diss., Princeton University, 1959.

Schroeder, Pat. *Champion of the Great American Family.* New York: Random House, 1989.

Scobie, Ingrid Winther. *Center Stage: Helen Gahagan Douglas: A Life.* New York: Oxford University Press, 1992.

Shadegg, Stephen C. *Clare Boothe Luce: A Biography.* New York: Simon and Schuster, 1970.

Sheed, Wilfrid. *Clare Boothe Luce.* New York: Dutton, 1982.

Smith, Hedrick. *The Power Game.* New York: Ballantine Books, 1988.

Smith, Margaret Chase. *Declaration of Conscience.* Edited by William C. Lewis, Jr. Garden City, N.Y.: Doubleday, 1972.

Spritzer, Lorraine Nelson. *The Belle of Ashby Street: Helen Douglas Mankin and Georgia Politics.* Athens: University of Georgia Press, 1982.

Stineman, Esther. *American Political Women: Contemporary and Historical Profiles.* Littleton, Colo.: Libraries Unlimited, 1980.

Tolchin, Susan J. *Women in Congress, 1917–1976.* Washington, D.C.: U.S. Government Printing Office, 1976.

U.S. Congress. House. *Memorial Services Held in the House of Representatives and Senate of the United States, Together with Remarks Presented in Eulogy of Edith Nourse Rogers, Late a Representative from Massachusetts, 86th Congress, 2d session.* Washington, D.C.: U.S. Government Printing Office, 1961.

___. Office of the Historian. *Women in Congress, 1917–1990.* Washington, D.C.: U.S. Government Printing Office, 1991.

White, Florence Meiman. *First Woman in Congress: Jeannette Rankin.* New York: Julian Messner, 1980.

Index

Page numbers in **bold** type indicate the main entries for the congresswomen profiled.